Mark M. Leach, PhD

Cultural Diversity and Suicide
Ethnic, Religious, Gender, and Sexual Orientation Perspectives

Cultural Diversity
and Suicide
*Ethnic, Religious, Gender,
and Sexual Orientation Perspectives*

THE HAWORTH PRESS
Haworth Series in Clinical Psychotherapy

Terry S. Trepper, PhD
Editor

College Students in Distress: A Resource Guide for Faculty, Staff, and Campus Community by Bruce S. Sharkin

Cultural Diversity and Suicide: Ethnic, Religious, Gender, and Sexual Orientation Perspectives by Mark M. Leach

Titles of Related Interest:

Alcoholism/Chemical Dependency and the College Student edited by Timothy M. Rivinus

Case Book of Brief Psychotherapy with College Students edited by Stewart E. Cooper, James Archer Jr., and Leighton C. Whitaker

Addressing Homophobia and Heterosexism on College Campuses edited by Elizabeth P. Cramer

Evidence-Based Psychotherapy Practice in College Mental Health edited by Stewart E. Cooper

Helping Students Adapt to Graduate School: Making the Grade by Earle Silber

College Student Suicide edited by Leighton C. Whitaker and Richard E. Slimak

Parental Concerns in College Student Mental Health by Leighton C. Whitaker

Stress in College Athletics: Causes, Consequences, Coping edited by Deborah A. Yow, James H. Humphrey, and William W. Bowden

Cultural Diversity and Suicide
Ethnic, Religious, Gender, and Sexual Orientation Perspectives

Mark M. Leach, PhD

The Haworth Press
New York • London • Oxford

For more information on this book or to order, visit
http://www.haworthpress.com/store/product.asp?sku=5680

or call 1-800-HAWORTH (800-429-6784) in the United States and Canada
or (607) 722-5857 outside the United States and Canada

or contact orders@HaworthPress.com

Published by

The Haworth Press, Inc., 10 Alice Street, Binghamton, NY 13904-1580.

PUBLISHER'S NOTE
The development, preparation, and publication of this work has been undertaken with great care. However, the Publisher, employees, editors, and agents of The Haworth Press are not responsible for any errors contained herein or for consequences that may ensue from use of materials or information contained in this work. The Haworth Press is committed to the dissemination of ideas and information according to the highest standards of intellectual freedom and the free exchange of ideas. Statements made and opinions expressed in this publication do not necessarily reflect the views of the Publisher, Directors, management, or staff of The Haworth Press, Inc., or an endorsement by them.

Identities and circumstances of individuals discussed in this book have been changed to protect confidentiality.

Cover design by Kerry E. Mack.

Library of Congress Cataloging-in-Publication Data

Leach, Mark M.
    Cultural diversity and suicide : ethnic, religious, gender, and sexual orientation perspectives / Mark M. Leach.
        p. cm.
    Includes bibliographical references and index.
    ISBN-13: 978-0-7890-3018-4 (case-13 : alk. paper)
    ISBN-10: 0-7890-3018-7 (case-10 : alk. paper)
    ISBN-13: 978-0-7890-3019-1 (soft-13 : alk. paper)
    ISBN-10: 0-7890-3019-5 (soft-10 : alk. paper)
    1. Suicide—United States—Cross-cultural studies. 2. Suicidal behavior—United States—Cross-cultural studies. 3. Suicide—Psychological aspects. I. Title.

HV6548.U5L422 2006
362.2808'0973—dc22

                                                                    2006016837

CONTENTS

Preface

This book is intended for clinicians and researchers who want to increase their consideration of cultural issues when working with or researching suicidal clients. It is not intended as a "what to do" reference when a client of any cultural background is sitting in your office and is clearly lethally suicidal. At that point commonly accepted suicide assessment and care procedures must be primary in order to maintain the safety of the client. There are standards of care that all clinicians should follow, regardless of the cultural background of the client (see Bongar, Berman, Maris, Sliverman, & Harris, 1998). However, culture can be considered when clients are not actively suicidal and may be considering suicide, whether recently or in the past. If a counselor is assessing for lethality, then culture becomes important because cultural and subcultural groups differ on their perturbation, or acceptance of suicide as an option. If a counselor is considering suicide risk factors, then asking about a variety of cultural issues may help in the decision-making and treatment-planning process. Understanding cultural nuances can assist with typical suicide assessment procedures to offer greater breadth and depth to the evaluation, thus assisting clinicians with their decision-making processes and interventions. This book presumes that the reader has an existing understanding of traditional suicide assessments. However, in the first chapter, there is an overview of traditional risk factors and a brief assessment model, just to refresh your memory. There are a multitude of assessment models already in the literature, and the interested reader should consult the literature for an overview (e.g., see Jacobs, 1999; Maris, 2001; Maris, Berman, & Silverman, 2000; Sommers-Flanagan & Sommers-Flanagan, 2002; White, 1999).

It is well-known that the number of persons of color will continue to increase in the United States and cultural influences, broadly defined, contribute significantly to a multitude of psychological issues. Suicide is no exception. In many ways clinicians already consider

Cultural Diversity and Suicide
© 2006 by The Haworth Press, Inc. All rights reserved.
doi:10.1300/5680_a

cultural influences when conducting suicide assessments, whether they are intentional or not. For example, clinicians understand that gender issues differ for persons who complete and do not complete suicide, that methods differ, and ideation may differ. Gender is a cultural variable because of its sociopolitical ramifications. What are often missing from other texts are issues such as the influence of gender identity on suicide. Many clinicians also understand that gay adolescents may be at greater risk than straight adolescents, but do not have access to studies highlighting possible reasons for these differences. This book summarizes some of the empirical and nonempirical literature on cultural issues in suicide, and speculates on areas that clinicians may wish to consider in their assessments and treatments. The reason for the speculation is that the empirical literature on culture and suicide, beyond fairly broad strokes, is limited overall when considering the total suicide literature. Most of what we know about suicide is derived from a dominant-culture perspective. Although some of this literature applies to many cultures, there are nuances and cultural variables that may need increased attention. For example, whereas numerous studies have discussed racial differences, very few studies have examined within-group variables such as racial identity and acculturation. Fortunately, the profession of counseling and psychology and the field of suicidology are moving toward increasing cultural diversity as an important factor.

We derive personal meaning through culture, because our cultures, broadly defined, help us determine who we turn to in times of stress, how we express ourselves emotionally, how our religious and spiritual faith influence our views of the afterlife, whether our level of acculturation allows us to seek out counseling, whether our level of racial identity helps us identify with similar people, and whether we fit into the surrounding cultures and subcultures. It is not these variables by themselves that *cause* suicide but they may contribute to suicide. For example, one study found that acculturative stress may account for a significant portion of increased suicide ideology within the Hispanic American community, but only in conjunction with other factors such as depression, self-worth, and gender (Rasmussen, Negy, Carlson, & Burns, 1997). Therefore, acculturative stress does not "cause" suicide (no one particular factor does) but does seem to increase suicide risk above and beyond depression, self-worth, and gender. Acculturative stress may then become a factor that counselors should consider with some of their clients.

Cultural issues can act as buffers to increased suicide risk. A client recently reported that she had seriously considered suicide "but would never do it because I'm Catholic." Religion and spirituality are cultural issues and should be weighed in a suicide assessment. My personal experience indicates that when a client has an intrinsic religious orientation ("I have a strong faith in God"), he or she is less likely to be placed at risk than if he or she has an extrinsic orientation (e.g., "I go to church and pray sometimes"). My experience is not better or worse than any other counselor and readers may not find the religious orientation statement to be accurate with some of their clients, but these are merely considerations. Recently, Greening and Stoppelbein (2002) found that intrinsic religious orientation, often correlated with religious orthodoxy, was related to decreased suicide beliefs of African American and European American adolescents. However, there is still little empirical data on the influence of religious motivations on suicide risk. The reader should also keep in mind that while I periodically offer opinions and clinical questions that I have utilized at times, they are simply opinions and may not be optimal for the client sitting in front of him or her. Counselors are advised to use their best judgment regarding cultural questions for clients based on their particular needs.

We should begin to increase our understanding of cultural variables in which clinicians can assist, such as cultural and social isolation and comfort with sexual orientation, as much as variables that we cannot change, such as age influences. Within cultural groups, little research is being conducted examining issues such as status within a cultural community, and whether the extent of risk factors (e.g., job loss, divorce) typically increasing suicide rates differs slightly based on cultural groups. Having taught, researched, and studied cultural influences on a variety of psychological and social variables for years, I will say that there is a lot of overlap among cultural groups. Therefore, hopelessness leading to suicide may manifest itself similarly regardless of culture. However, the nuances of culture need to be examined further with regard to issues such as how depression, a correlate of hopelessness, is viewed within specific cultures, how families respond to a clinically depressed member, cultural views of medication, and whether a hopeless and suicidal client will arrive for therapy simply because of a mistrust of the ethnically dissimilar therapist. The subtexts underlying each culture make them truly rich, yet are often overlooked in suicide assessment considerations. I consider culture a "background variable" from which decisions are made, and it can be considered in practically all contexts. The degree to which each counselor views culture as important to the client sitting in front of him or her will differ, but having the knowledge base is critical.

This book is delineated into chapters based on ethnic groups, but it highlights a multitude of within-group differences. Discussing a group of people from an ethnic categorical perspective is not optimal and cannot adequately capture the depth of personal experiences, but this was accomplished for two reasons. The first reason is that it offers a framework from which to study within-group variables. Many of the subheadings (e.g., gay/lesbian/bisexual/transgender issues, age, religion, prevention) could just as easily been introduced as major chapter headings, with ethnic information embedded in each of these chapters. This format was considered and eventually found to be extremely repetitive due to overlap among the ethnic groups. Second, we are constrained by our language. It is impossible, or at least overly repetitive and confusing, to consistently give caveats when writing the chapters. For example, most readers would find the following very confusing: "Asian American gay males from eighteen to twenty-four who live in New York, lack a religious background, and drink excessively are more likely to complete suicide than European American heterosexual males in the West who . . . ." I hope the reader can appreciate the book structure dilemma and understand that, while not optimal, the intent was to focus on the within-ethnic- group issues instead of offering ethnic generalizations.

The focus of this text is twofold. First, clinicians can begin to understand the role that culture plays in suicide assessments, regardless of whether someone is eventually considered high or low risk. This book is not intended to be a comprehensive review of all aspects of suicidology. To do so would be futile, as the suicide literature is massive. For example, I do not present the vast literature on psychopathology and suicide, specialty populations such as suicide in the justice system, or even all of the literature on prevention and intervention. Overviews are given to aid the reader with his or her own counseling, suicide assessments, and interventions, but to delve further into each of these and other sections would make this book unmanageable. Readers interested in greater depth regarding these topics can consult one of the multitude of texts and articles referenced in this book, or others that are deemed appropriate. This book is intended to simply assist the reader in adding cultural dimensions to their evaluations and treatments. I begin with the European American chapter because of the amount of research and clinical literature available and because European Americans have the greatest number of suicide deaths per year. The majority of information available about suicide in the United States has either focused on European Americans or discusses general variables that contribute to suicide (e.g., psychopathology, substance abuse). The European American chapter offers a framework from which to discuss the nuances and differences embedded within the other chapters.

Second, it is hoped that suicide researchers will begin to more fully consider cultural variables in their methodologies to determine the importance and strength of these factors. Much of this book is derived from empirically based writings. However, cultural variables such as ethnicity, religion, sexual orientation, gender, and age have not received the empirical attention necessary to fully understand the role of culture in the United States on suicidal ideation, attempts, and completions. Research into the cultural complexities of suicide is in its infancy, and researchers will find a wealth of research ideas embedded in the text. Adding culture as a component in all suicide research will yield fruitful results regarding the influence of culture on a range of suicidal ideations, attempts, and completed behaviors.

Chapter 1 presents an overview of how culture affects suicide, a brief history of suicide, and terms used throughout the book that the reader needs to become familiar with. These sections are followed by an overview of typical risk factors associated with suicide, including some cultural factors, a brief model of suicide assessment, and an overview of the necessity of this type of book. This chapter is designed to help the reader refresh his or her memory about various suicide areas, and to offer some interesting information, some of which may be new, and a framework from which to consider the following chapters.

Chapter 2 offers an overview of cultural variables often found in the literature, primarily from a European American perspective. As expected, given the number of European Americans in the United States and historical research foci emphasizing dominant culture philosophies, the majority of known empirical research includes the dominant group. This chapter is placed first for no reason other than the fact that the sheer amount of research conducted with this group helps frame the rest of the chapters. For example, most of what we know about gay/lesbian/bisexual/transgender (GLBT), age, gender, and religious issues associated with suicide are derived from studies of European Americans. There is nothing inherently wrong with this and many of the issues found within this ethnic group are consistent with issues found within other ethnic groups. Cultural issues in subsequent chapters will be compared in relation to this chapter, such as Christian European American influences on suicide (Chapter 2) versus Christian African American perspectives on suicide (Chapter 3), which we know less comprehensively. This chapter merely offers the foundation from which we can compare other groups, simply because of historical research emphases. The second chapter captures many of the within-group variables typically seen in both the suicide and multicultural literatures. It begins with numbers, followed by factors such as gender, age, religious groups, and GLBT issues. This section is followed by an overview of the traditional suicide prevention literature and traditional counseling approaches to suicide.

Chapter 3 offers an overview of cultural variables surrounding African Americans and their relationship to suicide with the European American studies. A growing literature has discussed buffers to suicide, especially with regard to the church and community. African American women complete suicide at a much lower rate than European American women and men (and most other ethnic groups), leading researchers to examine reasons for the low rate. Islam is included in this chapter because 90 percent of converts to Islam in the United States are African Americans. Others issues such as GLBT suicide and prevention efforts are included.

Chapter 4 examines the Asian American culture. Included in this chapter is information regarding death rituals and practices. The reason this literature is included is for the reader to gain an understanding of other norms and issues to be considered with the survivors should a suicide occur. An introduction into various spiritual philosophies such as Buddhism and Hinduism is included. In addition, this chapter includes a variety of within-group information, including suicide among Chinese Americans, Japanese Americans, Vietnamese Americans, Filipino Americans, Korean Americans, and Cambodian

Americans. Cultural nuances related to these within-groups will be presented, along with their relationship to suicide.

Chapter 5 presents Hispanic Americans and includes the roles of acculturation, suicide buffers, and cultural beliefs. The strength of Catholicism within the community is highlighted, along with unique cultural GLBT issues and prevention efforts. Where possible, ethnic groups such as Mexican Americans and Puerto Rican Americans are presented, though the overwhelming amount of research includes the category "Hispanic." Thus, the majority of information presented will focus on the Hispanic community.

Chapter 6 includes Native Americans, beginning with an overview of the very large diversity within the Native American culture. Adolescents account for the highest suicide rates among this group, and I focus on adolescents primarily in this chapter. Acculturation, the role of alcohol, tribal affiliation, and socioeconomic issues are presented. Spirituality is also included, along with existing prevention programs that have been implemented with Native American youths and adolescents.

I hope that the reader will begin to consider, or add to existing knowledge, the influence of culture on suicide. I believe that most readers and clinicians already include cultural knowledge while conducting suicide assessments, and perhaps this book will merely add to this knowledge. For others though, perhaps, some information presented in this book will infuse an interest which will allow them to incorporate a wide range of cultural considerations into their future assessments and treatment. I hope you enjoy the book.

ABOUT THE AUTHOR

Mark M. Leach, PhD, is Associate Professor in the Department of Psychology and Training Director of the Counseling Psychology Program at The University of Southern Mississippi. He also conducts evaluations and consults with a local mental health center. Dr. Leach has published in prominent journals such as the *Journal of Multicultural Counseling and Development* and *The Counseling Psychologist,* and has served on the editorial boards of these and other journals. He was a visiting scholar and adjunct instructor at the University if KwaZulu-Natal in Pietermaritzburg, South Africa, and an International Associate of the Pietermaritzburg Suicidology Project. Dr. Leach also worked in Newfoundland, Canada, and has taught courses in Mexico and Jamaica through the university's International Studies Program. He is a member of the American Psychological Association, Divisions 17 (Society of Counseling Psychology), 36 (Psychology of Religion), 45 (Society for the Psychological Study of Ethnic Minority Issues), and 52 (International Psychology). He serves on the Executive Committee of Division 16 (Counseling Psychology) of the International Association of Applied Psychology. Dr. Leach teaches courses in multicultural issues, individual and group practicum, and supervision, and his research interests include diversity issues such as racial consciousness and religious/spiritual issues in counseling, international ethics, forgiveness, and suicide.

Acknowledgments

A number of people have inspired and supported me throughout the writing of this book, most of whom did so unbeknownst to them. First, I would like to thank the multiculturalists over the years who exposed me to new ideologies, and taught me to constantly consider culture and broader contextual variables in all areas of research and practice. They also taught me that, like social movements, new ideas beget resistance, and that one can initiate new areas of research and teach topics initially unpopular among many others.

Second, I would like to thank the folks at The Haworth Press who were friendly, professional, and conscientious. Particular thanks go to Rebecca Browne, Kim Green, Peg Marr, Tracy Sayles, and Jason Wint. They made the process tremendously easy, and I recommend others to work with them and The Haworth Press.

Finally, I would like to thank my wife, Dawn, who edited the chapters and kept me balanced and focused when the book project became stressful and took unexpected turns. My life is clearly better with her in it.

Chapter 1

Introduction

Why not? I'm destined to go to Hell anyway.

Twenty-three-year-old European American Christian gay man
when asked how suicide became an option for him

I remember most of my actively suicidal clients and I am sure that most counselors do. Working with suicidal clients is considered to be one of the most stressful components of the job of most counselors, given the emotional toll involved with the counselor, client, and family. Of the therapists involved in direct client care, 20 to 30 percent will experience a client's suicide at some point during their career (Bongar, 2002; Greaney, 1995), whereas the number for psychiatrists increases to one-in-two (Chemtob, Hamada, Bauer, Kinney, & Torigoe, 1988). These clients are particularly taxing for most counselors-in-training, especially for early developmental level counselors and those who have not had significant experience with suicidal clients. In addition, graduate programs incorporating comprehensive and systematic suicide training are almost nonexistent (Westefeld et al., 2000). I teach graduate-level practical courses and conduct evaluations for a mental health center, and suicidal clients throw counselors-in-training into significant anxiety-filled emotional states. The level of responsibility for these clients and initial naïveté about what counseling entails often drives counselors to pursue other professional interests. The relationship between counselors-in-training and suicide becomes particularly difficult when considering that suicide, although rare nationally, is not rare for professional helpers (Bongar, 2002). In fact, approximately one in seven psychologists-in-training will experience a client who ultimately completes suicide (Brown, 1987).

Cultural Diversity and Suicide
© 2006 by The Haworth Press, Inc. All rights reserved.
doi:10.1300/5680_01

Suicide is complex and multifaceted, with few answers as to how suicidal individuals become so, and why some people complete suicide whereas others with similar levels of depression, diagnostic "severity," or alcohol intake do not. Suicide is a relatively rare event when considering actual numbers nationally, but when it does occur the impact can leave scars across family members and friends for years. For example, a few years ago an educated, forty-three-year-old European American male arrived at my office in a hospital, sat down, and immediately began to discuss how his brother-in-law drove to a lake a month prior and proceeded to use a gun to kill himself. My client felt responsible because "I should have seen it coming." His relationship with his wife diminished due to his depression and consequent level of responsibility, and his work became no longer enjoyable. Through counseling we discussed choices and responsibility and his lingering dysphoria until he could begin to separate his brother-in-law from himself.

HOW DOES CULTURE AFFECT SUICIDE?

Predicting suicide has always been a bane to clinicians, as it is impossible to be completely accurate and prevent all clients from completing suicide. However, researchers and clinicians obtain a better understanding of the factors that contribute to a completed suicide by studying three approaches to the assessment of suicide. First, sociodemographic variables are assessed to determine risk factors, such as age and gender. Many of these are outlined in this chapter. Second, clinical signs are assessed; these include previous attempts, social support deficits, and recent negative events such as job loss or spousal death. Third, psychological tests have been widely used to predict suicide, but as yet the results have been insufficient (Firestone, 1997). Suicide, regardless of culture, is probably best predicted by a conglomeration of biological, psychological, cognitive, and sociocultural factors. We know a fair bit about the psychological and cognitive factors, have an increased understanding of biological factors, and have learned some information about sociocultural (often demographic) factors.

Unfortunately, what we know about culture *as an important variable that influences suicide* is modest. The empirical literature on cultural influences on suicide is sparse at best, but we can translate areas within the broad cultural diversity literature into the suicide assessment and treatment literature. Culture by itself does not cause suicide. Nothing by itself causes suicide. It is the influence of culture in addition to other psychological, social, and biological issues that helps clinicians gain a more robust understanding of suicide. Many present studies include ethnicity, gender, or religion as a cultural variable, but results gleaned from several of these studies present broad strokes at best. Knowing that African American men are more likely than African American women to use lethal methods to complete suicide is important cultural information, but it is general. What other African American cultural influences play a role in buffering or guiding the decision to kill oneself? What factors are embedded in African American culture, particularly for women, that contribute to making it unlikely they will complete suicide? Some studies have suggested no significant ethnic differences between, for example, African American suicide attempters and nonattempters and European American samples, but I am more interested in understanding and presenting the subjective and qualitative differences among the ethnic groups. The subjectivity of causes, buffers, and reasons for suicidal behavior are in need of further study and increased clinical judgment. Berman (1991) indicated that suicide risk is very subjective and we must understand the client's experiences of stress, which stress factors are primarily overlooked by researchers and clinicians, and the personal meaning clients give to situations that may lead to suicide. Understanding individual and group meanings is difficult for both the clinician and the client. The clinician never fully understands what the client is thinking and feeling, and clients have different levels of what can be considered a "breaking point," which, as Shneidman (1999) argues, is lethality.

It is through culture that we begin to understand personal meaning, because culture offers the lens through which suicide factors such as coping styles, buffers, emotional expression, family structures, and identity can be viewed. The majority of studies currently published and the majority of clinicians interviewed over the years have included culture superficially with phrases such as "I've had a number of Hispanic clients . . ." or "He's a white male in his 20s . . ." Little is understood about the influence of within-group variables, such as acculturation, racial identity, extrinsic religiosity, gay identity development, and gender identity, on suicide. As the reader progresses through this book I am convinced that multiple research ideas will be conceived, and I have offered a few periodically in areas where virtually no research has been conducted. Clinicians will be able to see how the influence of culture may impact a present client, and direct sessions toward some of the culturally specific information found in this text. Researchers and clinicians who have examined some of these cultural factors in greater depth will be presented in this book.

Lester (1997a, 1997b) found that culture influences suicidal behavior and that we should focus on increasing our understanding of variables that are subject to change, such as social isolation, rather than those we cannot modify (e.g., age, sex). To extend his argument, we should focus on factors considered within the realm of cultural and social diversity, such as the status and respect associated with age within various cultural groups, the role of acculturative stress, racial identity instead of simply race, and gender roles instead of simply gender. Much of what we know about suicide is based on the dominant (European American) culture, which fails to highlight unique culture-specific experiences. What unique features of being European American add to the other typical risk factors that augment suicide in this country, especially since European Americans account for over 85 percent of completed suicides yearly? However, credit must also be given to the multitude of researchers and clinicians conducting studies on a variety of cultural variables. A growing number of cultural studies are being published, though the suicide and culture field is still in its infancy. The field appears to have matured sufficiently to the point of increasing its focus on examining a number of within-group variables, many of which will be presented in this book.

For example, what unique cultural factors contribute to Hispanic adolescent females engaging in nonfatal suicidal behaviors at a rate twice that of other ethnic adolescent groups? We know that many adolescents attempt suicide regardless of ethnicity and can easily say that failed interpersonal relationships, for example, contribute to these rates. However, we also know that, among other variables, the higher nonfatal rates among adolescent Latinas may be due to traditional gender role factors within Hispanic families (Kaplan, Turner, Romano, & Gonzalez-Ramos, 2000). Here, gender roles as a result of acculturation differences between parents and children become important within-group cultural variables in need of greater study. We also understand that middle-class adolescent Latinas are less likely to attempt suicide than those having backgrounds of lower socioeconomic status (SES), attesting indirectly to the role of economic viability as a cultural variable (often through parental education and subsequent child-rearing beliefs; Ng, 1996). Culture is a background variable that has the potential to influence and exacerbate suicide when conjoined with other well-established variables (e.g., depression, drug use, poor self-concept, mania, insufficient coping skills). For instance, what is the role of religion in the expression of depression and drug use among ethnic groups, and how do acculturation, generation in country, and language differences influence self-concept and coping, all of which impact suicide?

Clinicians generally accept the fact that religion, for example, may be an important variable to consider when assessing for suicide risk. The question is not whether religion is an influential variable, but of further refinement of our understanding of the segments of religion, its relationship to ethnic and cultural groups, and its relationship to suicide acceptability, which can help clinicians determine whether the person sitting in front of them is at significant suicide risk. As has been repeated many times, it is not whether someone is religious but *how* someone is religious (Spilka, Hood, Hunsberger, & Gorsuch, 2003). Similarly, knowing suicide rates among ethnic groups is important, but greater understanding of the role of acculturation within the Hispanic, Native American, and Asian communities and its relationship to suicide would be beneficial. Researchers have begun to examine the effects of acculturation on suicide ideation and nonfatal and fatal behaviors. It is hoped that they will continue to investigate the role of acculturation and identity on suicide so that clinicians can include acculturation into their decision-making assessment and treatment processes.

African Americans complete suicides at a rate lower than European Americans, but we know virtually nothing about the role of racial identity, or how people view themselves as racial beings, with regard to suicide risk. In fact, the only three studies assessing the influence of black racial identity on suicide found that increased black racial consciousness resulted in fewer completed suicides (Kaslow et al., 2004; Sanyika, 1995; Wells, 1995). Thus, the more developed the racial identity the less likely it is that one may complete suicide. We can only speculate on reasons why racial identity influences suicide because the research literature is very small. However, the consideration of racial identity during suicide risk evaluations leads to more robust assessments.

One of the earliest approaches to the study of suicide risk was to examine sociodemographic variables. Although clinicians should be considering these variables, many texts on suicide present only cursory glances at cultural issues embedded within them. For example, several texts have a section titled "Multicultural Issues in Suicide," which includes suicide rates by ethnic group, perhaps broken down by gender and age. However, in order to determine cultural factors that contribute to the rates readers must undertake rather extensive literature searches. It is the within-group variability that is difficult to piece together. This within-group variability is the unique feature of this book. My intention in writing this book was to organize much of the dispersed literature into some categorical form so that the reader can easily access cultural information related to suicide. Hopefully, I have gathered much of the pertinent literature into one book that highlights the cultural factors embedded with the major ethnic groups in the United States. Clinicians can not only examine the suicide rates of each ethnic group, but can also begin to consider nuances embedded within each ethnic group that may assist in determining whether the client sitting in front of them is at high suicide risk.

A BRIEF HISTORY OF SUICIDE

Recorded history has documented a multitude of suicides, with some of the most famous examples stemming from the Bible, the arts, and other literature. Among the notable biblical references is Saul, who asked his swordbearer to kill him but then fell on his own sword to avert capture by the Philistines. Some scholars also argue that the story of Samson is a story of suicide, in that after years of torment by the Philistines he destroys the city and kills himself in the process. Later, Shakespeare writes that Lady Macbeth killed herself due to her insanity, and in *Romeo and Juliet* the main characters each take their own lives after believing the other has died.

Clemons (1990a, 1990b) wrote a wonderful synopsis of the history of suicide, which will be condensed here. In the fourth to fifth century, the Catholic Church deemed suicide to be sinful, because people who attempted or completed suicide were considered demon possessed. For the next few hundred years it was not unusual for people who had completed suicide to be buried in nonconsecrated ground. Today some religious groups still choose to bury such individuals in unsanctified ground or on the outer edges of the cemetery or outside the grounds completely. The suicide-as-sin idea still resonates among many religious faiths because of the belief that the suicidal person chooses death, a decision resting only with God. Therefore, the suicidal individual is blaspheming God, the greatest Old Testament sin, and will spend eternity in hell. The Catholic Church has historically believed that the sixth commandment of "Thou shall not kill" applies to killing oneself, and many other religious groups have maintained this belief.

In the sixth century, three Church councils devised distinctive punishments toward not only the suicidal individual but also toward the families of those who completed the act. Because suicide was considered sinful, suicides' families were ostracized and persecuted for their family members' sins. Family members could not inherit estates, often relegating the family to a low economic standing. Although some readers may think of this policy as antiquated, many of today's insurance companies do not pay benefits to the family of a person who completes suicide—an idea inherited from deep historical cultural roots.

In the eighteenth century, Merian, a French physician, was the first to specifically adopt the notion that nonfatal and fatal suicides resulted from a mental disorder. By the late nineteenth century, through Durkheim's famous works (1897/1951), suicide came to be known as a result of an individual not adapting well to his or her society. It is through these papers that we begin to see glimpses of the cultural aspects of suicide, as many people who have engaged in self-destructive behaviors felt marginalized from their family and the larger society. Given the diversity of ethnic groups in the United States, most culture researchers now deem the acculturation process to be a significant factor that impacts individual stress levels, with feelings of marginalization associated with higher stress and potentially higher suicide rates.

In the early twentieth century, Freud hypothesized that suicide was a result of unresolved intrapsychic struggles between the id, ego, and superego, and Leenaars (1999) argued that suicide has both intrapsychic (e.g., cognitive constriction, inability to adjust) and interpersonal dynamics (e.g., rejection–aggression, identification–egression). Recently, work in neuropsychology has suggested that there are biological reasons for suicide, with much of the research focusing on a deficiency in serotonin associated with depression. In addition, evidence from family studies suggests that suicide tends to be more prevalent in some families, though whether it is biologically based or viewed as more acceptable in some families than others has not been fully determined. As the reader can surmise from the information presented earlier, perspectives on suicide are varied and multiple. Many of the theories include cultural components and it is on the cultural influences on suicide that this book focuses.

DEFINITIONS OF SUICIDE

Suicide is defined as an *intentional,* self-inflicted act that results in death. Suicidal behaviors are actions by which an individual places himself or herself in harm's way, and they may lead to self-destruction (Silverman & Maris, 1995). For example, driving too fast, drinking too much, and cutting one's wrists depict self-destructive behaviors, the first two examples being more unconscious than the latter. It is extremely difficult to adequately define suicide because of the difficulty in defining intent. Clinicians are very aware of clients who self-mutilate or are sensation seeking (Peterson & Bongar, 1989), probably without fully intending to die, though one can never be certain. One of the major research areas within the field of suicidology is determining the internal factors that may lead to suicide. What do people believe about suicide? What are their feelings prior to attempting suicide? Is there a neurochemical component to suicide? I will emphasize questions such as the following: Is suicide culturally acceptable? What prevents people from attempting or completing suicide? How do suicidal behaviors change depending on particular cultural groups? How does culture influence suicide completions, attempts, and behaviors? In order to give the reader an introduction or a refresher to the study of suicide, it may help to define terms and discuss the major risk factors.

Fatal Suicide

In the United States suicide is the eleventh leading cause of death, but among ten- to twenty-four-year-olds it is the third (Krug, Dahlberg, Mercy, Zwi, & Lozano, 2002). Suicides among adolescents and young adults account for more deaths than from eight other leading causes of death combined, including heath disease, cancer, and pneumonia. Overall, there are approximately 30,000 completed suicides annually in the United States, a number greater than the number of homicides. In fact, there are about three suicides for every two homicides nationally. The number of fatal suicides has stayed fairly consistent for years. Completed suicide is actually a fairly rare event when considering the total number of people within the general population, occurring in about 11 per 100,000 people (retrieved January 6, 2004, from http://www.mentalhealth.samhsa.gov/suicideprevention/costtonation.asp). Fatal suicides are differentiated from nonfatal suicides in that the person "completes" suicide. The term "completed suicide" instead of "committed suicide" has been used among suicidologists for a number of years due to several philosophical reasons, including the belief that committing suicide implies a form of criminal behavior. For example, one commits a felony or adultery, and although suicide can still be considered a legal issue in many states and locales, suicidologists are attempting to decrease its legal focus and increase public awareness of suicide as a mental health issue.

The term completed suicide has also recently been questioned on a number of philosophical grounds. The main issue is that "suicide" implies intent, and it is very difficult to establish individual intent in many cases, especially since the person is dead (the interested reader should consult Alston & Anderson, 1995, and Simonds, McMahon, & Armstrong, 1991, for more detailed explanations). This book will use the terms "fatal" and "completed" with regard to a suicide resulting in death that is presumed to have been intentional and self-inflicted.

Nonfatal Suicide

The number of people who engage in nonfatal suicides ("attempts") is much higher than people who complete suicide, with the former at approximately a 3 percent lifetime prevalence rate (Kral & Sakinofsky, 1994). There is a fine line distinguishing what is considered an intentional suicide attempt versus a client who unintentionally puts himself or herself in harm's way. Either way, such behaviors should be treated as a serious threat to self, and these clients are often considered to be difficult for many clinicians. Nonfatal suicide is self-destructive behavior that does not lead to death. The terms "nonfatal," "noncompleted," and "attempted" will be used interchangeably in this book because many clinicians are familiar with the term attempted, and it frequently becomes cumbersome to write using only one consistent term. Again, philosophical discussions among suicidologists regarding terminology are common, but I believe that the reader will understand the intent of the terms embedded within each chapter. Not all clients who physically hurt themselves want to die, as they may be seeking attention. In addition, they may not harm themselves severely enough to result in death. Research indicates that 80 percent of fatal suicides are by men whereas most nonfatal suicides are by women (Moscicki, 1995). In fact, women are more likely to attempt suicide than men regardless of ethnicity (Andrews & Lewinsohn, 1992; Garrison, McKeown, Valois, & Vincent, 1993), and this gender difference is almost a universal phenomenon.

Suicide completers may be qualitatively different from noncompleters, and show dissimilarities when compared with people who engage in suicide ideation without subsequent attempts. Canetto and Lester (1995a, 1995b) underscored some of the important differences among the groups, including ethnicity, preexisting factors, gender, and age. This text includes other factors, such as religious variables and gay/lesbian/bisexual/transgender issues, and attempts to highlight within-group differences between fatal and nonfatal suicides when possible. Shneidman (1991) argued that the differences between fatal and nonfatal suicides tend to lie within the subjectivity of perturbation (amount of "psychache," see the section Typical Risk Factors Usually Associated with Suicide) and lethality, making the job of the clinician difficult. The suicide literature has matured, differentiating repeat noncompleters from single-episode noncompleters (Boergers & Spirito, 2003; Vajda & Steinbeck, 2000). In general, repeat noncompleters are much more likely than single-episode noncompleters to possess more chronic symptoms, including greater impulsivity, greater likelihood of familial substance abuse, greater self-harm at younger ages, poorer coping skills, increased aggressiveness, and greater inpatient treatment histories (Kral & Sakinofsky, 1994; Kurz et al., 1987).

Self-Destructive Behavior

Persons who engage in risky behaviors may be considered by some clinicians to be engaging in suicidal behaviors, though the argument could be made that all humans engage in self-destructive behaviors periodically. Life-threatening behaviors are placed on a continuum ranging from thinking about suicide, to taking a significant behavioral risk, to completing suicide. For example, if one dodges oncoming traffic while crossing a busy street, it may be considered engaging in self-destructive behavior by some people. Riding in a vehicle without using a safety belt can be considered a self- destructive act. Engaging in sky-diving as a hobby is another example. However, the degree to which these behaviors are suicidal is debatable. Slashing one's wrists is self-destructive and quite possibly suicidal, though clinicians are well aware that some clients are more likely to engage in this behavior than others and may or may not be "serious" in their attempts. In this book self-destructive behaviors will be defined as those by which individuals place themselves in potentially harmful activities without consciously believing or intending the event to be a form of suicide.

TYPICAL RISK FACTORS USUALLY ASSOCIATED WITH SUICIDE

Looking for specific risk factors in the suicide literature becomes a daunting task, mainly because there is a plethora of risk factors reported that may play a role in suicide ideation and behaviors. For example, Slaby (1994) listed twenty-nine factors that contribute to suicide, including age, generation in country, intelligence, learning disorders, marital status, psychiatric disorders, stressful life events, substance abuse, and unemployment. No clinician or mathematical algorithm can accurately predict suicide in all cases. A fundamental problem encountered by every counselor is that for every suicide risk factor acknowledged, there are numerous people who experience the same traits or behaviors but do not kill themselves.

Many of the often-discussed risk factors are described here (impulsivity, substance abuse, psychopathology), and numerous other factors are listed in other writings. The critical piece for clinicians to bear in mind is that independent, individual suicide factors are not exceptionally meaningful, but the accumulation of factors increases the chances of suicidal behavior. It is the premise of this book that culture can both shield and augment suicidal behaviors in conjunction with various risk factors depending on the culture and its interpretation by clients.

Perturbation and Lethality

Shneidman (1991) provided a very useful suicide assessment model for clinicians, one that is based on the subjectivity of suicide. In his model, Shneidman indicated the combination of *perturbation* and *lethality* are necessary and sufficient factors when assessing a client's suicide risk. Perturbation does not kill in and of itself, as it is defined as the amount of dread, psychological pain, or hopelessness people experience. It is subjective and involves the client's psychache (Shneidman, 1993). Clinicians must determine how intolerable the perturbation has become, because intolerable perturbation often leads to lethality. Questions to consider might be, "On a scale from one to ten how much pain are you experiencing right now?" and "Has the pain become so bad that you're considering killing yourself?" Of course, not everyone who has significant psychache engages in suicidal behaviors.

Culture affects the degree of perturbation among some clients in that it may either potentially increase or decrease perturbation. For example, many African American clients of lower SES, who I have talked with during counseling sessions, have reported that they do not feel hopeless, despite seemingly overwhelming life stresses, because of their faith in God, a cultural belief that suffering is sometimes a part of life, and their understanding that their ancestors had a much more difficult time in this country than them. To kill themselves negates the suffering and disrespects their ancestors. Though African Americans share several religious beliefs with many European Americans, they tend to possess a stronger religious faith than European Americans on average (Spilka et al., 2003), leading to the hypothesis that both ethnicity and religion are important suicide-inhibitory cultural factors. Some authors (e.g., Gibbs, 1997; Marion & Range, 2003a) discussed the importance of religious beliefs as a cultural buffer dissuading African Americans from engaging in fatal suicide. Conversely, the psychache due to daily contacts of cultural racism and acculturation stresses may lead to increased suicide ideation above and beyond those who do not experience these stressors. Culture as a perturbation factor can both inhibit and exacerbate stress, either independently or as a concomitant factor, potentially leading to lethality.

Shneidman (1993) has argued that clinical factors such as depression (a factor associated with perturbation) do not cause suicide but may be a trigger toward suicide. Most clinicians will find this a rather obvious statement given the fact that the majority of clinically depressed clients are not actively suicidal. As indicated earlier, it is the contention of this book that culture influences perturbation. To be subjectively suicidal though, one needs another critical variable called lethality. Lethality does kill and is defined as the "conscious selection of suicide as a viable option" (Kral & Sakinofsky, 1994, p. 25). Clinicians can rate both concepts on a low–moderate–high scale. In order to help determine the odds of a client completing suicide, both concepts need to be considered. Lethality is also culturally based. For example, a client with a strong religious faith may not consider suicide an option because he or she believes God considers it an unpardonable sin. Or, it is less likely that a client might harm himself or herself if he or she is high in perturbation but low in lethality due to the fact that family responsibility is of utmost importance, and to leave his or her children without a parent would be unfathomable. As another example, ethnic groups differ in the acceptance of suicide. Japanese Americans and Chinese Americans seem to be more accepting of suicide than other Asian American ethnic groups, and Chapter 4 discusses cultural issues surrounding Asian American groups, such as the influences of age and religious beliefs. The degree of lethality has historically become embedded in some ethnic and cultural groups as compared to others.

Unfortunately, perturbation is often fairly easy to assess but lethality can be difficult (Leenaars, 1994). One reason for this difficulty is that once depressed clients decide that suicide is an important option, they often experience cognitive constriction or what is considered dichotomous thinking or tunnel vision (Rose & Abramson, 1992; Shneidman, 1993). Treatments often focus on how to reduce perturbation, as this leads to decreased lethality; however, recent research indicates that the reduction of lethality also decreases perturbation (Kral & Sakinofsky, 1994). Although many of the concepts presented in this text will focus on perturbation, particularly traditional factors listed later, many of the issues presented clearly fall in the lethality category. My argument is that we have overlooked a number of culturally related lethality (and perturbation) factors and should consider these along with many of the factors discussed later. Some cultural factors may increase psychache, such as the relationship of culturally based shame brought onto the family, or decrease lethality due to the fact that suicide is considered "a white thing" (Gibbs, 1997). Treatment approaches that are culturally consistent and reduce lethality on individual or small group levels have been developed. The chapter on Native Americans (Chapter 6) includes a section on a culturally sensitive intervention program for Zuni Pueblo adolescents, and there have been therapeutic successes with discussing racial identity and ethnic community connections among African American youths.

Shneidman (1987, 1989) presented ten common psychological characteristics of completed suicides: common purpose, goal, stimulus, stressor, emotion, cognitive state, perceptual state, action, interpersonal act, and consistency. Recently, Brown, Bongar, and Cleary (2004) reported thirty-five factors that have been associated with suicide risk in older adults; some of these factors are reported later in this chapter. A large amount of research on suicide risk factors has been conducted using European American college students, typically not discussed in cultural parlance, and the extent to which culture influences the common psychological characteristics and other factors listed later remains unknown. I will be the first to mention that many of the factors discussed here are important regardless of ethnicity, religion, gender, and sexual orientation. However, the amount of variance attributed to each factor may vary depending on the client and the specific accumulation of factors, particularly when cultural issues are considered. How some of these factors are culturally manifested influences suicide ideation, acceptability, attempts, and completions. For example, a client exhibits some suicidal ideation and the counselor attempts to determine inhibiting factors. Research indicates that if the client practices the Islamic faith, he or she is very unlikely to complete suicide. Being Muslim does not preclude suicide, of course, but it may reduce the chances of completing suicide and assist the counselor's determination in session. In addition, discussions including Islamic views of suicide may help dissuade clients from attempting, or act as a starting point from which to discuss perturbation. Again, to consider only one or two suicide risk factors is poor practice and possibly puts the client in danger, but the addition or subtraction of significant cultural, social, and intrapsychic factors helps determine risk. It is the aggregate of factors that may help the clinician assess a client's risk level in addition to unique, face-to-face decisions the clinician must make. As another example, the suicide rate among college students is significantly higher than that among the general population. That in itself is good information for the clinician to possess. However, include the fact that the GLBT population may attempt and complete suicide at a rate higher than the heterosexual population and the clinician may have a gay college client at greater risk for suicide, though being gay was not considered in the assessment previously.

Proximal and Distal Factors

None of the factors typically associated with suicide are good predictors by themselves, and the absence of these factors does not guarantee nonrisk (Sommers-Flanagan & Sommers-Flanagan, 2002). The majority of these factors have not changed much since the classic works of Durkheim (1897/1951), yet very few have been seriously considered within a contemporary cultural context. In order to offer a framework to consider risk factors it may be beneficial to think of them in of proximal and distal terms (Moscicki, 1995). Proximal factors are those that often act as precipitants and are connected temporally to the event. For example, a recent loss (job, family member) is considered a proximal event, one that clinicians often point to and consider important when clients have contemplated, attempted, or completed suicide.

Distal risk factors, on the other hand, are those that lay the groundwork and either increase or decrease self-destructive behaviors, sometimes depending on culture. Roy (2003) found that among alcoholics the distal risk factors of childhood trauma, family history of suicide, and impulsivity may increase suicide risk when combined with a proximal factor of depression. Distal factors may include an individual's cultural religious beliefs about suicide or reduced serotonergic activity. It may also include a person's cultural coping styles and susceptibility to stress. Some of these factors are sometimes missed by clinicians, particularly newer clinicians, who are focused on the immediate issues that a client may discuss. For example, many counselors-in-training whom my colleagues and I instruct often become narrowly focused on the client's immediate suicide ideation and miss many distal variables that may help them determine the degree of the client's suicidality. Many clients may eventually indicate they have suicidal thoughts but feel "I'd never do it because I'd go to hell," due to the religiously conservative geographic region of the country in which they live. Proximal and distal factors by themselves are considered necessary but not sufficient to lead people to complete suicide. However, a distal factor may act as a backdrop to the level of individual vulnerability to suicide, while a proximal one may act as a motivator for a decision to kill oneself. Consider the client who has a lifetime of difficulty in handling stress and whose father had completed suicide. He recently lost a good friend to an automobile accident and may lose his job due to corporate downsizing. The client may be at great risk for suicide because of his (distal) coping and stress histories, combined with the recent (proximal) losses of a friend and possibly his job.

Substance Abuse

The research has been clear for years that the risk for suicide increases dramatically for people who abuse alcohol and other substances (Ohberg, Vuori, Ojanpera, & Loennqvist, 1996). This risk is particularly significant if the person also has other risk factors such as being single, depressed, male, and in the upper socioeconomic class. Substance abuse is considered one of the most compelling factors associated with suicide, particularly for males, as it has been closely linked with more frequent attempts, increased suicide ideation, and greater lethality (Sommers-Flanagan & Sommers-Flanagan, 2002). Depending on the definition of suicide, some theorists believe all excessive alcohol and drug use is slow suicidal behavior, particularly when driving or engaging in other risky activities. Substances often act to chemically produce neurological depression, which contributes to suicide, and frequently lead to negative environmental effects (McBee & Rogers, 1997). In addition, they act as a disinhibitor, allowing clients to impulsively consider suicidal behaviors, inhibit problem-solving capabilities, limit hope for the future, and restrict attention to current situations (cognitive constriction) (McBee & Rogers, 1997; Sommers-Flanagan & Sommers-Flanagan, 2002). Support for the disinhibition hypothesis is extracted from research indicating that a significant proportion of homicidal behaviors are committed under the influence of alcohol or drugs.

Research is unclear as to whether previous inhibitions are modified and increase risk under the influence of drugs. For example, if a client believes that suicide is contrary to his or her previously held religious beliefs, does the influence of alcohol disinhibit this factor more than other distal factors? Unfortunately, much more research needs to be conducted. However, it would be in the counselor's best interest to assume that if the client has a history of using substances then the risk for suicidal behaviors increases. If the client is considered impulsive or possesses a family history of suicide or other concomitant suicide factors, then the likelihood of suicide increases even further with the addition of alcohol and drugs. About half of adolescent and young adult suicide completers have substances in their system, usually alcohol, at the time of their death, though other substances such as cocaine are commonly found during autopsies (Garrison et al., 1993; Marzuk & Mann, 1988; Marzuk, Tardiff, & Leon, 1992). A number of studies (e.g., Henriksson, Aro, & Marttunen, 1993; Rich & Runeson, 1992) have found that a large proportion of suicide completers have comorbid diagnoses, that is, either concomitant substance abuse and psychiatric disorders or multiple psychiatric disorders. Clinicians need to fully assess both recent and distant substance use and abuse histories, including a family history of substance use and abuse. Assessing for problem-solving abilities, previous coping strategies, and impulsiveness would also be helpful.

Affective Disorders

As every clinician is aware, affective disorders highly correlate with suicide ideation, attempts, and completions, but will be separated from the section on psychopathology later because of their historical association with suicide. Approximately 15 percent of people with a major mood disorder will complete suicide, a rate exceptionally greater than that among the general population (Kral & Sakinofsky, 1994). Perhaps the best-known predictor of suicide is depression (Coppen, 1994). Ask any clinician or layperson to discuss why an individual completed suicide and they will probably mention depression in the first sentence or two. There is some evidence that the relationship between depression and suicide is universal, and vegetative symptoms (e.g., sleeping and appetite changes) are found to be consistent with depression in practically all countries studied. Other factors frequently associated with depressed suicidal clients are anhedonia, panic attacks, alcohol abuse, and anxiety (Fawcett et al., 1990). Of course, not all people who complete suicide experience the same depressive symptoms, and not all depressed individuals complete suicide.

An extremely dangerous combination—one that cognitive-behavioral therapists emphasize—is a mood disorder in conjunction with cognitive constriction (Shneidman, 1987). Depressed people often become constricted in their thinking, becoming more linear and dichotomous, which narrows the perceived life options available to them. Hence, the lethality increases once constriction occurs, and it is a job of the clinician to expose the client to other options. I recently asked a client what she had to live for and she responded, "Nothing." I then asked her about her young children and she responded, "They'd be better off without me." I asked to project herself into one of her daughter's shoes ten years from now and discuss what her daughter would say about her mother (herself). She had great difficulty doing so because of the constricted thought and we ended the exercise. This information, along with previous information about intent to die, method, and likelihood, helped me determine that she was in significant danger to herself and we began discussing inpatient treatment. She and I determined two of the more important questions when assessing suicide risk, "Is suicide an option?" and "Is it the only option?" (constriction) (Kral & Sakinofsky, 1994). For her the answers were clearly affirmative.

Westefeld and Furr (1987) found that all college students who reported a previous suicide attempt also reported depression. A question that has arisen among suicidologists is "Can someone complete suicide without being depressed?" We will leave the answer up to the reader because it involves the reader's beliefs surrounding definitions of suicide, assisted suicide, rational suicide, martyrdom, and altruism. My belief is that humans can complete suicide without accompanying depression under specific circumstances, such as when suicidal thoughts surround an individual in the final stages of a debilitating, painful disease, or impulsivity grounded more in anger than depression (the relationship of which also depends on one's theoretical leanings). Readers can also consider their views of suicide and depression by taking into account destructive cults, such as the Branch Davidians, Aum

Shinri Kyo, Heaven's Gate, and Jonestown. There are no easy answers, and it is not the intent of this text to argue whether depression is a critical component of suicide. For those readers who work with people in their final life stages with a history of lingering, debilitating disease, the question whether someone can complete suicide without being depressed is one with which they must grapple.

The odds are that the overwhelming majority of a clinician's clients will exhibit some form of depression, and clinicians are generally aware that most clients who present with self-destructive behaviors have either long-standing unipolar or reactive depressive episodes. However, we cannot overlook the fact that many clients in states of mania place themselves at significant self-destructive risk. Whether it is suicidal behavior while in that phase is debatable because manic people generally feel very good by definition and are unlikely to be intending to die. The subsequent depressive episode lends itself to suicidal behaviors. Unfortunately, the bipolar–suicide relationship has not been studied as vigorously as the unipolar-depression–suicide link, yet the risk of self-destruction is high. Bipolar clients are at high risk for self-destruction (Goldring & Fieve, 1984), with rapid-cycle bipolar clients perhaps being at a higher risk than non-rapid-cycle bipolar clients due to greater depressive morbidity (Coryell et al., 2003). A client who I evaluated recently after his being detained in a holding facility clearly showed signs of mania (e.g., rapid speech, loose associations, distractibility) and was found by police walking down the middle of a busy street shouting at the top of his lungs. Whether self-destruction by walking down the street was intentional or not was not immediately determined, or even relevant, yet the client was clearly at risk of becoming severely injured or killed.

Hopelessness and Helplessness

It is rather obvious that not all depressed people engage in nonfatal or fatal suicidal behaviors. Therefore, there must be factors associated with depression that increase the likelihood of suicidal behaviors. Hopelessness and helplessness are two clinical indicators of suicide. In fact, Beck, Brown, and Steer (1989) and Beck, Steer, Kovacs, and Garrison (1985) found hopelessness a better predictor of suicide than depression. Outpatient clients who scored over nine on the Beck Hopelessness Scale (BHS; Beck, Freeman, & Associates, 1990; Beck et al., 1985) were eleven times more likely to kill themselves than clients with scores less than nine. Beck, Steer, Beck, and Newman (1993) found hopelessness, using the BHS, to be a better predictor of suicide ideation than depression using the Beck Depression Inventory.

Helplessness can be defined as believing in a future but not being capable of making change, whereas hopelessness can be defined as believing that the future holds no promise. Helplessness is often manifested through statements such as, "I'd like to die but I won't kill myself because of my kids," or "My family would be mad at me if I did it but I can't change things." Hopelessness is manifested with statements such as, "What's the point [in living]" and "I've always been this way so why not kill myself?" Of course there is overlap in the statements, and clinically I'm not convinced that determining the nuances between the types of statements will benefit counseling. What is important is listening for the intent of the client and the underlying meaning associated with the statements. Clients who see a future are less likely to kill themselves than people who see no hope at all. Clinicians should consider inquiring about the client's life plans, rejecting behaviors, and future options whenever possible (Kral & Sakinofsky, 1994). Although discussed in other chapters of this book, issues related to hopelessness and helplessness are manifested differently depending on cultural factors. For example, some Hispanic Americans have a worldview that includes *fatalismo*, directly translated as a fatalistic perspective. However, fatalismo is more closely tied within a deferring religious belief system and life decisions that are determined by God. Many non-Hispanic clients also adhere to a "helpless" worldview, such as those with very conservative religious beliefs. Many clients have indicated that much of their life is in God's hands and they manifest behaviors consistent with what might be incorrectly considered helplessness. Clients possessing this type of worldview may not be suicidal, though many comments may sound like helplessness due to their adherence to this religious tenet.

It serves clinicians well to discuss hope and hopelessness with clients who engage in self-destructive behaviors. Asking clients to rate their level of hope on a 1 to 10 scale is a popular way of receiving a gross idea about their level of hope and hopelessness. Assessment instruments such as those listed earlier and the short state and trait Hope Scales (Lopez, Snyder, & Pedrotti, 2003; Snyder, 2004) may yield beneficial results for clinicians in their assessment process. Hope instruments have not yet been validated as suicide assessment instruments, but counselors can easily administer the three- to five-minute instruments and discuss individual questions and subsequent responses with the client. Fruitful discussions are likely to evolve and may become a quick, beneficial means of assessing this facet of suicidality.

Previous Attempts

Past behavior is the best predictor of future behavior. The risk of suicide increases dramatically if the person has attempted suicide in the past, and previous suicide attempts are considered one of the primary factors clinicians should consider when evaluating suicide risk. Resnick (1980) found that almost 75 percent of persons who completed suicide had a history of nonfatal suicide in their past. Maris (1981) found suicide attempters more likely than suicide completers to make multiple low-risk attempts, with the latter group making fewer high-risk attempts. In addition, if there is a history of family or friends engaging in either nonfatal or fatal suicides, then the risk increases significantly. Suicidal behaviors often run in families, so an assessment of family history of suicide and the client's views of these suicidal behaviors is important to conduct. Simple questions such as, "Has anyone in your family or any friends attempted or died from suicide?" may help with the assessment process.

Questions regarding clients' previous suicide attempts are considered a common component in all suicide assessments (Rogers, Alexander, & Subich, 1994; Sommers-Flanagan & Sommers-Flanagan, 2002). When conducting involuntary commitment evaluations, I frequently assess people with suicide ideation. One of my "red flags" determining future attempts is a history, through case notes and/or by asking the person directly. I ask the client whether he or she has attempted suicide in the past and attempt to gather this information from case managers or family members. If no previous attempts have been made I probe further by asking about various self-destructive behaviors (e.g., alcohol and drug use/abuse). If previous attempts have been made I ask questions about dates (When was your last attempt? How did you attempt? Is the means still available?). Many clients will report, "Oh, it was years ago," which leads me into other questions such as "What is the likelihood that you would consider it now?" to look for inhibiting or exacerbating factors. Across all ethnic groups women are much more likely to engage in repeated nonfatal suicidal behaviors than men (Kachur, Potter, James, & Powell, 1995).

Psychopathology

Numerous clinical syndromes and disorders have been associated with suicide risk. Some examples are anxiety disorders (Khan, Leventhal, Khan, & Brown, 2002), schizophrenia (De Leo & Spathonis, 2003; Kelly, Shim, Feldman, Yu, & Conley, 2004; Radomsky, Haas, Mann, & Sweeney, 1999), bipolar disorder, and schizoaffective disorder bipolar type (Dalton, Cate-Carter, Mundo, Parikh, & Kennedy, 2003). As would be expected, clients experiencing comorbid schizophrenia and affective disorders are at greatest risk for killing themselves, and either disorder individually can be considered high risk (Resnik, 1980). For example, clients with a combination of psychotic and affective disorders such as schizoaffective disorder and major depressive disorder with psychotic features are often in jeopardy, and approximately 10 to 15 percent of persons with schizophrenia complete suicide whereas between 20 and 50 percent engage in nonfatal suicidal behaviors. Schwartz and Smith (2004) reported that increased knowledge of their illness, fewer years of treatment, and symptom severity increased the risk for suicide. Most clinicians who work with seriously mentally ill individuals can talk about clients who experienced auditory command hallucinations instructing them to kill themselves. One client whom I interviewed recently exhibited repeated visual hallucinations of a deceased family member directing him to join her. Command hallucinations are common among persons with psychotic disorders and should be closely monitored. Many of these clients may be in need of inpatient treatment for medication stabilization. Of course, a major depressive disorder with psychotic features also may place an individual in a high-risk category, particularly if there has been a suicide attempt previously. This is especially true if the client displays some impulsiveness.

Personality Issues

Other diagnostic behavioral disorders also increase the risk of suicide, and this is seen in the number of clients fitting the criteria for personality disorders such as being antisocial, borderline, and narcissistic, and having conduct disorders (Links, Gould, & Ratnayake, 2004). People diagnosed with these disorders are more likely than the general population to place themselves in risky circumstances, thus increasing risk for self-destruction. Blatt and colleagues (1995a, 1995b) have postulated that people with perfectionistic personality styles may have increased risk of suicide to a greater degree than people who report increased hopelessness. Dean and Range (1999) found that perfectionism predicted the level of depression that led to hopelessness in an outpatient population, while Donaldson, Spirito, and Farnett (2000) found that the focus may not be perfectionism itself but the self-criticism that accompanies it. It is too early to determine the extent of perfectionism on suicidal behaviors, but this line of research holds great promise and should be pursued vigorously. Counselors have noted that clients with perfectionistic tendencies are often "wound tight" and, by definition, see the world through a constricted, dichotomous lens. In other words, their worldview often consists of success or failure, with little gray area in between. They are also less likely to perceive their successes as actual successes than are persons without that style. Periodic or consistent "failure" often results in suicide attempts or completions.

Discussing a conceptualization of suicide signs, Firestone (1997) offers an interesting "syndrome of specific personality traits and behavior patterns that play a central role in all forms of psychopathology but that are particularly evident in suicidal individuals" (pp. 36-37), which he calls "inwardness." Inwardness is a retreat into the self as a way of defending against stress. In other words, inwardness is a means of coping when previous coping styles fail to be effective. It is characterized by seven factors:

> (a) a tendency toward isolation, (b) progressive denial of his or her priorities and withdrawal from favored activities and relationships, (c) use of additive substances or routines, (d) withholding personal feelings, (e) a preference for seeking gratification in fantasy in place of pursuing satisfactions in the real world, (f) marked feelings of self-hatred and cynical attitudes toward others, and (g) a lack of direction in life leading to a sense of despair and hopelessness. (p. 37)

Seasoned counselors can recall clients who fit into a number, if not all, of these categories, while newer counselors may want to consider these intrapsychic features in addition to the other behavioral, affective, and cognitive manifestations often exhibited by clients with severe pathology. For more information on his work on construction of suicide factors, see Firestone (1997).

Age and Gender

Age is a usually considered a factor when determining risk factors for suicide, but now clinicians cannot separate age and sex when considering risk factors. Anderson et al. (1995) found that males complete suicide at a rate four times higher than females. This fact has often been attributed to males using more lethal methods (i.e., handguns), but over 40 percent of females now choose handguns as their suicide method of choice. Suicides occur at a high rate for adolescents and young adults (ages fifteen to twenty-four) and for people, generally white men, over the age of seventy. Suicide is now the third leading cause of death among fifteen- to nineteen-year-old adolescents (Anderson, Kochanek, & Murphy, 1995). What is often overlooked is that these rates differ significantly depending on the ethnic group. For example, African American men do not show the same age pattern of suicide that European American men do, and African American women have very low rates of suicide across the life span when compared with other ethnic groups (National Center for Injury Prevention and Control, 2000). As a very general rule, completion rates tend to increase across the life span for European Americans, particularly men (though there is a slight drop from ages twenty-five to thirty-four), whereas completion rates for African Americans are generally low in early adolescence, peak in early adulthood, crest into the mid-thirties, and then decrease. Hispanic suicide rates tend to peak in adolescence and young adulthood and decrease with age. Native Americans have very high rates of youth suicide and very low rates after the age of forty. It is premature to indicate that age by itself is a significant risk factor for all ethnic groups, consistent with the other factors listed in this section. Even during the tumultuous teenage years when suicide risk increases significantly regardless of ethnicity, there are low completion rates among African American females, though suicide ideation is typically consistent with European American rates. Where suicide does appear to increase, though in part ethnically based, is in the over-eighty age group (generally European Americans). The elderly comprise just under 13 percent of the general population but account for 19 percent of the suicides (Conwell, 2001; Murphy, 2000). Less is known about "midlife" suicides (ages thirty to sixty-five) than during the younger ages among any of the ethnic groups, including European Americans, who dominate the suicide literature in general. A purpose of this book is to further delineate these ethnic differences and attempt to hypothesize why differences may occur in various ethnic communities. Therefore, in this book, the interested reader can consider age and other issues within different ethnic communities instead of merely a global factor.

Religion

Historically, religion has played a fascinating role in the study of suicide and has been considered a buffer against suicide (LoPresto, Sherman, & DiCarlo, 1994-1995; Martin, 1984). The extent to which religion actually acts as a buffer is unclear, and cross-national studies indicate that it may be more influential for women than for men (Stack, 1983). Rates differ depending on religious faith, and sometimes denomination, but recent evidence suggests that rates may be influenced more by an individual's degree of religious commitment than the faith affiliation (Neeleman, Wessley, & Lewis, 1998). Again, a critical issue is not whether individuals consider themselves religious, but how they are religious (e.g., attending religious ceremonies frequently, seeing members of the church/synagogue/mosque as a support system, reading religious materials). The overwhelming majority of U.S. research in this area has been conducted with Protestants and Catholics, while a few studies have included Judaic followers. International data indicate that Islamic nations have very low suicide rates, but less is understood about Islam and other faith groups and suicide in the United States. Both the Torah (Jewish religious text) and the Quran (Islamic religious text) strongly prohibit suicide, and research indicates that the Jewish and Islamic communities consistently show lower suicide rates than Christians (e.g., Bailey & Stein, 1995; Kok, 1988). Lower rates may be a result of increased orthodoxy or the infusion of religious devotion into the overall culture. Many of the studies comparing Jews and Muslims, for example, are reported from countries in which Judaism and Islam are considerably integrated into the legal, moral, and ethical cultural infrastructure (e.g., Israel, Kuwait, Egypt). Many Central and South American countries (e.g., Colombia, Mexico, Venezuela), which have laws and customs highly interrelated with Catholicism as well as high numbers of religiously devout people, also report very low rates of suicide (Lester, 1997b). Similar arguments have been offered regarding the African American and Hispanic American communities.

In the early part of the twentieth century, Durkheim suggested that predominantly Catholic-based countries would display lower rates of suicide than predominantly Protestant countries. Later research, however, failed to find such a connection, and some studies found that certain Catholic communities have higher suicide rates than some Protestant communities. Therefore, the evidence on national levels is considered inconclusive and the role of suicide in religious devotion nationally is unclear. However, the inconclusiveness may be a function of the questions asked and the research methods used. Some researchers have argued that church attendance and a closer spiritual and cultural connection with a higher power may help explain the relatively low suicide rates among the African American, Hispanic American, and Asian American populations. For example, when examining a European American and an African American group with equal church attendance, some clinicians (and many researchers) have argued that religion plays a greater embedded role within the African American community than within the European American community, though we cannot measure these qualitative differences well. These issues will be discussed further in the following chapters.

This text has major sections in each chapter that discusses religious influences on suicide within ethnic groups. Consistent with other variables discussed in this section, religion by itself may not predict suicide but is a factor to consider along with other variables. In other words, it is neither necessary nor sufficient as a unique variable, but important to assess nonetheless. Assessing for clients' beliefs about the afterlife is an important feature during a suicide assessment. For example, a recent African American client, who is an ordained Baptist minister, had been contemplating suicide for many weeks due to a bipolar disorder, a disorder he found debilitating. When asked about his views of the afterlife if he were to complete suicide he indicated that he would spend eternity in hell and would not attempt it. His current religious commitment was questionable, as he had recently lost some of his faith, yet his views of the afterlife were a significant suicide buffer in his life. His religious support system espoused similar views and helped him cope with his depressive episodes.

Ethnicity

This book is structured into different chapters based on ethnicity. Although ethnicity is a gross indicator of suicide, each chapter includes necessary within-group variations. Ethnicity itself has been considered a risk factor for suicide, though it is neither necessary nor sufficient. For example, on average, Native Americans are 1.5 times more likely to kill themselves than the general U.S. population (Kachur et al., 1995). However, there is wide variation in rates based on factors such as tribal group affiliation, acculturation level, living area, age, and alcohol consumption. European Americans have higher proportioned rates of suicide than Hispanics, African Americans, Asian Americans, and some Native American tribal groups. As an introduction to the role of ethnicity in suicide risk, Kaslow et al. (2004) found lower levels of ethnic identity contributed to increased suicide attempts. Other authors have found similar results, though empirical studies assessing ethnic identity and suicide are few. Gibbs and Martin (1964) introduced the concept of "status integration," meaning that social relationship stability and suicide rates are inversely related. Numerous authors (e.g., Sue & Sue, 2003) have identified ethnic groups as being marginalized from the majority culture, and some research indicates that the lesser the connection with a person's ethnic group the greater the feelings of marginalization, a factor associated with suicide. When considering ethnicity one must consider a multitude of additional factors such as cultural acceptability, age, gender, cultural means of suicide (e.g., firearms versus hanging), and afterlife beliefs (Range, Leach, & McIntyre, 1999). This book will attempt to integrate ethnicity with many of these and other factors in the chapters that follow.

Impulsiveness and Control

Other factors need to be considered when conducting a suicide assessment. For example, is the client impulsive? Have there been problems with impulsiveness such as explosive verbal outbursts or physical aggression in the client's behavioral history? Does the client's behavior indicate someone who enjoys attention and jumps from one topic to the next (with or without significant pathology)? Many counselors have clients diagnosed as borderline or histrionic whose pathology is connected with impulsiveness and nonfatal suicidal behaviors. Treatment often includes a focus on their impulsiveness and helping them reflect on their thoughts and behaviors prior to potentially acting on them. A colleague's client recently stated, "When you're dead, you're dead. At least I won't have to feel this way anymore." Fortunately she found him other reasons to stay alive after much discussion, including the impact of his death on others and views of the afterlife. It is critically important to determine both impulsiveness and control issues during assessments, and help the client reflect on long-term outcomes instead of impulsive, short-term ones.

It has been well established that proximity to lethal means significantly increases the risk of suicide (impulsiveness). For example, even after accounting for age, gender, alcohol abuse, and depression, the presence of a firearm in the home independently increases the risk of suicide (Brent, Kerr, & Goldstein, 1991). Clinicians versed in suicide assessments understand that asking clients whether their preferred means is available and accessible to them is a necessary component to a comprehensive evaluation. Additional factors that may increase impulsive behaviors include suicidal behaviors by friends or family (Davidson, Rosenberg, Mercy, Franklin, & Simmons, 1989), suicide clusters (Gould et al., 1990), and incarceration (Kerkhof & Bernasco, 1990).

The clinician must find buffers that prevent clients from actually acting impulsively but increase more healthy control over their lives. From my experience, for example, caring for children is often considered a buffer against impulsivity and suicide. The notion that the children may grow up alone or with a despised spouse or family member is enough to prevent many lethal actions. Religious issues, such as a belief in eternal damnation, are also mentioned with some frequency. I become more concerned when a client states no religious or spiritual belief and indicates that life is completely finite and espouses no afterlife beliefs. Connecting with others (e.g., friends, God) seems to be one of the critical factors that allow some clients to become more cognizant of how their current suicide ideation and self-destructive behaviors are impulsive.

Other Issues

Issues such as marital status, recent incidences of difficult life events, unemployment, personality characteristics, social support systems, cultural attitudes toward suicide, and access to means are important factors in addition to those listed earlier (Sarason & Sarason, 2002). For example, recently divorced or widowed people, particularly men, and never-married men are more likely to complete suicide than married men (Lambert & Fowler, 1997). Marriage appears to act as a buffer against suicide, particularly for European American males who are more likely to complete suicide than their females counterparts and males and females of other ethnic groups (Sommers-Flanagan & Sommers-Flanagan, 2002). In addition, living alone is sometimes considered a significant factor, but it may be associated feelings of isolation that directly contribute to suicidal risk. If true, then isolation can take many forms, including being culturally isolated and marginalized. Feeling marginalized is considered a cultural factor in the suicidal deaths of adolescents and the elderly, the latter of which has the highest per capita rates among European Americans, African Americans, and Asian Americans. Severe life events, including personal loss, increase the risk of suicide, particularly when social support systems are poor or nonexistent. Also, cultural attitudes play a large role in the acceptability of suicide as an option. These attitudes can vary by geographic region, religious influences, and ethnicity.

SUICIDE ASSESSMENT

Clients often present to clinicians with previous suicidal behaviors and/or current suicidal ideation. If a client arrives for a session and begins to hint at suicide, then clinicians must conduct a thorough evaluation and assess multiple issues surrounding a potential suicide. First, a mental status exam should be conducted in conjunction with suicide ideation questions. Clinicians should determine the person's level of psychopathology (e.g., hallucinations), judgment and insight, rational thought, alcohol and drug use, and affective range and mood state at the very least. Second, a psychosocial assessment needs to be conducted. This includes an evaluation not only of the risk factors described earlier but also of current living situation, medication compliance, coping strategies, potential social and personal buffers such as religious convictions, and social support. It is at this point that cultural issues can be introduced. Clinicians can listen for stresses related to internalized homophobia (e.g., "All of the other kids make fun of me and I'm tired of being this way"), acculturation issues, which are feelings of marginalization from the larger culture (e.g., "I just don't seem to fit in"), religion (e.g., "God let me down by taking my wife away from me; I've turned my back on the church and hope they all rot in hell"), age ("I'm just old and tired and all my friends are gone"), and racism ("I go to a mostly white school and don't have many friends there and some of them don't want me there").

M. Miller (1985) presented a model that has one of the more popular acronyms for assessing suicidal intent—SLAP. SLAP stands for Specificity, Lethality, Availability, and Proximity. Examples of each section of the model will be defined in the following paragraphs, but the reader should consult other models and authors, for example, Sommers-Flanagan and Sommers-Flanagan (2002), Bongar (2002), and White (1999), for a thorough overview of clinical examples and assessment procedures for suicide.

SLAP

Specificity

Specificity refers to the degree to which a suicidal client has considered the necessary components to complete suicide. There is a difference in specificity if a client says, "My father has a gun in his drawer and I'd use it" instead of "I think that I would probably blow my brains out, but maybe I'd just run my car off the road. I don't know, I just wish I were dead," as stated by a client recently. Either way more information is needed to determine a client's intent, but specificity helps the clinician determine the degree to which the client may complete suicide. A specific response should be considered as a significant sign of distress. Clients who are unwilling to inform the counselor of their means or intent and instead offer vague notions of suicide are often difficult to address and assess. A client who possibly has a specific plan in mind but also understands that mental health clinicians have to stop clients from completing suicide may respond with, "I've got a few ideas." The vagueness of the client's response calls for more clinical savvy and time to assess the degree of overall intent. This vagueness is also related to lethality.

Lethality

Lethality refers to the extent to which the method used would cause death. There may be a difference in whether a client would shoot himself or herself in the head or attempt to overdose on sleeping pills, though practically the clinician should treat each one as equally serious. Clinicians must assess the degree to which the means of suicide is lethal and the client's awareness that the means is lethal. Of course, even though the client may choose a method that is not immediately lethal, it does not mean that he or she is not in danger. The critical issue is the subjectivity of the suicide ideation or attempt. Further assessment is needed, such as the factors discussed earlier and throughout this book, and availability.

Availability

Availability is the extent to which the plan could actually be implemented. Clinicians can assess for availability by asking whether the client has a gun at home and whether he or she knows the location of the bullets. Does the client have enough sleeping pills at home or have the means to obtain enough to complete suicide? Of course, specificity and lethality lower the immediate risk if the gun or pills are not readily available. Again, the client may not be in immediate danger but should be continually assessed because environmental and personal factors can change quickly, and in many areas it is not difficult to acquire a gun or a variety of pills.

Proximity

Proximity refers to the location of helping resources, which may include friends, family, religious figures, neighbors, and twelve-step sponsors. Is there someone nearby on whom the client can rely to intervene should an attempt or significant suicide ideation be made? Does the client have a roommate? Does the client work alone or with others? Does the client attend church services? Research indicates that religion is inversely related to suicide, and many researchers have shown that much of this effect can be attributed to church attendance (e.g., Martin, 1984). People who attend church, whether religious or not, appear to gain benefit from the social or horizontal aspects of religion. Overall, the closer the proximity of helping resources, the less the significant risk involved.

Numerous authors and clinicians understand that during a clinical interview several key pieces of information should be collected prior to deciding the potential lethality of a suicidal person. Unfortunately, there is no magic assessment method, though there are integrative decision models that help with the process. Most decision-making models recommend that the clinician collect demographic information (e.g., race, gender, marital status), and also information about historical, social, situational, and psychological factors that may increase risk (e.g., definite plan, depression, alcohol use, family history of suicide, self-destructive impulses). The clinician may then assess risk further by using standardized testing measures (e.g., BHS and the Beck Scale for Suicide Ideation) and decide whether a client is at significant risk. Of course, consultation with knowledgeable colleagues or supervisors is always recommended. If significant risk is present, then various treatment strategies such as involuntary or voluntary hospitalization, day treatment programs, or assiduous outpatient care are possible.

Consider an overview of a conglomerate of decision-making models and how culture may be beneficial to address. First, most models begin with some consideration of demographic factors when determining the risk level for suicide. As indicated earlier, women are less likely to complete suicides than men overall. That information alone is good to know and may be a factor to consider with some potentially suicidal clients. However, it may also be helpful for clinicians to understand that Hispanic American women are much less likely to complete suicide than European American women. Gender and ethnic issues should necessarily be considered; yet questions that arise are "Why do they complete suicide at a lower rate than men?" and "What cultural factors are important within the Hispanic community that lend themselves to lower suicide completion rates among women?" Similar questions hold for other cultural groups as well. What cultural factors are associated with gay young men that may lead to increased suicide rates? Why is it that persons of the Muslim faith are much less likely to attempt and complete suicide than Christians?

Second, what kind of historical and clinical (social, situational, and psychological) factors may contribute to suicide risk? Historical factors often include family history of suicide or previous attempts, and these are critical factors. What about the combination of historical and cultural factors? Consider the second-generation Hispanic male who feels marginalized from his own culture, or even alienated from society. Persons considering suicide often describe feelings related to being on the outskirts of society or not fitting in with society, essentially discussing the acculturation factor called marginalization. These people may have attempted to maintain a cultural heritage but feel peripheral to their cultural group. The client's first-generation parents are less likely to include a family history of suicide, yet increased acculturation difficulties may lead to greater suicide ideation for the second-generation client (there is some evidence that suicide rates increase with the length of the duration of residence of some immigrant groups in the United States). Cultural marginalization leading to suicide has been given only minimal attention, yet it is a potentially strong sociopsychological factor. When conducting a suicide evaluation the clinician may want to ask questions addressing acculturation and the level of comfort felt within the majority and familial cultures.

SUICIDE PREVENTION

In this section I will present an overview of general suicide prevention efforts. Some of the efforts addressed apply to all clients, regardless of cultural background. For example, after-school programs may be very useful and help reduce the occurrence of suicide. However, it is my argument that programs should include culturally relevant segments when possible, such as focusing on ethnic history and relationships to the past, and on the values and traditions of cultural groups. Therefore, although general after-school programs may apply to the majority of adolescents, there are instances in which they should include culturally sensitive materials. The majority of prevention studies have either focused on European Americans or have applied a European American perspective onto other ethnic groups and have not included culture-specific prevention concerns. In this chapter I offer an overview of programs. Ethnically specific prevention issues will be addressed in the following chapters where appropriate, and when research evidence indicates that specific cultural issues can be beneficial with clients.

Suicide prevention programs have generally fallen under the categories of primary, secondary, and tertiary. *Primary prevention* involves the improvement of psychological health before significant suicide issues arise. It involves impeding suicidal tendencies and is the most difficult of the three to implement because it presumes that we know what factors lead to suicide (Lester, 1994b). Although we have some very general ideas of concurrent factors, we are nowhere near fully understanding why one person completes suicide while another does not though they may appear to have similar diagnoses, thought patterns, social support, family background, and the like.

Primary prevention programs may include preventive psychotherapy or the use of appropriate medications for affective and other disorders. Other examples include programs designed for the prevention of alcohol and drug abuse. After-school programs often fall within this category. School education programs for primary, secondary, and postsecondary students have been studied and implemented with varying degrees of success (e.g., Cecchini, 1998; Mishara, 1999; Shaffer, Garland, Gould, Fisher, & Trautman, 1988). Examples of other primary prevention programs include intervening with postpartum women (Spinelli, 1999), adolescents who have experienced some loss (Hetzel, Winn, & Tolstoshev, 1991), and child abuse victims (Buzi, Smith, & Weinman, 1988), though there are many others. Lester (1990) made a culturally consistent argument when he reported that people who had not bonded well with their community and family had higher rates of completed suicide, consistent with Durkheim's (1897/1951) theory of social integration.

Secondary prevention is early intervention for suicidal people. These people have considered suicide and may have significant ideation but have not attempted suicide. Some of these programs have been assessed to a greater degree than primary prevention programs, yet there is still some dispute as to the degree of their effectiveness (Frankish, 1994). These include identifying high-risk groups, crisis centers that include suicide hotlines, personal crisis counseling, and restricting access to means of suicide. Lester (1994d) listed a number of societal and personal ways by which we can reduce access to potentially fatal means of completing suicide, including detoxifying domestic gas, cleaning up automobile gas emissions, and increasing the number of states with gun ownership waiting periods (Clarke & Lester, 1989).

Tertiary prevention programs involve interventions for people who have been or are currently suicidal, and would have died had it not been for tertiary interventions. Counseling, psychotherapy, and medication are the most popular intervention programs (Leenaars, Maltsberger, & Neimeyer, 1994). Counseling and psychotherapy use a range of approaches consistent with the treatment of other psychological disorders. The use of some medication has been shown to be effective in reducing suicidal behavior because of their reduction of depression and other negative psychological and physical symptoms (Montgomery, Montgomery, Green, Bullock, & Baldwin, 1992). With the advent of new classes of antidepressants (e.g., Prozac, Zoloft) and antipsychotics (e.g., Geodon, Zyprexa), it will be interesting to determine whether suicide rates decrease, because some research has indicated that the newer classes of medication are not significantly better than the older ones (e.g., tricyclics) in reducing depression and suicide (Glenmullen, 2000). For example, Tueth (1994) found that for a subset of depressed clients Prozac may induce akathisia due to it adversely affecting serotonergic neuronal discharge. These clients may be more likely to consider completing suicide due to the visible nature of the side effect than if they had been prescribed another antidepressant. There has been speculation as to whether the newer classes of antidepressants decrease depression to a greater degree than the tricyclics, yet they do have fewer side effects. Thus, its specific effects on suicide have yet to be determined and it is purely speculative at this point.

Lester (1994a) offered means of examining prevention strategies used by other program types (e.g., drug abuse prevention, crime prevention) and implementing them into suicide prevention programs. For example, he indicated that drug abuse prevention programs are much more direct and frightening than suicide prevention programs by including tapes of those who died from cancer or the dangers of cocaine. He reported that suicide prevention programs could emphasize the long-standing problems that occur when suicides are not successful, such as organic brain syndromes and spinal cord injuries. Churches could also discuss their opposition to suicide, though church leaders have informed me that they are unlikely to tackle this topic for two reasons: (1) bringing up the topic might increase suicide rates (though we know this is false) and (2) it is a difficult or irrelevant topic for many to hear and they have to "fill the collection plate." Regardless, Lester's (1994a) point that a more direct approach may be more beneficial than what has typically occurred with suicide prevention programs is well-taken.

Suicide prevention programs focusing on GLBT issues can be presented, particularly for school-aged individuals. McDaniel, Purcell, and D'Augelli (2001) indicated the peer-based prevention approaches may be most appropriate for grade school through high school age groups, particularly since some research indicates that some current school-based programs may not be helpful (Muehrer, 1995). Prevention programs aimed at younger age groups can help offset future problems associated with being a GLBT teen. Schools can emphasize decreasing discrimination and discussing concurrent behaviors that are often associated with feeling ostracized (e.g., substance abuse). Some schools now include instruction that being gay is one of many sexualities and should be considered normal. Many regions have now organized GLBT dances and other activities for youths, which can help develop healthy relationships. It is hoped that by the increased acceptance of GLBT issues feelings of marginalization and depression will decrease, resulting in decreased suicide rates. It is clear that research in this area can be fruitful.

CRISIS INTERVENTION AND CULTURE

Crisis Intervention

I recall a client who entered my office for the first time and quickly pronounced that he was suicidal. I immediately switched from what I thought would be a typical initial counseling session to a crisis intervention mode of thinking. The two have very different purposes. With counseling the treatment may have multiple goals. Crisis intervention, though, has one unique goal—to keep the person alive (Leenaars, 1994). The purpose of crisis intervention with suicidal clients is to expand their options and help them connect emotionally with anyone or anything. As discussed earlier, suicidal people engage in cognitive constriction, or the idea that the world is narrow and options do not exist. Suicide becomes the only way out of a seemingly impossible situation. The job of the counselor is to help the client realize that options do exist, and it is always better if multiple people are involved (e.g., colleagues for consultation, physicians for medications, friends for support and supervision, pastors for spiritual guidance).

Leenaars (1994) discussed a five-step model that is used by many clinicians, and it will be briefly summarized here. Readers should consult this or other crisis intervention articles and texts for further information. I will add cultural information that may be useful even during crisis intervention using a systematic model. The first step is to establish rapport, and the quicker the better. The client must be able to trust a nonjudgmental and compassionate counselor so that future options can be pursued. Often, suicidal clients believe that "no one cares for me and I'd be better off dead." Establishing a relationship is critical to showing that the counselor (and probably others) cares about their future. As with general counseling, it is wise to consider whether rapport can be established because of ethnic or gender differences. For example, I recall an African American client who was lethally suicidal and with whom I had difficulty building rapport, even minimally. She responded vaguely to questions when she would answer them at all. As with many clients, I asked how she felt sitting in the room with me. She responded that since I was white and a male she couldn't trust me because a white male had raped her. We spent some time discussing my whiteness, how she has known other white men who did not rape her, and that I was not the man who raped her. It is not likely that "full" rapport will be established during this first session, but enough rapport to move on to the next steps can be formed. Of course, rapport is not a static step and occurs throughout the session(s). Because of my willingness to discuss our ethnic differences my client's cognitive constriction began to diminish.

The second step is to explore the client's perception of the problems and his or her worldview. Counselors with cultural sensitivity will listen for cultural content from their clients. What is the client looking for in life and which needs are not being met? Are the issues shared by practically all humans, such as relationship loss, or are they more culturally specific, such as loss of status in the community or shame? Other questions might be, "Where is the pain located in their body?" "Who has hurt them the most?" If I believe that a client has underlying anger toward someone that may precipitate suicidal behaviors, I will ask, "If you were to kill yourself who would you want to find you?" This question serves two purposes: first, to indicate to the client that suicide is only one of many options and, second, to determine with whom they may be most angry.

The third step is focus, which involves helping the client gain some control over the situation by working on something tangible. Questions such as "What would you like me to do?" and "How can I help you the most right now?" may be helpful. At this point the counselor should not begin further treatment with the goal of in-depth counseling or psychotherapy but aim to make sure that the client can leave the office with a plan of returning in the future. If no plan can be made, hospitalization is the likely option.

The fourth step is to develop options and constructive action with the client. Reframing clients' thoughts and helping them derive options is critical in this step. Consistent with Leenaars (1994), I have discussed suicide as an option with clients, but only an option. If counselors quickly maintain that suicide is not an option then rapport and expanded thinking will be more difficult to establish. The intent is to help clients realize that suicide is a choice but not the only one. Depending on the client I have said, "Suicide is an option, but perhaps it is not the best option today. Let's come up with some other options that may be better for you in the long run." By stating "in the long run," I am trying to plant a seed alluding to a greater time frame than the client is presently considering. If the client cannot imagine other options, I will mention future counseling. By doing so, I have now created an option. If a client still cannot develop options to suicide I may add something like "You could go walking." If it becomes an option, then that is movement (though we clearly remain in crisis mode and the session does not end there). If they inform me that walking is not an option, then I have still created another option but they choose not to engage in that behavior. What behaviors would they like to engage in? Choices are discussed and plans are made prior to the termination step. In this step both the counselor and the client summarize the treatment and choices that have been planned. Included in this step are emergency contact numbers and follow-up procedures, either with the present therapist or another counselor.

TRADITIONAL COUNSELING
AND PSYCHOTHERAPY APPROACHES

Once the client is out of immediate danger it is helpful to engage in counseling. Most of the major theoretical systems of change discuss suicide, yet it is rarely addressed in this manner in graduate-level training programs. It has been well established that many of these theories have focused on white, middle-class clients primarily, with little addition of culturally important factors (cf. Leach & Carlton, 1997; Leach & Sullivan, 2001). The majority of treatment approaches have focused on the dominant culture, and the few suicide-specific interventions that have been developed from the major theories seem to utilize a dominant culture philosophy. Recently, there have been authors who have included culture as an important factor when considering suicidal clients. For example, in Leenaars et al. (1994) some authors appropriately discussed gender and age issues, yet critical cultural issues such as gender identity, gender roles, ethnicity, and acculturation were not emphasized. Canetto and Lester (1995a) saw this limitation in the literature and added diversity issues to their book on women and suicide, including multiple chapters that address cultural-specific issues. In contrast, other authors give a passing glance to suicide from a cultural perspective but primarily focus on the culture itself and do not include therapeutic issues to address in order to engage in primary, secondary, or tertiary prevention.

The major theories do address suicide specifically to various degrees. For example, cognitive therapy focuses on the cognitive triad (self, world, future; Beck, 1987), irrational beliefs through faulty appraisals, cognitive rigidity, pessimism, hopelessness and other thought patterns, and the assumptions that undergird client thinking. Clinicians may focus on the suicidal client's view that life will *never* get better and that he or she will *always* be alone and have a poor job. Therapy would involve the client becoming more aware of the relationship of these thoughts to those of suicide, and attempt to get the client to view these thoughts more objectively and with greater distance. They may focus on whether the thoughts are rational and have clients test their beliefs cognitively and behaviorally. They may also discuss the idea that suicide is often based on an impulsive decisions and that these decisions can be faulty.

Behavioral therapists are likely to focus on reinforcement schedules and social coping skills to offset client learned helplessness. Persons considering suicide are often asked to keep thought and behavior logs, consistent with cognitive therapies, and often sign no-suicide contracts. Clinicians may implement assertion, anger management, and family interventions that increase reinforcers. Persons in inpatient or partial care programs may be offered work-related activities or given tokens or points for various behaviors. Many of these programs attempt to give the person a sense of purpose, hope, and worth.

Feminist theories often focus on the inequitable role that women play in society. Enns (1997) has written extensively on the role that personality plays in Western and non-Western societies, including coping styles as they relate to self, relationships, emotion, and achievement. She has also discussed four different types of feminist ideologies and their relationship to therapist preferences, interventions, and diagnostic practices (Enns, 1992, 1997). In brief, feminist therapists work on empowerment and the limitations that society places on individuals, which may lead to frustration, depression, suicide, and numerous other social and psychological ills. Whereas the major therapies implicitly have at their core the notion of empowerment, feminist models are more direct in looking at the client's place in a social structural hierarchy and working toward diminishing oppression by reconceptualizing health, pathology, identity, roles, and relationships. Therapists are more likely to act as advocates for their clients and are more likely to take a sociological perspective on suicide treatment than some of the intrapsychically or intrapersonally focused therapies (Radov, Masnick, & Hauser, 1977).

The psychodynamic foundation of suicidal behavior can be conceptualized from perspectives of drive theory, ego, the self, and object relations. Psychodynamic theorists point to increased aggression and narcissistic vulnerability as central to suicidal behaviors. Traditional psychoanalytic approaches to suicide focus on the ego-splitting that occurs through the loss of an introjected love object. In essence, we receive benefits from others through desires, and if a loss occurs, we may experience self-directed aggression. Other related hypotheses include disturbed ego functioning and pathological object relations (Ivey, 1999). Kaslow et al. (1998) found strong support for an object relations hypothesis in a sample of suicide noncompleters in that they possessed more primitive object relations than a control group.

D. Wasserman (1988) found more unstable object relations due to parental loss among suicide noncompleters. Treatment approaches with suicidal people must address cultural influences. It is not enough to understand that someone is depressed, but what does that depression mean to a person culturally? Is it a sign of weakness? Is medication readily accepted? Some ethnic groups are less willing to take synthetic medication than others, for example, traditional Native Americans (Paniagua, 2005). Is rational suicide an option for a client and what are his or her views on rational suicide? These views are, in part, culturally driven. Based on the maturity of the diversity field, particularly its relationship to suicide, my approach is to use one or more of the major models and include diversity issues when appropriate. For example, I will inquire about their religious beliefs and views of the afterlife, listen for the relationship of being gay or African American or a woman to stressors in their life. Other more specific cultural approaches to suicide will be presented in the following chapters when possible.

Theories of multicultural counseling have emerged over the past fifteen years, each focusing on nuances of individual and collective cultures while simultaneously acknowledging similarities among cultural groups. They center on certain basic assumptions such as multiple realities, cultural awareness of the counselor, expanding therapeutic repertoires beyond that restricted to only one or a few traditional approaches, pluralism, internalized culture, and complex cultural interrelationships, to name a few (for an extended summary of multicultural counseling, see Fuertes & Gretchen, 2001; Ponterotto, Fuertes, & Chen, 2000). These models are worldviews that supplement other counselor interventions and traditional models of therapy. They include sociopolitical influences on the individual and the collective, and emphasize multicultural constructs that inform all counseling, regardless of client. Thus, multicultural counseling is an approach with different philosophical underpinnings, which is used in conjunction with traditional approaches. Making the adjustment to a multicultural framework can be difficult for some clinicians, though most include cultural issues in their counseling routines. In order to give a reader who is less than familiar with some multicultural vernacular, a brief introduction into some of the terminology presented in this text, a few terms will be discussed in the following section.

ADDITIONAL TERMS DISCUSSED
THROUGHOUT THE BOOK

Ethnicity and Race

Although the U.S. public tends to attribute cultural differences to race, I want to avoid using the term *race* where possible because of the wide disagreements regarding its practical usefulness (Jones, 1991; Phinney, 1996; Zuckerman, 1990). It has been accepted for years that there is more within-group than between-group variation among ethnic groups in terms of personality, culture, and biology. Biologists have shown genetic similarities between biological races, largely due to thousands of years of global migration and interracial marriages. I prefer to use the term *ethnicity* to describe the groups of people mentioned in the following chapters, and the multicultural field has moved toward greater acceptance of the term ethnicity, instead of race. The term race will be used only when psychological models specifically focus on race or sociorace (e.g., Helms, 1990). Phinney (1996) indicated that the term ethnicity has been defined differently depending on the writer and specified three key aspects of ethnicity: (1) cultural norms and values, (2) the strength, salience, and meaning of ethnic identity, and (3) the experiences and attitudes associated with minority status. These three areas are dimensional and not categorical classifications. However, merely knowing the ethnic background of an individual does little to help the clinician understand an individual's specific mental health outcomes, reactions to grief, and sociocultural norms. Ethnicity in this book is used to guide the reader in understanding cultural nuances associated with suicide.

Racial and Ethnic Identity Formation

The past fifteen years has seen an explosion of literature addressing racial and ethnic identity formation. Consistent with Phinney's (1996) belief in the salience of ethnicity for the individual, identity models have been devised for numerous ethnic and nonethnic groups such as Asian Americans (Sodowsky, Kwan, & Pannu, 1995), Hispanic Americans (Casas & Pytluk, 1995), biracial Americans (Kerwin & Ponterotto, 1995), European Americans (Helms, 1990; LaFleur, Rowe, & Leach, 1995), GLBT Americans (Cabaj & Stein, 1996; Garnets & Kimmel, 2003), women (Ossana, Helms, & Leonard, 1992), feminists (Downing & Roush, 1985), and multiple identity dimensions (Reynolds & Pope, 1991; Robinson, 1999). The majority of these models tend to share features such as a developmental focus (moving from least mature to most mature stages or statuses), views of self, perceptions of one's ingroup and outgroup, and various sociopolitical underpinnings. These models have added to our understanding of racial and ethnic identity significantly, and it is difficult to understand the importance of a client's ethnicity without understanding the ethnic stage or status of the client. These models also allow us to look at within-group variation and the individual's amount of acculturation, which may lead to a better understanding of suicide. Some people may feel marginalized from society, thus contributing to depression and hopelessness, which can lead to suicide. For example, GLBT adolescents who feel marginalized may be more likely to attempt suicide than GLBT students who are more comfortable with their sexual orientation. Research indicates that older GLBTs are less likely to complete suicide than the younger ones, possibly because of greater sexuality identity comfort. More investigation is needed in this area to determine the impact of marginalization on identity and suicide.

Helms's People of Color Racial Identity Model

A major component of racial identity development is overcoming negative self and other group conceptions, and internalized stereotypes (Helms, 1995). Helms proposed a five-stage model in which views of self and internalized stereotypes are impressed. There are numerous other models of racial and ethnic identity, but the Helms model will be used to offer an example. It should be noted that research has yet to delve significantly into the relationship between racial identity and suicide, though some hypotheses will be presented here. In the *conformity* (pre-encounter) status, people of color devalue their ethnic heritage, are unaware of their sociopolitical histories, and hold European standards of merit. Racial issues are not prominent components of their lives because they believe too much emphasis is placed on race in this country. It is hypothesized that people in this status would probably be at higher risk for suicide based solely on racial identity due to greater conformity to "European American" standards. European Americans have higher rates of suicide than persons of color. People sharing the *dissonance* status exhibit confusion about their racial group and their own ideas of racial self-definition. There is disorganization and anxiety, and a belief that they don't conform to a European American social group but have yet to connect with their ethnic community. Risk of suicide may increase because of a lack of ethnic connection. The third status, *immersion/emersion,* is demonstrated by people of color denigrating the dominant group and idealizing their own group. There is often dichotomous thinking—that standards set by their own group are good and that European American standards are bad. This status is defined by black consciousness, or an awareness and knowledge of heritage and current social plights and strengths of black Americans. It would be predicted that suicide risk decreases for people holding this identity status because of the perceived connection with their own ethnic group historically and at present. Sanyika (1995) found that African Americans with greater black consciouness were less likely to complete suicide than those with decreased black consciousness. The *internalization* status is manifested by a positive commitment to one's own socioracial group and more objectivity toward the dominant group. Thinking is much more flexible and analytical. Finally, in the *integrative awareness* status, people value their own collective identities and other group identities for the sake of more global, humanistic expression. Suicide risk would be hypothetically less likely for an individual in this status. The reader should keep in mind that the hypotheses are merely speculative based on theory, and studies have yet to fully determine their validity.

Phinney's Ethnic Identity Formation

Phinney (1996) offered four coping outcomes used to navigate ethnic identity struggles, and her research is largely based on the *process* of identity development instead of the *content* of ethnic identity development. The focus in on how identity develops instead of what is manifested. Individuals become *assimilated* when they adhere to the dominant cultural group norms and do not adhere to their own ethnic cultural backgrounds. Consistent with Helms (1995), persons in this category are at higher risk for suicide simply based on ethnic identity. *Alienated/marginalized* individuals do not adapt to the majority culture and have also distanced themselves from and denigrate their own cultural group. Though minimally studied, people in this status would be at higher risk for suicide because of marginalization. Individuals who are *withdrawn/separated* are distanced from the dominant culture and idealize their own ethnic group, thus having less suicide risk on average. Finally, *integrated/bicultural* individuals maintain their ethnic culture but also learn the necessary skills needed to adapt to the dominant culture. When considering adolescent development, the adolescent moves from initial unawareness of his or her ethnic identity, through a stage of increasing awareness and exploration of identity largely as a result of racism, anger, and anxiety, to a final stage in which he or she has explored identity issues, feels comfortable with, and has come to terms with his or her ethnic identity. The greater the comfort within identity, the less likely it is that the individual will complete or consider suicide (e.g., Chandler, Lalonde, Sokol, & Hallett, 2003; Walker, 2003). Yuen, Noelle, Nahulu, Hishinuma, and Miyamoto (2000) found that Native Hawaiian adolescents were more likely to attempt suicide than non-Native adolescents due to a reduction in cultural affiliation. Issues such as depression and substance abuse were also strong predictors, and future research could determine the extent to which depression and substance abuse are associated with ethnic and cultural identity diffusion. In the following chapters, ethnic identity contributes to the assessment and treatment of suicidal individuals, especially for persons of color. On average, the greater the connection to their ethnic group the less likely it is that the person will attempt or complete suicide. However, there are notable exceptions, such as the fact that elderly Japanese Americans are at higher risk for suicide *because* of cultural influences.

Acculturation

Acculturation can be defined as the degree to which new cultural patterns can be integrated into the old ones (Dana, 1993; Grieger & Ponterotto, 1995; Paniagua, 2005), and the process can be defined as either internal or external. Internal acculturation occurs when cultural patterns change due to moving from one region to another in the United States. For example, approximately 70 percent of African Americans live in the southeastern United States. An African American from Birmingham, Alabama, who has shared cultural values with other southern, large-city African Americans may have a difficult transition to Lincoln, Nebraska, whose population consists of fewer than 5 percent African Americans. Values and attitudes toward African Americans may not be consistent between the areas and the process of fitting in may be difficult. As another example, I had (and continue to have) difficulty adjusting to living in the South, even though I have lived in various geographic regions both within and outside the United States. There is evidence that the acculturation process may be more difficult when adjusting to a place similar to your own culture than one very different. Cultural differences are more blatant and expected when moving to very different areas. Moving to the South appeared at the outset to be consistent with my Midwestern roots. However, rules of engagement, etiquette, and social norms differ in subtle forms. The first time I saw a "traditional southern" female client for counseling after having moved to Mississippi, I asked her about anger during the first session, which she deemed inappropriate. It was not proper to ask a traditional southern woman about anger in the first session. As it was explained to me later, "You can be glad and you can be sad, but you can't be mad." My Midwestern upbringing allowed me to express myself frequently and allow others to do the same, and my client later informed me that she thought I was quite rude in asking about anger so quickly. Although this is not the case for all southern female clients, cultural views of anger can differ and adjustments must be made.

External acculturation is what most people imagine when considering acculturation. An individual moving from his or her country of origin to the United States may have a sense of culture shock and navigate through a transition period. Having poor English language skills is often considered to be the greatest deterrent to acculturation. However, we also know that some people from other countries fit into U.S. culture easily, largely because of the diversity of people and the pockets of cultures encountered in various areas of the country. For example, a person from China who moves to San Francisco and does not speak English can survive well if he or she moves into Chinatown. The same is true of Mexicans who move to border towns such as Brownsville, Texas, or Las Cruces, New Mexico, and Cubans who move to Little Havana, Miami, or Puerto Ricans who move to New York City.

To borrow from Berry (1990), levels of acculturation can be depicted as a two-by-two grid. Berry described four types of acculturation: assimilation, or maintaining beliefs and actions consistent with mainstream culture; biculturalism, or maintaining beliefs and actions consistent with two or more cultures and being able to move easily from one to another; traditional, or maintaining values consistent with the original culture; and marginalized, or the feeling that one does not belong to any culture. Other models that expand the number of acculturation factors have been presented, but the reader will get a general understanding of acculturation from the Berry model, and the terms used in this text will follow his model.

As a clinician it would be beneficial to assess for acculturation upon seeing any client for the first time. In fact, clinicians informally assess acculturation levels naturally, often by determining the consistency between the client and themselves. This assessment can be accomplished informally by evaluating traditional interactional patterns, command of the English language, religious background, dress, and geographic history, or through more formal methods (e.g., acculturation inventories such as the Suinn-Lew Acculturation Scale and the African American Acculturation Scale). It is unlikely that the average clinician will see a traditional client for therapy (unless in a crisis situation; see Paniagua, 2005), as they tend to rely on other resources such as family, community, and religious figures for support. However, it is not unusual for court-ordered traditional clients and those who have already received family and community support services to arrive at your office. Traditional clients often respond well to traditional approaches to treatment, and clinicians should be well aware of the traditional ceremonies, become involved in the culture, and work closely with the local community (Paniagua, 2005). It is more likely that the average clinician will see bicultural, assimilated, or marginalized clients in therapy or through prevention programs. Clinician awareness of traditional values, beliefs, and ways of engaging clients is still important and should be incorporated into therapeutic interventions.

Chapter 2

European Americans

DATA

European Americans have the highest numbers of completed suicides in the United States, though this should not be unusual given that they also comprise the majority of its population. They constitute over 85 percent of all suicides in this country. Given that approximately 30,000 people complete suicide in the United States each year, European American suicides account for over seventy-five deaths a day, or the equivalent of over 27,000 deaths a year. European American men account for almost three-quarters of the completed suicides nationally. Internationally, women in general are more likely to engage in nonfatal suicidal behaviors to a much greater degree than men, and this fact is true for European American women as well (Kushner, 1995).

GENDER

Historically, the literature on suicide attributions has differed among men and women. Women were thought to complete suicide for physiological, emotional, and interpersonal reasons, whereas men were more likely to do so for financial and social, or egoistical reasons, often in conjunction with alcohol (Canetto & Lester, 1995b). The emphasis on the study of suicide traditionally has been on mortality issues; thus, the major foci have been on assessing, predicting, and treating predominantly male behaviors. However, Kushner (1995) pointed out that although there are still differences in completed suicides among men and women, the gap has narrowed over the past century. Overall, European American men complete suicide at a rate

Cultural Diversity and Suicide
© 2006 by The Haworth Press, Inc. All rights reserved.
doi:10.1300/5680_02

of 19.4 per 100,000 and fall behind only Native American men proportionally, and European American women complete suicide at a rate of 4.7 per 100,000, just behind Native American women (National Strategy for Suicide Prevention, retrieved January 6, 2005, from http://www.mentalhealth.samhsa.gov/suicideprevention/diverse.asp). Women are about two to four times more likely to engage in nonfatal suicidal behaviors than men (Canetto & Lester, 1995a). They are more likely to use less lethal methods than men, but the methods are changing dramatically. European American women have increased their use of firearms as the preferred method of suicide over the past decade, almost equaling the use among men, at over 50 percent (Holinger, Offer, Barter, & Bell, 1994). As mentioned earlier, suicide has historically been considered masculine (Canetto, 1991), and it will be important to determine whether female completed suicides increase using "male methods" (e.g., firearms, hanging) as traditional social roles and responsibilities continue to blur. Thus, clinicians relying on the traditional view of suicidal women using pills to engage in suicidal behaviors are mistaken. If a female client hesitates when responding to questions about a method of suicide, it would behoove the clinician to ask about access to firearms along with other methods.

AGE

Adolescents and Young Adults

Among European American adolescents (ages fifteen to nineteen), suicide is the second leading cause of death in the United States, and the third leading cause for persons aged fifteen to twenty-four. The reason for the age differences is that the National Center for Health Statistics (NCHS) reports epidemiological data in five- and ten-year age groups. About 10 percent of all adolescents reported engaging in nonfatal suicidal behaviors (Ritter, 1990; K. Smith & Crawford, 1986). European American males account for almost three-quarters of all suicides in the fifteen to twenty-four age group. Males account for five times more completions than females, and European Americans in this age group are about 2.5 times more likely than African Americans to complete suicide (Berman & Jobes, 1995). The older age group is much more likely than the younger group to complete suicide, and the rates for both groups have risen significantly over the past fifty years. Reasons for the increase include greater exposure to alcohol and other drugs, increased affective disorders, impulsivity, marginalization, increased access to firearms, more family dysfunction, increased conduct disorder (among males), and poor problem-solving skills (Berman & Jobes, 1992). Unlike other ethnic groups, there is a fairly linear trajectory across the life span among European Americans who complete suicide, except for a slight dip from the mid-twenties to the mid-thirties. In other words, except for the dip, on average, the older one gets the greater is the suicide completion rate. For example, elderly European American men are much more likely to complete suicide than elderly African American and Native American men.

Elderly

The European American elderly population comprises the highest proportion of completed suicides among all age groups, with the highest rate among people in their eighties. The primary factor for contemplating and completing suicide among this age group (and many others) is depression. Approximately 25 percent of all completed suicides yearly are those above the age of sixty-five, though older Americans constitute less than 15 percent of the population. These figures become particularly disconcerting since the average age of the U.S. population, the life span expectation, and the number of people over sixty-five continue to increase. By 2030, over 20 percent of all Americans will be over the age of sixty-five, resulting in over 65 million people. Of course, not all of these people will be European American, as the data also suggest that by the year 2030 approximately half of all people in this country will be European American, whereas the other half will be persons of color. Suicide rates differ depending on ethnicity; hence, the influence of current mainstream acculturation factors becomes particularly important. As people begin to assimilate to mainstream U.S. culture will suicide rates among persons of color increase accordingly? Regardless, the rates among European Americans increase with age and the importance of intervening with this population before suicide occurs cannot be overstated. Clemons (1990a) argued that religious communities should address the concerns of the aging population including the reality of suicide. Unfortunately, many religious leaders are not likely to discuss suicide, even during private moments, due to a variety of concerns including lack of training, myths about increasing suicide if discussed, and frightening parishioners.

RELIGION

Religion versus Spirituality

In the psychology of religion research literature it is generally well accepted that, regardless of study, approximately 95 percent of those asked report a belief in some form of a God (e.g., Zinnbauer, Pargament, & Scott, 1999). The variability of their God differs tremendously though, particularly when people discuss their religious beliefs in terms of religion or spirituality. Religion is often considered to be a more formal, organized system of faith, which includes rituals, traditions, and worship (Zinnbauer et al., 1999). Unfortunately, the study of religion is extremely difficult because of its multidimensionality, and the fact that there are over 2,100 religious groups in the United States (Keller, 2000; Melton, 1996). Therefore, when assessing the role of religion in a suicidal client's worldview, it is imperative to determine his or her understanding of faith. For example, if both the counselor and client are Southern Baptist the counselor cannot assume that they share the same religious worldview, though there is probably an initial impulse to do so. For example, some Southern Baptists believe that suicide is an unforgivable sin (because there is no potential for atonement), whereas others take a less stringent position. Although there may be significant overlap in the counselor's and client's general religious groundings, there is still wide variability in the interpretation of a number of topics as they relate to their respective faith group.

While the overwhelming majority of people in the United States believe in a God or Higher Power, there is an increase in people who self-identify as spiritual. Consistent with the term religion, spirituality includes a multidimensionality that can be perceived as more nebulous than religion. Spirituality is usually associated with a relationship to a transcendent power (Fukuyama, 1999) and is considered to have more depth and breadth than religious definitions. It seems to have more to do with the depth and breadth of human existence and the willingness to believe in a power that is transcendent and all-encompassing. Spirituality is often associated with creativity, courage, compassion, growth and development, and a connection to others through transcendence (Fukuyama & Sevig, 1999).

Researchers have had a difficult time delineating the empirical relationship between religion and spirituality. If one examines the pencil-and-paper instruments that include both religion and spirituality, they often appear to be measuring similar factors. Of course, there is overlap between the constructs, but it is difficult for the counselor to use these instruments effectively with any valid way of delineating the degree of client religiosity and spirituality. Clinically, perhaps a more relevant issue surrounding both religion and spirituality is the client's adherence to a more literal or conservative translation of the Bible (or Quran, etc.) (the Bible is the literal word of God or was influenced significantly by God) or a sociohistorical perspective (the Bible is interpretable and must be considered in context; an extended discussion apears later). Although no known research has been conducted comparing the two understandings to suicidal intent, it would make intuitive sense to state that conservative, literal translations are less likely to lead to suicide.

The relationship of religious ideation, faith, and behaviors to nonfatal and fatal suicide has been examined from multiple theoretical and empirical perspectives, and clinical knowledge of the different religions, faiths, and belief systems can help clinicians who work with potentially suicidal clients. It should be acknowledged initially that people of all ethnic groups can belong to any of the religions noted in this and subsequent chapters. The following introductory information about Christianity, Judaism, and The Church of Jesus Christ of Latter-day Saints (LDS) are placed in this chapter because, quite frankly, it is impossible to place religions in a chapter in which they would fit perfectly. Other religious faiths are placed in other chapters. The only other option would be to include a separate chapter on religion, but after serious consideration I concluded that it would detract from the structure of the book and would make for repetitive reading across chapters. It is hoped that the reader appreciates the dilemma, and I ask for your understanding. Obviously, some Asian Americans, Hispanic Americans, African Americans, and Native Americans are Christian, Jewish, or LDS (Mormon), for example, just as some European Americans are Buddhist, Muslim, or Confucian.

Christianity

It is impossible to summarize any religion succinctly and still give it the respect and justice it deserves. This brief introduction is meant to offer only a general framework from which to understand Christianity. The Christian faith is probably one of the broader religions, meaning that there are numerous subgroups with specific beliefs and rituals, though most share a belief that Jesus Christ is the Son of God. The Bible is the religious text that most Christians believe contains or was inspired by the word of God, sectioned into sixty-six books comprising the Old and New Testaments. Sharing some books and beliefs with Judaism and Islam, the Old Testament contains God's word prior to the birth of Jesus Christ, whereas the New Testament revolves around the life of Jesus and the future of the world. It is also probably the religious text most interpretable of the major faith groups, meaning that it is the most studied book of all time and, unlike many other religious texts, lends itself to multiple interpretations over a multitude of topics.

Controversy Within the Christian Church

Perhaps the most controversial issue surrounding the church is not the inclusion of GLBT or women's issues but how pastors and churches interpret the Bible. Religious leaders vary in their acceptance of the literal interpretation of the Bible, which has direct implications on their (and their congregation's) views of suicide and the afterlife. Because of the interpretive variability, scholars and laypeople alike disagree on the passages of the Bible that represent suicide. These interpretations largely rest on whether one considers suicide to be self-murder. Broadly discussed, if an individual is conservative in his or her religious beliefs and believes that suicide is self-murder, then it may be likely that the person has a negative view of suicide (barring potential client issues such as deserving to spend eternity in hell due to shame). These negative views may act as buffers against suicide, assisting the counselor in determining the likelihood that the client will engage in suicidal behaviors. Often there appears to be a religious relationship between murder and the afterlife; therefore, if one completes suicide then one is going to hell. Biblical issues surrounding suicide can be discussed with clients, particularly views of suicide and the afterlife. If suicide is not considered self-murder, then the person may be more likely to consider it an option and a different biblical approach may be necessary should biblical issues arise in treatment. If a client is contemplating suicide and has Christian religious or spiritual leanings, it is critical that the counselor understand the client's perception of suicide and the afterlife.

As counselors it would not be helpful to discuss the nuances of suicide in the Bible with clients, but unfortunately, many clinicians are wary of discussing religious issues with clients at all, as they often misinterpret religious discussions as equated with religious arguments or religious persuasion. Many clients arrive believing that suicide is morally and biblically wrong and a sin against God. It is likely that they are unfamiliar with the specific biblical passages discussing suicide, and instead rely on indirect passages such as "You shall not kill." Many church leaders have interpreted the sixth commandment to mean "You shall not murder, including yourself." Obviously, as therapists it would be a mistake to argue the point with your client if you believe that the passage does not apply to suicide. However, I have spoken with people who have struggled with the sixth commandment because of their being in the latter stages of life-threatening illnesses. One client in the early stages of amyotrophic lateral sclerosis (ALS; "Lou Gehrig's disease") arrived at my office wanting to discuss "getting my affairs in order" prior to the inevitable physical immobilization that he would eventually experience. These included financial issues, leaving his job, discussions with his children and other loved ones, etc. He was not suicidal during our time together but had considered making arrangements for suicide and believed that God's love would override the sixth commandment. Clinicians who have been involved in similar situations know the moral and ethical dilemmas that cross one's mind and are based partially on one's own religious beliefs. For example, the counselor may handle the future suicide consideration differently based on personal religious or spiritual beliefs. Holding to my professional ethics I discussed with him the hope that he would not complete suicide, particularly since it may become assisted suicide and involve others if his condition worsened quickly; yet having seen the agonizing debilitation involved with this disease, it was difficult for me disagree with his possible choice.

Helminiak (2000) stated that there are at least two ways of interpreting the Bible, the *literal reading* and the *historical-critical reading*. The first is consistent with fundamentalist views, following the belief that every word in the Bible is either inspired by or taken literally as the word of God, whereas the second takes a social context approach and leaves room for more biblical interpretation. The type of interpretation espoused by both client and counselor may determine their ability to work together on religious issues and suicide. For example, let us return to the popular fundamental passages allegedly condemning suicide—Exodus 20:13 and Deuteronomy 5:17, "You shall not kill." A client who believes in a literal translation may believe that the passage is extended to the self, therefore, you shall not kill yourself (self-murder). The reason that killing yourself is not justified is because only God can give and take life, and one is blaspheming the Holy Spirit or taking control away from God. Some people also believe that it blasphemes God through the first commandment, "You shall have no other Gods before me," with the idea that humans act as God when completing suicide. The Catholic Church also believes that self-murder is the only sin in which there is no opportunity to ask for forgiveness, although a change in canon law in 1983 allowed for people who had completed suicide to receive full funeral rites in some instances. These instances often include the idea that a person cannot be mentally healthy and complete suicide. Therefore, since the person was not mentally healthy then they were not fully sane and cannot be held accountable for their actions. Conversely, a client taking a historical-critical stance may believe that the murder passages do not extend to the self, or that God's love is all-encompassing and will prevail, or that suicide is biblically justified in certain circumstances. For example, prior to his inevitable capture, Saul fell on his sword, an act that led to his martyrdom (1 Samuel 31:1-13; 2 Samuel 1:1-16).

Religious and anthropological scholars have argued that views of an afterlife determine an individual or society's views of suicide. The earliest identified text discussing suicide is titled *The Dialogue of a Misanthrope with His Own Soul*. This Egyptian document views the afterlife as a positive place and therefore death is seen as attractive (Clemons, 1990b). In early church history there was a belief that only martyrs would reach paradise, because *martyr* is a Greek word originally used to describe people who professed their faith to Jesus Christ publicly. Soon after the death of Jesus Christ numerous people completed suicide in the name of martyrdom, and over the years martyrs became closely associated with Christian death by persecution, though it was not originally intended as such (Clemons, 1990b). Augustine argued that suicide is a form of homicide, and thus prohibited by the sixth commandment as sinful. Suicide is perceived as a sin not only because of the inability to ask for forgiveness but also because the person is selfish and cannot continue community service. Thomas Aquinas agreed with Augustine and wrote that suicide is both a sin and a crime. Of course, there are variations in the perceived consequences of suicide based on Christian denominations, and even within denominations. Some people believe that the only nonpardonable sin is the nonacceptance of Jesus Christ, whereas others believe that suicide is equally unpardonable. Although attitudes toward suicide tend to be increasingly charitable, it is still usually considered to be a sin according to the Christian faith.

It was not until Durkheim (1897/1951) that suicide was examined empirically, particularly in relation to religious ideation. Durkheim believed that Catholic European countries had lower suicide rates than Protestant European ones because the former had stronger social bonds. Bainbride and Stark (1981), however, did not find differences in suicide rates based on religious influence, and differences of religious influence on suicide are generally considered to be reserved for religiously conservative persons versus those who are not. Durkheim's theses have garnered numerous studies and arguments, though no consensus has been found. It may not be the particular religious faith (e.g., Catholic versus Protestant) of the client regarding suicide acceptability but the degree to which the client espouses that belief. Historically, the Catholic faith has imposed "vastly heavier theological and social sanctions against suicide than most Protestant groups" (Stark, Doyle, & Rushing, 1983, as quoted in Shopshire, 1990). However, there seems to be a flaw in the statement that the degree of religious conservativism is the primary factor in suicide acceptability, because of cultural issues. As will be outlined in other parts of this book, various religious faiths *as a group* have different rates of suicide, and it is hard to believe that everyone who espouses those beliefs are firmly and conservatively committed to their faith. For example, evidence indicates that people who espouse the Islamic faith are much less likely to complete suicide than Christians, though it should be noted that there is a smaller body of research on Islam and suicide.

What Does the Bible Say About Suicide?

Interpretations of biblical verses regarding suicide are numerous, and I will present specific popular verses to assist the counselor in understanding the religious worldview of his or her client. A problem with delineating biblical passages is that definitions of suicide differ. According to Clemons (1990b), an excellent text from where much of the following sections have been derived, there are three types of biblical text regarding suicide: (1) direct, specific passages that show an individual's suicidal behaviors as an act of martyrdom or heroism, (2) indirect, nonspecific passages that have been interpreted to condemn the act of suicide, and (3) indirect, nonspecific passages that have been interpreted to condone the act of suicide, which usually rely on human values and Jesus' teachings. The only direct passage of suicide discussed in the New Testament is that of Judas Iscariot, the betrayer of Jesus. This suicide passage has been described as repentance for forsaking Jesus, and therefore his death is considered acceptable, though there is no specific text condoning or condemning Judas's suicide (Matthew 27:5). An indirect passage of nonfatal suicide occurs in the New Testament in which a jailer who believed he had allowed Paul to escape prison was close to killing himself with his sword before Paul yells to him that he has not escaped (Acts 16:23-28).

Specific Biblical Accounts of Suicide

Specific accounts of suicide are reported primarily in the Old Testament, particularly with respect to martyrdom. The majority of the following information is derived from Clemons (1990b) who offers a brief, well-researched, and poignant account of suicide in the Bible. The Old Testament offers six direct accounts of suicide. Saul is perhaps the most prominent figure in Hebrew scripture to complete suicide. He was badly wounded and had lost all of his men and his three sons in a battle on Mount Gilboa. When he determined that the enemy would soon capture him, he asked his armor-bearer to kill him with a sword. When his armor-bearer would not do so, Saul fell on his own sword. The Philistines stripped his body of its armor and hung his body along with those of his sons on the wall of Beth Shan.

But when the inhabitants of Jabesh-gilead heard what the Philistines had done to Saul, all the valiant men arose, and went all night, and took the body of Saul and the bodies of his sons from the wall of Bethshan; and they came to Jabesh and burnt them there. And they took their bones and buried them under the tamarisk tree in Jabesh, and fasted seven days. (1 Samuel 31:1-13)

Saul's body was retrieved out of respect, and there is no mention that suicide was considered dishonorable and that he should be condemned. Further, upon hearing how the men of Jabesh-gilead honored Saul, David (2 Samuel 2:4-7) asks the Lord to bless the men for their allegiance to Saul, thus underscoring the fact that there was no condemnation for community members who honored the suicide. However, in 1-2 Chronicles, written 300 to 400 years after Samuel, Saul is viewed as being unfaithful to God and therefore died through suicide at the hand of God, thus leaving the kingdom to David. The act of suicide was not condemned by the author of Chronicles, however.

There are five other direct accounts of suicide in the Old Testament. In 2 Samuel (17:23), after being rejected Ahitophel hangs himself and was buried alongside his father. In 1 Kings (16:15-20), Zimri sets fire to his house in the city prior to being besieged. In Judges (16:28-31), Samson asks God for the strength to raze a Philistinian house and invoke revenge for years of torment, and dies with the Philistines. In Judges (9:52-54), Abimelech is close to death after his skull is crushed at the hands of a woman. He asks his armor-bearer to kill him with a sword, which he does, in order to avoid the embarrassment of being killed by a woman. Finally, in Jonah (1:12-15), Jonah asks his men to throw him into the sea during a severe storm in order to calm the raging waters, which they do. He does not die and eventually saves the city of Nineveh, and God's nature is revealed through him (Clemons, 1990b). In none of these scriptures is suicide specifically condemned (or condoned) by either God or the community. It is unlikely that clients have knowledge of these passages, but if they believe suicide can be justified biblically then more general contemporary therapeutic topics may be necessary, such as discussing their influence on future generations and on their immediate family. For example, families with someone who has completed suicide are much more likely to have multiple suicides in their family lineage even if the person was not known to another family member. Suicide as an option increases when someone has completed suicide in the family, and discussing the client's impact on future generations may be helpful. In addition, it is always a good idea to discuss the suicidal client's beliefs about the afterlife, though many clinicians are wary of discussing this area because of concerns about their competency in dealing with religious or spiritual issues or inflicting their values or beliefs on the client. However, if counselors are uncomfortable with this topic then their omission may be considered unethical.

Nonspecific Biblical Accounts Condoning Suicide

I agree with Clemons (1990b) that it is difficult to be "pro" suicide except in extraordinary circumstances. As clinicians we understand that life improves for most people contemplating suicide if they do not complete the act. There has been some discussion occurring in the United States about the merits of rational suicide, and these have typically been closely associated with inevitable death and pain issues. It should be noted that even though Clemons discusses biblical passages that allegedly condone suicide, he uses the term "condone" to mean "to pardon" or "to excuse" (p. 51). A number of biblical passages have been associated with condoning suicide, usually in conjunction with God's unabiding love for humans (e.g., "And surely I am with you always, to the very end of the age," Matthew 28:20), human rejection of the present state of affairs on earth and nirvana in the afterlife (e.g., "Whoever finds his life will lose it, and whoever loses his life for my sake will find it," Matthew 10:39), and martyrdom (e.g., "Very rarely will anyone die for a righteous man, though for a good man someone might possibly dare to die," Romans 5:7). These passages refer to suicide only indirectly, and clinicians would be well served to listen for passages such as these (or modern alternatives such as "I believe that I'll end up in heaven anyway because God loves me") as a means to justify suicide among clients.

A severely depressed client once mentioned that the only true sin is not believing in God, and since God gave him free will then God would not remand him for completing suicide. This discussion eventually turned to the client's views of God and what God's plan was with regard to family and friends. Cognitive-behavioral researchers have noted for years that persons who are significantly depressed, including those considering suicide, exhibit tunnel vision and constrict their worldviews. By helping the client expand his or her worldview to include family, friends, and the community, it is more likely that the person will not complete suicide. However, after discussing the impact of her death on family and friends, a client remarked that she would not care because "they don't care about me anyway." Through counseling we delved into her anger toward her family, which eventually helped relive her suicidal ideation, though the first few weeks were extremely difficult. I have found that asking a client, "If you were to kill yourself who would you want to find you?" gives a clinician a good indication of whom the client is upset and angry with. I am most concerned about the client who states, "I don't care if anyone finds me" because their suicidal ideation may be more introjective than interjective.

Nonspecific Biblical Accounts Condemning Suicide

The biblical condemnation of suicide has been discussed widely, and generally revolves around God being the only creator and thus the only one who can take life (e.g., "The Lord brings death and makes alive; He brings down to the grave and raises up," 1 Samuel 2:6), God allegedly forbidding suicide (e.g., "Do you not know that your body is a temple of the Holy Spirit, who is in you, whom you have received from God? You are not your own," 1 Corinthians 6:19-20), and the certain biblical figures who did not attempt suicide though given great tribulations (the story of Job or the story of Jesus' temptation by the devil). If your client is considering suicide, whether in a crisis or longer-term clinical situation, then discussion of these and related passages can be considered if the conversation turns to general religious faith, God images, and the afterlife. The caveat is that arguments over passage meanings should be avoided, as it may lead to the client becoming increasingly upset and decreasing counselor credibility and empathy. However, general discussions of the client's views of various passages can be a therapeutically useful tool.

Heaven and Hell

Most Christians believe in an afterlife, often referred to as heaven and hell, though their descriptions may be vague and unsettled. Images of heaven and hell are as varied as the number of people you talk to. Some Christians believe the soul rests in one or the other permanently, whereas others believe that even in hell there is a chance of attaining heaven if the individual repents and accepts God. Numerous conceptions of hell, from Dante's levels of hell to the depiction of hell in the Hollywood film *What Dreams May Come,* with Robin Williams, depict ideas of the afterlife. The traditional Western conception of heaven popularized in the media may consist of bliss, peace, clouds, and freedom. Hell may consist of a variation of the fire and brimstone theme, largely through church sermons denouncing the fires of hell. Pope John Paul II initiated study to move the conception of hell from fire to a place without God, consistent with the Hollywood depiction where Robin Williams's wife in the movie is rescued from a lonely and dark place. Heaven, conversely, is a place where God is present. Some recent religious revisionists have suggested that both heaven and hell are states on earth, wherein people create their own heavens and hells. It may be interesting to interview suicidal individuals who accept the revisionist version of heaven and hell, because the threat of hell has been a suicide deterrent throughout history.

It is critically important to gather an understanding of the client's conception of the afterlife and what happens to the soul if one completes suicide. Afterlife views can be a deterrent to suicide, though the clients who worry me the most as a therapist are the ones who say, "There is nothing after death" or "I don't care if I end up in hell. I deserve to go there anyway." However, if I am conducting a suicide assessment and these types of statements are made, it often assists in the clinical direction taken. In my experience most of these clients need to be committed to an inpatient facility. Straightforward questions such as, "What happens to you after you've died?" and "What are your family's views and how will their views affect them after you're gone?" can garner important information, which may allow the counselor to understand the client's intentions better.

Case Example

Stephen is a thirty-year-old white male who was raised Catholic and considers himself Catholic but tends not to attend church or practice his faith in other ways. He has been clinically depressed for over a year since his wife of five years left him after she had an extramarital affair. He had attempted suicide recently but also believes that he will go to hell if he does succeed. He was partially paralyzed from an automobile accident that occurred about three years ago and walks with a cane. Stephen arrived at the counseling clinic as part of an aftercare program upon his release from a local regional psychiatric hospital. The counselor, a non-Catholic, eventually pursued the reason for his attempt given the client's religious beliefs. Stephen indicated, "I am in hell now anyway and God is punishing me while on earth, so why not kill myself and accept my fate." They discussed his anger directed toward God for placing him in this situation and his anger toward his wife. However, he also indicated that he deserved this fate since he had "not been a good Christian," and still is not a good Christian because of the anger he is experiencing. He mentioned that his wife was probably right to leave him because "I'm not the man she married." He was speaking about his physical disability. A suicide assessment was completed while Stephen was in session and he indicated that he would not attempt suicide during the week. All other significant indicators were also negative. However, the counselor recalled that the anniversary of her leaving him was approaching within the upcoming two weeks. Do you as a counselor trust that he will not attempt suicide this week? How much emphasis do you place on his comment about already being punished and in hell. Does this factor override the suicide assessment which found that he did not have a current plan or means? The counselor and he made a plan for contact at prescribed times prior to the next session, and he agreed to continue the Wellbutrin prescribed by the hospital psychiatrist.

Stephen was fairly consistent with arriving for his weekly therapy sessions. The counselor and he worked on his anger, the outcome of which changed his views of his wife. The attributions placed on God were modified as they worked on his adjustment to the accident. The counselor recommended that he receive concurrent supportive group therapy for this adjustment, through a local hospital. Weekly, the therapist would assess, either directly or indirectly, Stephen's level of depression and suicide ideation. After six months the ideation had all but vanished, though there were periodic thoughts. His depression level had decreased significantly, though it still existed. Sessions with the individual counselor were reduced to bi-weekly, and he continued to be involved in group therapy monthly.

Intrinsic/Extrinsic Religiosity

One of the most salient and researched variables discussed in the psychology of religion literature is intrinsic and extrinsic (I/E) religiosity. Allport and Ross (1967) were early proponents of the idea that Christians hold diverse and broad religious beliefs with various motivations and it would be a mistake to categorize people simply on the basis of their denominations or faith groups. For example, they believed it more important and relevant for clinicians and researchers to consider an individual's type of religious commitment instead of whether they consider themselves Catholic, Methodist, Baptist, or

Lutheran. Intrinsic people are those who have a strong relationship with God and "walk the walk." They have a strong commitment to their core beliefs and their actions are often consistent with their beliefs. Extrinsically religious people have a relationship with God, but probably not quite as strong as intrinsics, and may attend church for other reasons. In other words, intrinsics live their faith and extrinsics use their faith. Although many other religious constructs have been presented in the literature, I/E has gained much empirical attention and is considered one of the fundamental variables in the study of the psychology of religion. Unfortunately, some of the instruments measuring this construct have difficulty discerning intrinsic beliefs from orthodox or fundamentalism beliefs. Other variables such as "quest" (those people with a strong faith but who still question parts of their belief system) have been developed as an optional means of studying religious faith development but will not be highlighted here with regard to suicide. The comparison of I/E and quest among suicidal clients may present fruitful and important results, and more research delineating these variables with the suicide spectrum is valuable.

Why is the I/E construct important in the assessment of suicide? Numerous authors have found strong relationships between I/E and suicide, with stronger faith and intrinsic (or sometimes orthodox) beliefs acting as buffers against suicide. For example, Greening and Stoppelbein (2002) found that religious orthodoxy emerged as the strongest correlate as a suicide buffer after controlling for other buffers among European American and African American adolescents. Nisbet, Duberstein, Cornwell, and Seidlitz (2000) found intrinsic religiosity inversely related to the occurrence of suicide among people over fifty years of age. African Americans are more likely than European Americans to possess greater intrinsic faith, a factor that many authors have attributed to lower suicide rates (e.g., Bender, 2000; Greening & Stoppelbein, 2002). As indicated earlier therapists should consider client beliefs in suicide and the afterworld. Though a crude indicator, research indicates that persons espousing intrinsic beliefs are less likely to consider suicide a viable option than those with extrinsic beliefs. Caution should be noted. No research to date has determined the relationship of I/E on suicide as depression, substance abuse, or other suicide correlate factors increase. Overall, as a single factor, it is likely that intrinsic religiosity acts as a buffer against suicide, though its buffering influence when adjoined with other psychosocial factors is in need of significant empirical research. In other words, how much of the buffering variance does intrinsic religiousness account for when compared with other psychosocial factors?

Case Example

Julia, a thirteen-year-old European American female, was raised in a conservative Seventh-Day Adventist community and began "acting out" prior to being enrolled in a Seventh-Day Adventist boarding school by her parents. A number of the adolescents at the school were sent for similar reasons and group counseling was conducted with eight of the students. During one session Julia indicated that "I should just go ahead and kill myself." She had been diagnosed with oppositional defiant disorder and displayed significant histrionic traits. Her anger stemmed from her defiance of the church's teachings, which she perceived as highly restrictive and antiquated. On numerous occasions she reported multiple sexual exploits, drinking, and dancing as an anger response toward her parents and upbringing. She began experimenting with her sexual identity, including have sexual relations with other adolescent young women. Her parents began to distance themselves from her, an issue that the counselor addressed with them on separate occasions. She continued, however, to eat specific foods deemed appropriate by her faith, while denying other faith beliefs. Counseling evolved into her decisions regarding pleasing God by eating the foods and praying, but she had not considered the idea that she may not be pleasing God because of her other behaviors. Her worldview had become one in which most of her faith was outdated and her parents were restrictive. Her conflicts led to suicide ideation in order to run away from the religious confusion. By helping the parents understand her dilemma and working with Julia in family counseling they eventually settled on a compromise. She ended up being allowed to engage in specified behaviors and as her anger diminished her sexual promiscuity diminished.

Judaism

Most followers of Judaism fall into one of three denominations—Orthodox, Conservative, or Reform—depending on the level of adherence to traditional Judaic teachings. Differences among the denominations are numerous, but they all share common bonds that define them as Jewish. Judaism can be considered a religion because there are specified rituals and behaviors that Jews share, regardless of denominational differences. Judaism can also be considered a community tied together by thousands of years of shared history and ancestry, thus fitting the definition of an ethnic or cultural group (Rabinowitz, 2000). People who follow Judaism have two main texts that guide the faith, the Torah and the Talmud. The Torah (meaning "Law" or "Path") is made up of the Pentateuch, or the first five books of the Bible given to Moses. The Talmud (a written tradition on the explanation and interpretation of the scriptures), which offered more specific laws, was developed as society became more complex (L. Miller & Lovinger, 2000). Because there is similarity across the types of Judaism, and because very little empirical research discusses psychosocial differences among the groups, I will present the information in aggregate form. However, differences will be noted when appropriate, particularly with burial and mourning practices.

Research using both U.S. and international statistics indicates that Judaic persons complete suicide at rates lower than Christians but slightly higher than Muslims. Therefore, Judaism may be viewed as a buffer against suicide. It should be noted that the overwhelming amount of religion-and-suicide literature in the United States has focused on Christian groups. Above all else, Jewish tradition considers honoring the dead *(kibud ha-met)* and comforting the mourner *(nihum avelim)* to be the two most important directives when a death occurs.

Judaism and Suicide

Life is sanctified in Jewish tradition, and thus it is never appropriate to complete suicide. In fact, according to the Talmud, Jews are not allowed to hasten death in any way. There are a few exceptions however, such as if death is considered inevitable and absolute or if the individual maintains life only through artificial means, then one is sometimes permitted to instruct the physician to "pull the plug." Depending on the faith tradition and the degree to which the person has traditional beliefs though, even "pulling the plug" may occur only after consultation and the blessing of the rabbi.

The Talmud considers suicide to be self-murder and the person who completes suicide is also considered to have committed sacrilege because he or she has decided to take control of his or her own soul, instead of leaving the decision to God (Lamm, 1969). Persons completing suicide cannot receive heavenly rewards because they have decided their ultimate fate. Some Jews believe that suicide is a worse sin than murder because the murderer has the possibility of altering future deeds and asking forgiveness. Further, the person completing suicide has left family and friends and committed a selfish act, which will adversely affect numerous generations until their own death. Finally, suicide is an act against the Jewish people as a whole, since Jews often have a responsibility to continue the faith across the world. As Lamm indicated, "they have refused the rightful share of their duties in this world" (p. 216).

Suicide is prohibited because the individual gives up the opportunity to continue to accomplish good deeds and help others, and has willingly destroyed the soul that God gave him or her. Note that for the purposes of the Jewish faith, suicides are not always officially ruled as such by police or a physician or a coroner. Only a rabbi can deem a death a suicide according to Jewish law. Consistent with recent thought in the Catholic faith, most rabbis now believe that the only way an individual can complete suicide is if he or she in the throes of a mental disorder and is therefore not considered mentally healthy. This decision, though solely resting on the shoulders of the rabbi, often includes input from law and mental health professionals. Decisions to consider whether a death may be deemed a suicide include whether there was concomitant involvement of depression, anxiety, or alcohol or drug abuse. Other rabbinic considerations include whether the person may have had a last minute change of attitude, the possible motivation of the act, and whether the death was truly planned. Therefore, the individual may not be responsible for his or her actions. Because of this belief, many people who appear from the outside to have died of self-inflicted wounds can be considered accidental death victims. Therefore, the deceased have all of the rights and privileges accustomed with traditional mourning and burial customs if deemed a suicide from one of the mentioned factors.

Mourning

It is hoped that clinicians will never have a client complete suicide, but since the data indicate a good chance that a client will complete suicide while in your care, mourning and burial rituals are discussed in this section. This section is included because most readers are familiar with Christian services and rituals, but fewer are acquainted with Jewish practices. Rituals from other religious groups will be offered in other chapters.

Upon the death of a loved one, it is proper to show grief for the living by tearing a garment *(k'riah)* that he or she is wearing. This garment is worn during *shiva,* the seven-day mourning period following burial (Donin, 1972; Levine, 1998). If the deceased is a parent, the tear is often made over the heart, or over the right side of the garment if another relative. At this time a blessing is conveyed: *Baruch ata adonai elohainu melech ha-olam dayan ha-emet* ("Blessed art Thou, Lord our God, the true Judge"). Although controversial among Judaic scholars, it is generally accepted that mourners rend the garment even when the person has completed suicide.

There is no honor in suicide according to Jewish tradition, and this belief is carried over into parts of the mourning, burial, and observance periods. First and foremost, although the person completing suicide is to be admonished (assuming that it was not rendered an accident or the individual was considered to be mentally ill), respect for the family is still shown. Unlike nonsuicidal deaths in which the family is responsible for making funeral arrangements and caring for the deceased, the whole community is responsible for making arrangements if the death is considered a suicide. The reason behind this difference is that the Jewish community, and Judaism as a whole, treats the suicide as an abhorrence. The usual immediate mourning rituals do not generally apply either; however, respect is paid to the family through visitation. The mourning period called *aninut* (the time between death and burial) applies only until the funeral arrangements have been made and not until the interment, as is traditional (Lamm, 1969).

The usual procedures for burial are followed (e.g., shroud, casket, grave). No eulogy is given at the funeral home for a person who completed suicide, and a tombstone is permissible but without the benefit of eulogy (again, if not deemed an accident or mental illness). If the cause of death is determined by a rabbi to be an intentional suicide, the individual cannot be buried within six feet of another in a Jewish cemetery, and is usually placed in a separate area or near the perimeter. Sons of the person who completed suicide still recite the Kaddish (Jewish prayer; see later) but if Orthodox must recite it for twelve months, instead of the customary eleven months of recitation, in order for the deceased to receive full redemption for his or her act. Of course, the process and time frame for reciting the Kaddish for family members will vary depending on the level of faith expressed by your clients.

Much of the following information pertains to Orthodox and Conservative Jews, though certain rituals are followed to various degrees by the majority of mourning Reform Jews. As with many ceremonies and traditions, the degree to which one follows many of the Jewish traditions is dependent upon the beliefs of the individual. It is best for the counselor to follow the client's lead regarding ceremonial rituals, but the reader is given a general background of some of the rituals here.

There are three periods of mourning following burial in Jewish tradition, regardless of the type of death. The first, *shiva,* occurs during the first week (three days for Reform Jews) and is observed by the father, mother, spouse, son, daughter, brother, and sister. Comforting the mourner as an outsider does not begin until after the burial in order to give the grieving family enough time to show their fullest amount of grief. Consistent with Ezekiel 24:17, the mourners' first meal after burial (the "Meal of Comfort") is provided by someone outside of the family. In Orthodox tradition, no greetings are exchanged upon entering the house, as the mourner initiates the conversation. However, Conservative and Reform Jews allow for the expression of condolences to the mourners upon arrival. Visitors should also not divert the conversation onto another topic because that decreases the chances of the mourners expressing their grief appropriately. Upon leaving, the mourners say: *Hamakom y'nahaim etkhem b'tokh sh'ar availai tziyon vee-yerushalayim* ("May the Lord comfort you with all the mourners of Zion and Jerusalem"). Following tradition, mourners sit on low stools or the floor, and engage in rituals such as not wearing cosmetics, not bathing, and not shaving. Mirrors are often covered so mourners cannot focus on themselves, although there are various interpretations as to the origin of this ritual.

The second period of mourning, lasting thirty days, is called *shloshim* (thirty), and concludes the mourning for everyone except for the mother and father. Rituals are respected such as not cutting one's hair and not attending parties. The third period, lasting for the rest of the year, is called *avelut* (mourning). Joyous occasions are avoided during this mourning period, and sons recite the Kaddish prayer at religious services. The Kaddish is recited daily because in times of distress there may be a tendency for mourners to strike out against God, and this ritualized prayer helps the sons maintain contact with a loving God. A *minyan,* or quorum of ten Jewish males, is required to recite the Kaddish, though this is not always practical. The sons recite the Kaddish each year on the anniversary *(Yahreit)* of the death, and mourners light candles that burn for twenty-four hours (www.jewfaq.org/death.htm). The *Yahreit* is also a day to perform acts of kindness.

Prior to death, Jews believe that life is measured by the deeds one does and by whether the person has fulfilled his or her potential. The time before death (such as resulting from terminal illness) should be a time during which one reflects on his or her life's works. Some people at this time leave *ethical wills,* which are documents through which individuals pass along values, beliefs, and hopes to younger generations (Levine, 1998).

Jewish Views of the Afterlife

The Torah emphasizes immediate and definitive rewards and punishments while on earth, instead of abstract future rewards and punishments (e.g., Leviticus 26:3-9, Deutronomy 11:13-15). However, the Torah also acknowledges that specific passages denote loved ones will be reunited upon death and the wicked will be separated from their loved ones (these people experience *kareit,* or spiritual exclusion), indicating that there is an existence after death. Some who espouse the Jewish faith believe in an afterlife whereas others do not. Examples of passages acknowledging the postdeath existence can be found in Genesis 25:8 ("Then Abraham breathed his last and died at a good old age, an old man and full of years, and he was gathered to his people") and Deuteronomy 32:50 ("There on the mountain that you have climbed you will die and be gathered to your people, just as your brother Aaron died on Mount Hor and was gathered to his people").*

There are common misperceptions by non-Jews of what Jews believe happens after the body dies. To confuse the issue more, there are as many beliefs about the afterlife among Jews as there are among other religious faiths. The general belief is that upon death the soul returns to God, is immortal, and has consciousness, similar to beliefs in

---

*New International Version of the Bible.

other religions such as in Christianity. This spiritual place is referred to as *Olam-Haba,* and this also refers to the future time in which God will reign over the land and the souls of the dead will rise (Levine, 1998). Olam-Haba is a time during which all people will be judged and decisions will be made on their soul's final resting place.

At the time of death, a time of purification of the soul occurs, which may take anywhere from a brief time period for a righteous person to over a year for an evil individual. Some Jews believe that the evil person will return to the dust from which he or she came, whereas others believe that an angel appears for each bad deed performed. These angels then torment the soul for the length of time needed to cleanse it. Upon cleansing, Jews who follow the Sephardic tradition (Jews descended from Spain, the Middle East, and Africa) believe that the soul rests in *Gan Eden,* in the presence of God for eternity. Those Jews who follow the book of Ezekiel believe that upon death, the soul rests and waits for the coming of the Messiah during the Final Judgment. "Thus said the Lord God: I am going to open your graves and lift you out of the graves . . . and bring you to the land of Israel. I will put My breath into you and you shall live again" (Ezekiel 37:12-14).

Life is considered to be so precious that deliberately taking or hastening a life is considered morally wrong. Within the Jewish community though, there has been recent debate about whether Jewish law (the Talmud) prohibits taking someone off medical life support, for example. Orthodox Jews generally believe that the decision to take an individual off life support is counter to the Talmud, while Reformed Jews may believe that this choice may be appropriate in certain circumstances (Levine, 1998).

Burial and Autopsies

The process of caring for the dead until burial is performed by only the most admirable of the Jewish community members, and for some families people sit with the dead body and are considered keepers, or *"shomerim."* Embalming and removing bodily organs from the body is strictly forbidden. Keeping the body whole is valued; therefore, blood and organs are considered to be a part of the person. The body is to be buried as soon as possible, but never on the Sabbath or on the first day of traditional Jewish festivals, and closed caskets are considered honorable. Cremations are generally forbidden, but if cremation occurs and the ashes are not returned to the earth then the family is not required to observe *shiva* (Donin, 1972). Autopsies are prohibited unless there are unusual circumstances as determined by the rabbi. Often, exceptions are made by the rabbi if an autopsy would save another life, or in some cases of law. Specific rules do apply though and it is highly recommended that a family member consult a rabbi prior to an autopsy agreement (www.jewfaq.org/death.htm).

Of course, it serves the clinician well to have a general understanding of some of the basic traditions surrounding death and suicide should he or she be working with family members and friends. Those interested in learning more about Jewish views of the afterlife are directed to three excellent texts: *The Death of Death: Resurrection and Immortality in Jewish Thought* by Neil Gillman, a Conservative rabbi at the Jewish Theological Seminary, and *Jewish Views of the Afterlife* by Raphael, a Reconstructionist rabbi. Counselors interested in reading about Orthodox traditions are directed to the definitive text *The Jewish Way in Death and Mourning* by Maurice Lamm.

The Church of Jesus Christ of Latter-day Saints

Followers of the LDS tradition believe in a unique blend of Jewish and Christian doctrines in combination with the teachings of the modern prophet Joseph Smith. Joseph Smith was fourteen years old in 1820 when he received the first of several appearances by messengers from God who informed him that he would have a special role in the church. Three years later, he received a second vision indicating this messenger was one of the authors of buried ancient scriptural writings engraved on metal plates. These plates contained information about the 1,000-year spiritual history of two Israeli families that eventually became two civilizations. Joseph Smith translated these plates through spiritual guidance, thus creating the *Book of Mormon: Another Testament of Jesus Christ*. The Book of Mormon is considered to be an additional word of God in conjunction with the Bible. It is more respectful for clinicians who are not LDS to call their clients LDS rather than Mormons for two reasons: first, Mormon was a term used by early enemies of the church, and second, the LDS designation highlights the role of Jesus Christ in their faith (Ulrich, Richards, & Bergin, 2000).

LDS and Suicide

Latter-day Saints followers are the least likely of any of the major religions to complete suicide, and this religion has one of the longest life expectancies of any religious group in the United States. Latter-day Saints do not condone suicide but leave judgment up to God. There is no specific reference in the Book of Mormon that discusses suicide, but there are biblical references, as discussed earlier. According to The General Handbook of Instructions (1998), a life-guiding text within the LDS church, a person who takes his own life may not be responsible for his acts. Only God can judge such a matter. In addition, although the "Thou shall not kill" commandment is accepted by the LDS church to include killing oneself, it has explicitly extended it to include self-destructive behaviors that may lead to suicide deaths (e.g., reckless driving leading to death, drug abuse). A person who has considered suicide seriously or has attempted suicide is often counseled by the bishop and may be encouraged to seek professional help. If the client is already seeing a non-LDS counselor, then collaboration with the local bishop may be fruitful. As always, it would be extremely beneficial for the counselor to become familiar with the tenets of the LDS faith.

The church believes that life is a gift from God and taking one's own life is sinful. The short time that a person exists on earth determines his or her eternal existence and acts as a testing period, similar to other religious doctrines. Therefore, no one has the right to kill themselves because life is a test from God and a person who completes suicide behaves against the will of God. Further, the LDS faith is consistent with others in that one does not have a right to complete suicide because it affects many others. Therefore, one's life does not belong solely to that individual, but also to the numerous people who will be affected by his or her suicide. The LDS church does, however, allow that mentally disturbed people are not responsible for their suicides, consistent with other religious traditions (e.g., the Catholic faith). People who complete suicide will not be received into the Celestial Kingdom, the highest level in the afterlife, and therefore will spend time in hell prior to possibly gaining access to the Telestial Kingdom.

LDS Views of the Afterlife

According to LDS doctrine, death is merely a separation of the spirit and the body. Individual qualities (e.g., personalities, abilities) are carried into the afterlife. People who followed the teachings of Jesus Christ will continue to do so in the afterlife, whereas those who have not will enter the spirit world. The *postmortal spirit world* is a place where the person is placed in the hands of God. After the mortal physical death, the spirits of all men, whether they are good or evil, are taken to God (Alma 40:11).* They are then assigned, after judgment, to a place in paradise or a place of hell, depending on their behavior in their mortal life. The postmortal spirit world is a place of continued learning, and there is a continuation of work, life, and activities (Mosiah 4:6; Doctrine and Covenants [D and C]† 33:1).

God is considered to be fair and loving, and each person is judged by the willingness to follow the works of God. After judgment, people will be placed into the appropriate Kingdom, which is described later. Followers of the LDS church believe that individuals are judged not just by God but also by the apostles. Other saints and prophets also assist in judgment, creating a hierarchy of the judged, with Jesus sitting at the throne. Judgments of eternal damnation are conducted by Jesus alone.

The LDS church does not believe in a singular heaven but instead believes that the saved are placed in one of three Kingdoms of Glory, depending on the person's lifestyle while on earth. The apostle Paul spoke of three glories (1 Corinthians 15:40-41), and Jesus intimated multiple glories when he said, "In my father's house are many mansions" (John 14:2). The first two are named *celestial* and *terrestrial* by the apostle Paul whereas the third was unnamed. Prophets Joseph Smith and Sidney Rigdon experienced a vision on February 16, 1832, and reported the third glory as *telestial*. The Celestial Kingdom, the highest glory, is reserved for those who embrace the gospel of Jesus, are baptized by immersion, repent for their sins, and receive the Holy Ghost by the laying on of hands (Dahl, 1992). They will spend eternity in the presence of Jesus and God. Only those who follow the word of God and engage in a temple marriage between a man and a woman

---

*Much of the information is taken from chapters from the Book of Mormon.

†Doctrine and Covenants: A collection of works not translated but given by God to modern prophets. It is used in conjunction with the Bible, the Book of Mormon, and other religious texts.

are capable of attaining the highest degree of glory. Those who attain this highest level in the Celestial Kingdom become gods, receive exaltation, and are joint heirs with Christ (cf. Romans 8:14 17; D and C 76:50-70; 84:33-39; 132:19-25) (Dahl, 1992). Due to the requirement that only heterosexual couples can enter the Celestial Kingdom, there are some concerns for those who are GLBT. This dilemma will be addressed later.

The Terrestrial Kingdom is reserved for people who have generally followed God's law but have not been fittingly virtuous to obey all of the principles of the gospel (D and C 76:71-80). They do not receive all of the benefits of the Celestial Kingdom but are sufficiently rewarded in heaven based on their acts while on earth (Dahl, 1992).

The Telestial Kingdom is reserved for those who have not received and abided by the gospel of Christ. This kingdom is for those who have lied, committed adultery, murder, and other sins but did not repent. The majority of people end up in Telestial Glory. These people are judged unworthy of entering the Kingdom of God and must spend time in hell during which they must repent and come to understand God's word. However, they still do not receive the fullness of the gospel. The Telestial Kingdom is still considered to be a glory that surpasses all understanding (D and C 76:81-90; 98-112; 88:100-101).

The LDS church believes that there are at least three impressions of hell. First is the sense of misery while on earth as a result of disobeying God's laws. These people can be rescued while still on earth through the teachings of Jesus Christ and through the seeking of atonement. Second, there exists a temporary state of spirit misery while preparing for the resurrection, in which cleansing of the soul occurs. The majority of souls in this state will eventually receive the Telestial Kingdom. Third, the permanent state for those who commit blasphemy and who cannot be cleansed through atonement. They remain in hell even after the resurrection. Everyone will hear the gospel of Christ, whether on earth or in the postmortal spirit world, and acceptance or nonacceptance determines his or her chances of achieving glory.

LDS Funerals and Mourning

Outward displays of mourning are considered appropriate and expected, as it shows the amount of affection toward the deceased. As with many funerals, LDS funerals are solemn occasions. However, there is also a spirit of hope because of the belief of a future reunion with the deceased after this mortal life (Madsen, 1992). The funeral usually takes place in the LDS chapel or a mortuary under the guidance of the bishop of the ward. Latter-day Saints members who complete suicide are not dishonored and, if in good standing with the church, can be buried in temple clothes following normal funeral services. Funerals usually begin and end with a hymn and a prayer by a family member. There are often reminders that the difficulties on earth are temporary and following the word of God will bring eternal joy. The funeral consists of eulogies and sentiments, and often people will speak about the Atonement, Resurrection, and other doctrines. Typically, the graveside ceremony is attended by family members and a few intimate friends.

GAY/LESBIAN/BISEXUAL/TRANSGENDER ISSUES

Case Example

Kelly, a twenty-four-year-old European American, college-educated, religiously conservative lesbian female, arrived for counseling services because of her belief that she was going to hell. Her father, an Episcopalian minister, has suspected that she was lesbian but Kelly never told him or other family members. She grew up in a strict household in which rules were made and were not to be broken. Kelly was instructed to attend church two times a week at her father's church. During her teenage years she recalls hearing her father rile homosexuals and indicate that they were going to hell. Kelly wanted to "come out" to others, especially her family, but was afraid to do so. She made an appointment for counseling because she had recent thoughts of suicide in order to save her family the embarrassment of having a lesbian daughter. Upon her arrival at the counseling clinic a formal suicide assessment was completed by the counselor and discussion occurred about her shame of disappointing her family and her inevitable future after her death. She was not found to have suicidal ideation that day and indicated that she would contract for six weekly sessions with the counselor. Renegotiation of the contract would occur after six weeks. Part of her treatment involved alternative ways of reading the Bible, moving away from a more literal to a more historical-critical perspective. This new perspective allowed her to interpret her prior teachings in a broader light, but also added anxiety because her religious beliefs and worldview were challenged. In essence, she began to see that her learned interpretation of biblical suicide was just that, an interpretation. However, she also began to have increased anxiety because she relied on her faith for much of her life and her worldviews in a number of areas began to be challenged. Treatment focused on broadening her worldview in many areas. Her anxiety eventually increased to the point where she had more frequent suicidal thoughts, but also presented a sense that she should continue in treatment. Therapy was renegotiated and work began on discussing her being a lesbian with her family. As a therapist, what other issues might you consider?

There has been little empirical research on the relationship of GLBT issues and suicide across the life span. However, because of high rates of suicide ideation, attempts, and completions among GLBT youths, the limited empirical literature available has focused primarily on youths, with decreased emphasis on middle and late adulthood. Therefore, I will emphasize the literature on GLBT adolescents in this chapter. The little research there is on adult GLBTs indicates an inverse relationship between suicidal ideation and age. In other words, the older one gets the less likely it is that social influences resulting from sexual orientation become an important factor in self-destructive behaviors. Many clinicians and researchers believe that this inverse relationship is related to the fact that most GLBT clients are out of the closet to one degree or another by the time they are in their late twenties or thirties, and feel more comfortable as sexual beings than younger GLBT clients. More research clearly needs to be conducted to better understand the relationship of sexual orientation and suicide, particularly studies focusing on related issues such as internalized homonegativism and basic developmental sexual identity issues. Comfort with sexual identity is often considered to be grounded in developmental theory. Understanding the within-individual nuances of identity maturity may help lead to increased understanding of the effects of stressors and environmental influences on GLBT persons based on their individual developmental levels.

Of course, many GLBT clients come out at different times during their lives, and this can be stressful regardless of the age. For example, during an evaluation I spoke with a male client in his mid-forties who was in the process of coming out. His greatest source of stress was informing his parents, both of whom are conservative Southern Baptists and believe, according to the client, that gay individuals will enter hell. Though he was not suicidal during the brief time that I saw him, he indicated that he had considered it within the past six months. During the short period of time that I spent with him, we discussed his parents' potential reactions upon hearing that he had completed suicide versus their reactions to the information that he is gay. Neither reactions were positive, but there were qualitative differences in the responses and I recommended that his counselor consider focusing on these areas.

General Issues and Youths

Most of the research conducted on the percentage of GLBT youths who engage in nonfatal (including ideation) and fatal suicidal behaviors has consistently shown rates in excess of 30 to 50 percent. Beginning with Gibson's (1989) now widely cited document on GLBT suicide, studies indicate that GLBT youths are much more likely than heterosexual youths to engage in nonfatal and fatal suicidal behaviors. Gibson suggested that the primary cause of the suicides was internalized homophobia. More recent studies (e.g., D'Augelli, 2002; Goldston, 2003) have found and reported similar results.

The importance of being GLBT as a separate suicide risk factor is a debated topic, as it has political ramifications (Garland & Zigler, 1993). Gay youths often cite similar reasons to those given by heterosexual youths for nonfatal suicidal behaviors (e.g., family dysfunction, low self-esteem, relationship problems; McDaniel et al., 2001), leading to questions about the role that being GLBT plays in suicide. In a review of the literature, McDaniel et al. (2001) indicated that GLBT youths may be at higher risk for maladaptive risk behaviors that may be associated with suicide, thus supporting the idea that GLBT issues are important factors to consider among some members of this age group. Savin-Williams and Ream (2003) recently concluded that sexual orientation did not predict suicidal behaviors but gay-related stressors did help predict these behaviors for a subset of their gay youth sample. Of course, there is nothing inherent among GLBTs that "cause" them to become more suicidal, but clinicians must consider different processes concerning self-destructive behaviors that may have root in being GLBT. Family and community nonacceptance, hate crimes, and personal discomfort may lead to increased self-destructive behaviors such as drug use or unprotected sex. Clinicians need to discuss sexual orientation issues, particularly with suicidal GLBT clients, to determine the level of confidence, comfort, developmental level, and stability with being GLBT. It is important for clinicians to understand some of the research data in order to aid in the assessment of suicide among GLBT youths, as being gay in America may increase the likelihood of at least suicide attempts, if not suicide completions.

Among adolescents, males are much more likely to report suicidal thoughts and attempts than females (a reversal from the heterosexual literature), and are also more likely to attempt suicide than heterosexual males and females. McBee-Strayer and Rogers (2002) found that almost 41 percent of their GLBT respondents significantly considered suicide, including identifying a specific suicide plan, or had made a serious attempt in the past. Almost half indicated that there was a chance for future suicide attempts. Abuse, identity issues, and social acceptance were reported as significant factors of suicidal ideation, and males were more likely to include substance abuse as a notable factor. Remafedi, Farrow, and Deisher (1993) found that 30 percent of their GLBT participants had attempted suicide at least once, with 50 percent of them reporting multiple efforts. A disturbing yet critical finding in the study was that the majority of these youths used more lethal means, which could eventually result in decreased rescue opportunities.

A number of other studies (e.g., D'Augelli & Hershberger, 1993; Rotheram-Borus, Hunter, & Rosario, 1994) found high nonlethal rates among their samples. The Youth Risk Behavior Studies found that, on average, gay male youths were three to four times more likely to attempt suicide that requires medical attention than heterosexual males. It was estimated that between 25 and 40 percent of gay male youths have engaged in nonfatal suicidal behaviors and over 50 percent have considered suicide. Of those who have engaged in nonfatal behaviors, almost 45 percent were repeat attempters. It should be reiterated that the majority of gay youths do not engage in self-destructive behaviors, and even if they did, being gay by itself does not predict attempts (Remafedi et al., 1993). However, being a sexual minority may be a concomitant factor given the stressors that often occur due to being gay. The numbers, though not as high for female youths, are still significantly higher than for the heterosexual population.

A few studies have considered the relationship of suicide with being GLBT on college campuses. Westefeld, Maples, Buford, and Taylor (2001) found strong relationships among depression, loneliness, reasons for living, and suicide in a GLBT college student sample (see also Westefeld et al., 2000). Sexual orientation by itself was not the critical factor, but the resultant isolation, by prejudice, and loneliness contributed to suicide risk. Other authors (e.g., Berrill, 1990; Norris, 1992) found similar results, denoting higher rates of prejudice against GLBT students resulting in increased emotional isolation and negative affectivity. Therefore, being GLBT in America is considered a high risk factor for suicide attempts, particularly for younger age groups. As gay Americans age, there is an inverse relationship between psychosocial problems and a homosexual identity (Remafedi, 1987). In other words, GLBTs become more comfortable with their sexuality as they age and are less likely to consider and complete suicide than younger GLBTs.

Unique Factors for Counselors

There are unique factors that the counselor should consider when considering gay client suicide risk. First, McBee and Rogers (1997) reported that identity confusion may play a role in the high rates of suicide among the gay and lesbian youth population, as coming out of the closet frequently welcomes negative behaviors from society, leading to feelings of inferiority, role confusion, and depression. There has been much speculation by researchers and clinicians that the usual identity issues corresponding with normal adolescent development are compounded by sexual identity confusion in gay youths. Teague (1992) reported that homosexual stigma leads to feelings of isolation, shame, and guilt. A reason for the difficulty in adjusting to society's norms is because of the still tight sex-role expectations. For example, Lamke (1982a, 1982b) found that masculine and androgynous roles (using the Bem Sex Role Inventory) resulted in healthier self-esteem among gay boys and girls, while feminine and undifferentiated roles resulted in increased psychosocial and adjustment difficulties. Gibson (1989) speculated that the earlier the gay or lesbian adolescent becomes aware that he or she is considered "different," the earlier potential problems may occur. This awareness and the corresponding problems may increase the rate of suicide attempts and completions.

Second, family dysfunction increases the risk of suicide (Kourany, 1987; McBee & Rogers, 1997; Schneider, Farberow, & Krucks, 1989). Family dysfunctional issues, such as poor role models and divorce, seem to be precipitating factors of gay and lesbian suicide attempts. These factors contribute to suicide attempts regardless of sexual orientation, but the counselor may want to be particularly vigilant of these factors when they occur in combination with adolescence and a gay sexual orientation. A correlate of family dysfunction is the degree of acceptance the gay adolescent receives from family members during the coming out process. Reactions from family members range from permanent, severed relationships to a parental process that has been aligned with the grief process. On the severe end of the spectrum, research consistently indicates that a significant number of gay homeless youths (often runaways) did not receive acceptance from family members after initially coming out. These teenagers were rejected from their homes or ostracized at school. The number of GLBT adolescents forced to leave home permanently though is low. At the other end of the spectrum are parents who run through a gambit of emotions consistent with death and dying grief models (e.g., shock, denial). Usually, parents will come to terms with their adolescent's homosexuality, with some accepting their child but not his or her behavior, whereas others eventually become completely accepting of their child's sexual orientation. It is the rare parent who accepts the child and has few or no concerns upon learning that their child is gay. Many parents suspect that their child is gay prior to the coming out process. It is extremely important for counselors to work with the family unit, and not merely the individual at this critical point, when the adolescent has decided to come out (or has recently). Poor reactions by family members increase the risk of suicidal behaviors.

Third, the severance of social ties increases the risk of suicide. The majority of Americans view homosexuality negatively, ranging from a religious sin to moral unacceptability and disgust. During the 2004 elections eleven states voted on a range of gay-marriage-union issues and all were soundly defeated, while many other states had previously held similar votes. Conservative religious figures such as James Dobson and Jerry Falwell consider homosexuality to be not only sinful but also a threat to family values. Other, less visible people have conflictive attitudes toward gays and lesbians, with thoughts such as, "I have no trouble with gays, but I'm glad that my son is not gay," or "I believe strongly in equal rights, but I reject the idea of gay marriages." Once the person has come out, previous social networks often collapse, increasing the need for counselors to be available and accepting of the gay client. Friends, family, and close associates often reject the individual, thus throwing the adolescent into a social identity crisis. Saunders and Valente (1987) indicated that withdrawal and severe depression may occur when the gay adolescent cannot talk to friends during especially burdensome periods, particularly as relationships dissolve (McBee & Rogers, 1997). Research consistently indicates that the loss of a significant relationship is a major contributor for gay males and lesbians seeking counseling services. Some clinicians and clients have reported that intimate relationships become more important in homosexual relationships than heterosexual relationships because of the social isolation often felt outside of the relationship. Many of the factors mentioned earlier contribute to nonfatal and fatal suicidal behaviors regardless of sexual orientation, but the counselor may want to be particularly vigilant of these factors when combined with adolescence and a gay sexual orientation, as they appear to be qualitatively different.

Fourth, if you are gay in America, you are likely to hide your homosexuality for a number of reasons. You are more likely to lose a job, be ridiculed publicly, and attacked verbally and physically than heterosexuals. Staying in the closet maintains a deceitful identity and is not necessarily the opposite of coming out. It is well accepted that coming out is a process that may take many years to conclude, if ever. Many GLBT persons have invented opposite-sex partners to avoid detailing the truth, avoid "coupled" social gatherings, and maintain secrecy surrounding their GLBT social and personal networks.

For gay persons who live in fear and secret, this can cause unique problems when a partner or friend dies. Unlike in heterosexual relationships, grief must be hidden, and one cannot talk about the loss to family, straight friends, neighbors, and co-workers. Counselors must also keep in mind that grief is often kept in check at the funeral of a GLBT individual if the deceased was in the closet. The natural family may not be aware of their child being gay, and the secret is maintained through stilted grieving at the funeral in order to show respect for the deceased. In addition, given various religious views regarding premarital sex, religious leaders may frown upon allowing the individual a funeral ceremony. This is further compounded when the deceased took his or her own life during the course of AIDS (Saynor, 1988).

Religious Faiths' Views of GLBTs

Christianity and Homosexuality

As always, both counselors and clients must consider their beliefs surrounding their interpretation of the Bible. As a counselor, are you somebody who takes the Bible literally, or do you consider the historical-critical context of the book? Recent evidence suggests that your response may differ depending on the topic one is considering (Leach, Levy, Denton, & Owens, 2004). Your response to this question when considering GLBT issues may help to assist with or detract from your effectiveness when working with a gay client who has been told through Christian churches that he or she is defective, a sinner, and going to hell. There are numerous passages in the Bible that some consider God's testament on homosexuality, with the scripture readings denoting anti-homosexuality. Many counselors have encountered clients with traditional religious beliefs who say, "Why don't I just kill myself since I was born defective and will spend eternity in hell."

In addition, because of the doctrine in some churches, many GLBT clients have repeatedly understood that God condemns homosexuality and they are not welcome in either church or heaven itself. I believe that since some of your gay clients in various stages of identity development believe they have been condemned, either directly or indirectly by the Christian Church, it is critically important for the counselor to be aware of the most frequently mentioned passages regarding homosexual acts. The reader will notice a bias of mine toward a more historical-critical, or culturally consistent view of the biblical texts, meaning that one cannot read the Bible without considering the culture and context in which it was written. Much of our contemporary society has determined that numerous biblical passages are not applicable in today's world and "picks and chooses" what works in the particular situation (Leach et al., 2004). For example, the majority of our society does not literally follow many of the rules outlined in the Old Testament such as one cannot touch a woman who is menstruating (Leviticus 15:19-24), work on the Sabbath (Exodus 35:2), or eat shellfish (Leviticus 11:10). Therefore, I take the position that homosexuality in the Bible must be considered within the context of the day. I also understand and respect readers who espouse more traditional or literal beliefs regarding homosexuality and the Bible.

Which biblical passages are said to deal with homosexuality? Much of the following information is summarized from Helminiak (2000), a scholar who has written extensively on homosexuality and Christianity. I have found that gay clients who have learned a more traditional religious approach to homosexuality are frequently surprised to learn that there are alternative interpretations for biblical text supposedly admonishing homosexuality. Some of the more frequent biblical scriptures and stories are discussed here, with the less-frequently mentioned alternative interpretations now gaining increased respect among many theologians. Suicidal gay clients may wish to discuss their traditional Christian beliefs surrounding being GLBT, particularly since they have often grown up hearing they are flawed and an abomination. Counselors familiar with these and other biblical passages can discuss client beliefs from an alternative angle, and it is highly recommended that counselors read interpretations of biblical text from alternative perspectives. Clients can often find relief from discussions that allow reinterpretation of previously held beliefs. A major concern is not whether clients are willing to discuss their religious beliefs but whether the clinician feels comfortable discussing religious issues. The following biblical text passages are commonly considered to relate to homosexuality.

The story of Lot in the geographic area of Sodom and Gomorrah is frequently mentioned as a primary biblical reference condemning homosexual behaviors. It should be noted that biblical writers were unaware of the differentiation of sexual orientation and behaviors and thus described behaviors only. In Genesis (19:1-11) Lot was sitting at the gateway of Sodom when two male angels appeared to him. Shortly after inviting them into his home, all of the men in Sodom surrounded the house and questioned Lot as to the identity of the men. They asked Lot to bring the men out "so that we may *know* them" (Genesis 19:5; italics added). The interpretation of this passage is that the men of the town wanted to have sex with the angels. Lot went out and said, "I beg you, my brothers, do not act so wickedly. Look, I have two daughters who have not known a man; let me bring them out to you, and do to them as you please; only do nothing to these men, for they have come under the shelter of my roof" (Genesis 19:7). The men of Sodom approached the door to break it down, but the two men (angels) inside reached out their hands and brought Lot back into the house and blinded the townsmen.

The verb "to know" occurs almost 1,000 times in the Old Testament, and this is one of the ten times scholars believe that it is considered to have a sexual connotation (Helminiak, 2000). Helminiak and other more liberal biblical scholars have argued that the sin of these Sodomites was not the homosexual act implied in the passages but that they would break the cultural duty of hospitality. Why would Lot offer his daughters at great personal and economic cost given that his daughters were considered valuable commodities? A cardinal rule of Arabic, Semitic, and Lot's culture was the belief that God expects one to protect and offer shelter to anyone who asks, even if the person is an enemy. By allowing the townsmen to intrude on the houseguests, Lot would have broken God's law of hospitality. Although some may balk at this interpretation, many scholars believe that Ezekiel (16:48-49) has final authority by indicating that the sin of Sodom was not sexuality based but a matter of not helping the poor and needy. In this passage of Ezekiel there is no mention of sin concerning sexual behaviors. Therefore, it does not appear that the sin of Sodom was homosexual acts but that they failed to welcome needy travelers. Other passages such as those in Wisdom (19:13) connote that the sin was a hatred of strangers, resulting in inhospitality, which denied Jewish law. There are other passages that biblical scholars have used to admonish homosexuality whereas other interpretations have argued that they have nothing to do with sexuality. They indicate that the Sodom account is about injustice, oppression, partiality, adultery, lying, and encouraging evildoers. Adultery is the only sexual sin listed here, but many historical scholars believe that the sin still was not sexual, but a sin against justice since women were considered the property of men.

Other historical scholars have argued for another perspective that places same-sex behaviors in a more tempered light. Western history has indicated that it was not male-male sex that was despised, but the forced taking of the unwilling partner, thus creating a power differential. For example, both St. John Chrysostom (fifth century) and Peter Cantor (twelfth century) indicated that same-sex behaviors were acceptable if the partners were active (Helminiak, 2000). If one was receptive only he was considered unmanly. If there was any objection at all it was not that the sexual behavior occurred but that one of the men was considered effeminate. That attitude has transferred to various modern ethnic groups such as the Hispanic and Asian communities. As the Hispanic American and Asian Americans chapters indicate, sexual orientation can be viewed differently from mainstream European American and same-sex behaviors can occur, though the passive individual (usually male) is often the only individual considered effeminate or gay. The power differential involved in the story of Lot (a mob of men versus two visitors in Lot's home) attests to an additional nonsexuality theme.

Another popular writing used to condemn homosexual acts is found in Leviticus 18:22: "You shall not lie with a male as with a woman; it is an abomination." There is additional punishment in Leviticus 20:13: "If a man lies with a male as with a woman, both of them have committed an abomination; they shall be put to death, their blood is upon them." Historical-critical biblical scholars indicate that numerous acts, including swearing at one's parents, were considered sins punishable by death (Helminiak, 2000). Engaging in homosexual acts had a very different meaning in the days of Leviticus. To participate in homosexual acts was not considered condemnable because of sex but because engaging in this sex meant acting as a Gentile or a non-Jew. Therefore, homosexual acts were condemned by Leviticus not because of the actual sexual act but because it was considered to be religious treason. In fact, Leviticus does not specifically make any statement about the morality of homosexual acts. Therefore, Helminiak indicates that one cannot condone or condemn present-day homosexual acts based on Leviticus because they are discussing two different ideas.

Some scholars also argue that the term "abomination" carried a different meaning in ancient Israel in the days of Leviticus. Although today we may use the term to describe something horrific, Leviticus (20:25-26) suggests that the term may be simply another word for unclean and therefore a violation of the purity rules of Israel. This code was designed to keep the Israelites separate from other people.

Considerations for counselors. Homosexuality is a difficult topic for many counselors-in-training, as well as for many professional counselors. The difficulty often stems from religious beliefs, including many of the passages described earlier. It is my belief that if counselors feel so strongly about conservative or literal interpretations of these biblical passages when their suicidal clients hold similar beliefs, then they are much less likely to benefit the client. Often, counseling includes a strong emphasis on the role of biblical text with these clients. If at all possible, counselors should become familiar with various interpretations of biblical references to assist clients in considering alternative, less self-defeating attitudes.

As shown earlier some biblical scholars offer interpretations not often discussed in churches across the country. It is easy to understand why many GLBT suicidal clients carry thoughts of condemnation because of religious upbringing. Most congregants and many religious leaders have not considered multiple perspectives on homosexuality, particularly if their beliefs are conservative and their translation of the Bible is literal. Discussing alternative interpretations with a client who believes that he or she is defective and going to hell may cause initial dissonance yet could reap potential long-term benefits. This type of work can be accomplished if the client is not in immediate danger and is working on identity and self-esteem issues. Of course, the belief about going to hell can also be considered a buffer with some suicidal clients; hence, reinforcement of that idea may be in the client's immediate interest. Numerous books discussing the Bible and homosexuality in modern America are now obtainable, and these may be helpful for some clients to become aware of alternative explanations. Many clients (and students) with whom I have shared books such as the one by Helminiak (2000) have found it immensely freeing and useful because frequently they had not considered alternative explanations to their traditional religious upbringing.

LDS and Homosexuality

Unlike some of the other major religions, it is extremely difficult to be gay and maintain strict membership in the LDS Church, or at least maintain many of the beliefs espoused by the Church. As alluded to earlier, it is impossible to be gay or lesbian and attain the Celestial Kingdom in the LDS Church. The Church requires that only people who fully receive the gospel, have faith in Jesus Christ, repent for their sins, are baptized by immersion, and have entered into the *covenant of marriage performed in the temple* (sealing) can gain access to this Kingdom. Since the LDS Church considers engaging in homosexual behaviors to be contrary to God's will, it is impossible for a gay couple to receive a temple marriage, and therefore they cannot attain the highest degree of glory. In addition, the role of women in the afterlife has been the cause of some debate within the LDS Church. It is generally accepted that men who have been received into the Celestial Kingdom are reunited with their wives. Since gay couples are not man and wife, they cannot arrive at the Celestial Kingdom. It may be helpful for the clinician to discuss the client's God images and the degree to which he or she holds conservative LDS beliefs. Gay male and lesbian clients may have to focus increased attention on God's love and grace more than the specific teachings of the Church, consistent with many others who must separate that part of their identity from their respective faith groups. At some point the client may have to significantly modify beliefs about what the Church has taught them and what being gay means to him or her.

These modified beliefs also hold true for gay allies who belong to various religious groups, as they may reject the Church's stance on homosexuality yet maintain Church teachings in other areas. Faith, death, the afterlife, how the LDS Church and other faith groups view homosexuality and suicide, and their legacy should they complete suicide are considered important topics and are often discussed. For example, some clients respond to other faith groups' ideas about being gay and eventually residing in heaven. Most of the mainstream religious organizations in the United States officially denounce homosexuality, yet some individual religious figures and parishioners hold less stringent views. Recently, the Presbyterian Church of America held a conference with much volatility over GLBT issues in the church, and a recent ruling over the ministry of a lesbian pastor in the Pacific Northwest Conference (Washington State) has divided many people from the Methodist tradition. Regardless, clients can often benefit from the understanding that not all faiths treat homosexuality in similar fashion and espouse the same beliefs as the LDS church. Consistent with most suicidal clients engaging in tunnel vision thinking, it is the hope that the counselor can expand the client's religious beliefs without denying the individual.

Judaism and Homosexuality

According to Orthodox tradition, the Torah does not mention homosexual orientation (sexual orientation was unknown at that time, unlike behaviors) but does strictly forbid sexual relations between men (e.g., Leviticus 18:22), considering homosexual behavior among men as abhorrent. The Torah considers homosexual sex as a grievous sin, one of the few sins described in very strong language. However, the Torah delineates sexual behavior based on gender. In Leviticus 20:13, sexual relations between men is considered a sin and punishable by death, as are adultery and incest. Female homosexual relations, however, are not explicitly forbidden by the Torah, and very few discussions of female homosexuality exist in the Talmud. Halacha (Jewish law) does indicate that women should avoid sexual relations with each other. However, as with many religious traditions struggling with issues surrounding GLBTs, the Jewish community also possesses diverse thinking on the topic.

Some Chazal (the rabbis) interpret "to lie" in Leviticus 18:22 ("Do not lie with a man as one lies with a woman; that is detestable") as meaning anal sex. While there is controversy over the interpretation of this term, some Jewish gay men believe that it is therefore acceptable to engage in other forms of sexual relations (e.g., mutual masturbation, oral sex). Some Jewish clients may arrive at the counselor's office with the belief that they cannot be both gay and *frum* (a religiously observant Jew). Therefore, their belief may suggest that they cannot attend the synagogue or practice Judaism if they are gay. Their identity or sense of self may become jagged, thus leading to depression, anguish, fear, and potentially suicide. How they interpret the Torah is of utmost importance, but many Orthodox Jews now believe that if homosexuality is genetically based, then they may not be responsible for their actions (members.aol.com/GayJews/FAQ/html). Overall, it is acceptable to be gay and Jewish, to even think about sexual relations with another man, but Jewish law prohibits sexual relations between homosexuals. It would be helpful for non-Jewish counselors to understand the various interpretations of the passages, along with receiving consultation from a rabbi, in order to offset a potentially lethal situation with a client. Counseling can be accomplished in conjunction with a rabbi perhaps, currently an underutilized counseling resource.

The Central Conference on American Rabbis (CCAR), through the Reform movement, has had a long history of supporting equal rights for gay and lesbian Jews. In 1977 the CCAR called for an end to the criminalization of homosexual acts between consenting adults, and in 1990 the Conference adopted a policy allowing gays to become full members of the rabbinate. This view was consistent with the recently adopted policy of the Hebrew Union College-Jewish Institute of Religion (HUC-JIR), which allowed for all HUC-JIR graduates to be welcomed into the CCAR upon application, regardless of their sexual orientation. However, at that time, it was unclear as to whether CCAR would acknowledge a homosexual relationship as *kiddushin* ("Jewish marriage"). In 1996 a resolution resolved to support the rights of Jewish gay men and lesbians to receive all of the benefits of a civil marriage. The concept is that all Jews, notwithstanding their sexual orientation, are religiously equivalent. However, two ad hoc committees within the CCAR were formed to determine whether a ceremony could be considered *kiddushin*. In 1997 the Union of American Hebrew Congregations adopted a resolution to support secular proposals to legally legitimize same-sex marriages and for congregations to honor these marriages. By 1998 both committees of the CCAR reported their findings: the Ad Hoc Committee on Human Sexuality indicated that the ceremony performed would qualify as *kiddushin,* whereas the Committee on Responsa reported that a committed relationship would not qualify as *kiddushin*. Recently, Rabbi Yoffie of the CCAR stated that the Conference in Greensboro, North Carolina, affirmed through Jewish ritual the union of a homosexual couple (Yoffie, 2000). This resolution allows rabbis to officiate at these marriage ceremonies, though there is considerable opposition to the resolution. The resolution does not compel a rabbi to perform such a ceremony, does not outline the rituals to be performed, and does not indicate that the ceremony should be considered a "marriage." Rabbinic participation is left to individual congregations but is a historical step of the Jewish faith toward accepting gay men and lesbians. Although many disagree with the following statement, Rabbi Yoffie (2000) voted for the resolution.

> I did so because of my belief that our gay and lesbian children, relatives, and friends are in great need of spiritual support; that the Torah's prohibition of homosexuality can reasonably be understood as a general condemnation of ancient cultic practice; that loving, permanent homosexual relationships, once difficult to conceive, are now recognized as an indisputable reality; and that in these relationships, whether or not we see them as "marriages" it is surely true that God and holiness can be present . . . if there is anything at all that Reform Jews do, it is to create an inclusive spiritual home for all those who seek the solace of our sanctuaries. And if this Movement does not extend support to all who have been victims of discrimination, including gays and

lesbians, then we have no right to call ourselves Reform Jews. (http://www.faqs.org/faqs/judaism/FAQ/10-Reform/section-19 .html)

SUMMARY

The majority of research studies and clinical interventions have been developed with the majority culture in mind, particularly since European Americans comprise nearly 90 percent of all confirmed suicides in the United States. However, there is a need for culture-specific prevention and intervention programs since the noncompletion and completion rates of members of other groups of color is increasing. Efforts developed and validated with primarily European American samples can be transferred, in part, to other groups. For example, it is unlikely that the relationship of substance abuse or the effects of family dysfunction differ significantly among group members. The differences occur through cultural nuances, such as whether racial identity and acculturation factors influence the treatment of depression, which may lead to substance abuse or family dysfunction. Some ethnic communities are more or less accepting of GLBT issues than the European American community and may lead to decreased or increased feelings of alienation. By including a range of ethnic, religious, and other cultural groups, we will be better able to identify not only critical factors for persons of color but also culture-specific factors for European Americans. Researchers must continue to determine the within-group cultural differences of the European American community also. For example, to what extent do conservative and less-conservative Christians and Jews rely on religious coping during times of extreme stress, and what factors determine the extent to which this coping occurs? What processes lead to suicidal ideation for young GLBTs who experience discrimination? The list of questions is endless. It is hoped that researchers and clinicians will concurrently consider cultural variables in their projects and interventions to gain a more robust understanding of what works for which clients and under what conditions.

Chapter 3

African Americans

"You're going to put me in the hospital again, I just know it."
"Why do you say that?"
"Because you're white and I'm black."

An interaction with a thirty-eight-year-old
African American woman, previously suicidal,
who had been stabilized for months on antipsychotic
medication and was not presently suicidal

Much has been written on the underreporting of African American suicides and the difficulties in establishing long-term trends in suicide rates (e.g., Joe & Kaplan, 2001; Lester, 1998). Although suicides among all ethnic groups are probably underreported, it becomes particularly salient when considering African Americans. In fact, Phillips and Ruth (1993) suggested that African American rates were misclassified more than any other ethnic group. The first issue—the role of the church and family when classifying suicide—is cultural. Classifications often get changed to "accidental death" for a multitude of reasons. Second, until the 1960s and early 1970s suicide rates were generally classified as whites and nonwhites, thus combining all persons of color into one category. Third, the idea of "victim-precipitated suicide" has been discussed in the literature. This term refers to deaths in which people, usually discussed in the literature as African American youths, place themselves in harm's way and officially die from homicide, though it can be argued that the death can be ruled a suicide. At the very least it is self-destructive behavior. The argument could be made that a segment of youths of all ethnic groups may

Cultural Diversity and Suicide
© 2006 by The Haworth Press, Inc. All rights reserved.
doi:10.1300/5680_03

engage in these behaviors though, and future research should expand beyond the African American designation.

DATA

Suicide within the African American community is often "described as an epidemiological paradox" (Watt & Sharp, 2002, p. 236). African Americans have historically experienced low suicide rates, despite a history of social and legal oppression such as segregation, slavery, and poverty (Chance, Kaslow, Summerville, & Wood, 1998; E. E. Griffith & Bell, 1989; Lester, 1998). Researchers have historically attempted to account for the suicide rates among the African American community by aligning the rate with risk factors such as poverty, racism, interpersonal and family dissension, and a host of other occurrences. As Baker (1988) indicated, this "African-American family deficit theory" is biased since it assumes that African American families cannot meet the needs of their members. It should be reiterated that suicide rates within the European American community are much higher than that within the African American community; hence, the deficit theory may need modification toward the European American community if it is maintained at all.

GENDER

The rate of suicide completion among African American males is about half that of Native Americans and European Americans per 100,000 people (approximately 11.2 compared to 20.9 and 19.4, respectively), whereas the completion rate for African American females is 1.9 per 100,000 (National Strategy for Suicide Prevention, retrieved January 6, 2005, from http://www.mentalhealth.samhsa. gov/suicide prevention/diverse.asp). In fact, the rate for African American females has dropped during the 1990s (National Center for Injury Prevention and Control, 1999), resulting in the lowest rate for ethnicity-by-gender groups (along with Hispanic women). As Baker (1994) reported over the lifetime, an African American male is 50 percent less likely to complete suicide than a European American man, and an African American woman is 270 percent less likely to complete suicide than a European American woman. However, the rate for African American male teenagers (ages fifteen to nineteen) has increased significantly over the past twenty years, with the rate being around 14.8 per 100,000 (Kachur et al., 1995). Lifetime prevalence attempt rates among nineteen- to twenty-two-year-olds is 5.3 to 6.6 percent per 100,000 people (Ialongo et al., 2002). Overall, suicide completion rates within the African American community are much lower than that of the European American community. In fact, suicide is the only means of death for which African Americans have lower mortality rates than European American (Lester, 1998; Rogers, 1992).

AGE

In the European American community, there is a fairly consistent trajectory of completed suicides across age groups. European Americans, particularly men, begin with a relatively high rate of completed suicide during adolescence and young adulthood, dip briefly during the late twenties and early thirties, and increase throughout the lifespan. African Americans, however, show completion rates similar to European Americans within the fifteen to nineteen age group, which rise during young adulthood, peak during the ages of twenty to thirty-four, and then decrease with age (Gibbs, 1997). Once past early adulthood the rates stay fairly flat and lower than European American rates. Suicide completion rates for African American males have increased since the early 1980s, though rates for other groups have also increased. The age group of twenty-five to thirty-four possesses the highest rate for African American male suicides. African American female rates, however, have declined slightly over the past twenty years. Because of the higher rates, I will focus on adolescents and young and middle adults primarily in the next sections, followed by a discussion of elderly African Americans.

African American Adolescents

Suicide is the third leading cause of death among African American youths (Kalafat & Elias, 1995). Statistics from the CDC indicate that African American adolescents attempted more suicides than European Americans, though the completion rates were lower (Lester, 1998). Unfortunately, the number of completed suicides among African American adolescents has increased since 1980, and the number of attempts since 1990 has grown fairly linearly. For African American male adolescents, the rate of completed suicide is now almost consistent with European American rates. Between 1980 and 1995 the rates of completed suicides for African Americans aged ten to nineteen more than doubled, from 2.1 to 4.5 per 100,000 people. This rate is low when considering the total population, but the over 100 percent increase is significant given a mere fifteen-year span. As expected, firearms accounted for almost 60 percent of completed adolescent suicides, with males using this method 87 percent of the time (Joe & Kaplan, 2001). Females are more likely to use drug overdoses or jumping as their means of suicide, though the rate of death by firearms among young women is quickly increasing. Joe and Marcus (2003) and Watt and Sharp (2002) reported that from 1991 to 2001 African American and European American nonfatal suicidal rates among adolescent females were also similar. Consistent with other ethnic groups, young African American women are more likely to attempt suicide than young African American men.

Risk Factors Among African American Adolescents

A number of risk factors have been associated with suicide within the African American community, particularly among youths. Many of these factors are consistent with youth risks in general, including feelings of hopelessness, impulsive behavior, and easy access to alcohol, illicit drugs, and guns (Garland & Zigler, 1993; Watt & Sharp, 2002). Other contextual factors include partner and community violence, family unit breakdown, economic changes, psychopathology, sexual abuse, and personal isolation (Hewitt, Newton, Flett, & Callander, 1997; Kaslow, Thompson, Brooks, & Twomey, 2000; King, Hovey, Brand, Wilson, & Ghaziuddin, 1997; Lewinsohn, Rhode, & Seeley, 1996; Pastore, Fisher, & Friedman, 1996). Some of these are cognitive and psychological factors whereas others can be conceptualized as social stressors. For example, Ialongo et al. (2002) found that African American youths living below the poverty line were more likely to have reported previous suicide attempts and ideation when compared with the youths living above the poverty line. They also reported that few African American adolescents who had attempted suicide previously had received subsequent mental health services. Koenig, Ialongo, and Wagner (2002) found similar results and indicated that they may be due in part to greater negative caregiver strategies and younger parental ages. Although the risk factor correlates among ethnic groups may not always be unique, there has been very little recent research examining the cultural processes occurring between groups. In essence, which of these and other factors contribute to suicidal behaviors among African American and European American youths, and do they differ based on ethnicity? For example, why are previous suicidal attempts a stronger predictor of suicide completion among European Americans than among African Americans (Bagley & Greer, 1972; Joe & Kaplan, 2001)? Why is it that depression seems to be a stronger predictor of suicide completion among African American females than among African American males? More research is clearly needed in the study of African American suicide, especially the relationship among cognitive, social, pathological, and cultural factors.

Strains

Watt and Sharp (2002) investigated the role of predictive social strains among African American and European American adolescents. They briefly summarized the theoretical literature attesting to whether African Americans and European Americans respond differently to status (i.e., economic mobility issues) and relational (e.g., relationship to family, church) strains. For example, Durkheim (1897/ 1951) and R. W. Maris (1969) argued that African Americans are less likely to respond to status strains than to relational strains, whereas European Americans showed the opposite pattern. Others have indicated no significant differences in suicide correlates among African and European Americans (Gunnar, Guest, Immerwahr, & Spittel, 1998). In their study of African American and European American nonfatal suicide adolescents, Watt and Sharp (2002) found process differences. African American adolescents were confronted with more status strain than European Americans, yet were less responsive to that strain than European Americans. If differences do exist in the process of suicide, then interventions that emphasize the different processes of African American and European American suicides can be devised. It is still premature, and perhaps incorrect, to design completely different interventions based on ethnicity alone, largely because of the commonalities that exist in other suicide areas (e.g., alcohol abuse, access to weapons) and the paucity of research in this area. The majority of these studies have focused on adults and not on adolescents. Regardless of the sometimes contradictory nature of social-strain research, when confronted with various strains it is clear that African Americans are still less likely to attempt and complete suicide than European Americans. It is clear that research in the area of African American youth suicides (and all age groups for that matter) should be increased. In particular, research is needed on the processes involved in nonfatal and fatal suicide behaviors to help refine and add specificity to suicide interventions among all ethnic groups.

CULTURAL BUFFERS

Given the historical oppression of African Americans it is necessary to identify reasons for the low suicide completion rates, as higher numbers would be expected intuitively. Consistent with other ethnic groups, comorbidity with psychiatric disorders is prevalent among African Americans that engage in nonfatal and fatal suicidal behaviors. Although there are psychodynamic and psychosocial explanations (see Chance et al., 1998, for a brief overview), a number of sociocultural hypotheses have recently been presented which may help in understanding the low rates of suicide when compared with other ethnic groups. Gibbs (1997) summarized five African American cultural values that diminish suicidal risk. These factors include (1) the church, (2) the central role of women, (3) elders, (4) the extended family and kin networks, and (5) cohesion within ethnic neighborhoods. Each of these factors will be discussed in greater depth in the following pages.

The Church

The African American Christian Church has long been considered to be a source of support for the African American community (Gibbs, 1997; Paniagua, 2005), and conjointly, the Church has proposed that suicide is a sinful act and therefore unacceptable. In this section, I will discuss suicide and its relation to the African American Christian community, followed by an overview of Islam and its views of suicide. The latter is included because the overwhelming majority of converts to the Islamic faith in the United States are African Americans. Though Gibbs was referring to the Christian Church, it is nonetheless important that the role of the Islamic faith be also included in this chapter.

Christianity

African Americans are more likely to hold intrinsic views of religion, engage in more personal devotion, are more conservative religiously and more frequent church attenders, and hold more rejecting attitudes toward suicide than European Americans, all correlated with decreased suicide behaviors (Greening & Stoppelbein, 2002; Neeleman et al., 1998). Some researchers (Billingsley, 1992; Gibbs, 1997) have indicated that because of the history of oppression in the United States, African Americans may have a collective resiliency or fortitude, which considers suicide a weakness and a stain on the Church. Some African American clients have indicated that suicide has historically been associated with "letting the man win" based on both cultural and religious ideas. The premise is that it is better to struggle because other African Americans endured significantly worse hardships, and the struggle is rewarded in heaven. Suicide is simply not an option for many African Americans because of the resiliency factor. Even when Stack (1998) reported the role of the African American church may have been overestimated with reduced suicide acceptability, church attendance was considered an important correlate.

Early and Akers (1993) interviewed a group of southern community pastors and each believed suicide to be an unpardonable sin resulting in eternal damnation. These pastors considered there to be no legitimate excuse for suicide. Suicide was considered "a white thing" and an unacceptable alternative to distress due to African American culture and resiliency (p. 288). This resiliency grew from oppressive historical and present-day events by which African Americans are continually reminded of and faced with negative prejudicial attitudes. During days of slavery laws, many of the songs sung while completing forced labor were comprised of biblical themes, which maintained a sense of collective identity.

The pastors interviewed considered it strange to be discussing a topic such as suicide because it was considered unusual in the African American community. However, these pastors also indicated that as

African Americans become more acculturated or mainstreamed into U.S. culture, suicide rates may increase. In a recent study, Walker (2003) found that low ethnic identification and acculturation stresses lead to increased suicide ideation among African American men with low religious identification. While there is no direct evidence yet that increased acculturation may lead to rising rates, it is interesting to note that the African American teen suicide rate has increased significantly in the past twenty years. This rate may be indicative of a growing trend, though we also know that suicide rates have increased among teens during this time period regardless of ethnicity.

Although there is a strong negative relationship between church attendance and suicide (Martin, 1984) for both African American and European American groups, African American women attend church at a higher rate than their European American counterparts. Therefore, religion, as measured by church attendance, may mitigate suicide rates and act as a suicide buffer. Other research indicates that African Americans are more likely to incorporate more internal and orthodox religious beliefs into their worldviews than European Americans (Greening & Stoppelbein, 2002). In addition, African American church leaders became community leaders and were critical players in the civil rights solidarity movement, which offered the community strength and hope. African American pastors still maintain high status within the community and their teachings on suicide still carry weight.

The literature on religion and suicide among ethnic groups is not clear though. Some of the confusion rests on whether one is discussing suicidal attitudes or behaviors and studying imagined circumstances surrounding suicide or actual nonfatal and fatal behaviors. For example, Marion and Range (2003a), in their study wherein African and European American women imagined themselves in various circumstances, found religion to correspond with negative attitudes toward suicide regardless of ethnicity. Overall though, the overwhelming majority of studies have found the African American Church to be an important component in suppressing suicidal behaviors. Clinicians may want to include a spiritual component to the treatment of most clients, particularly African American clients. This component may not include church attendance, but the addition of a historical familial connection, which can be spiritual.

Case Example

I was called to conduct a commitment evaluation of a twenty-one-year-old African American female who had made a suicide attempt. Prior to arriving at the holding facility, the only information available was that she had consumed an excessive number of pills of unknown type. Most states require either two physicians (usually psychiatrists) or a physician and a psychologist to conduct the evaluations. After the evaluation, the client proceeds to court and a judge determines whether he or she should be committed to an inpatient unit for further treatment. The psychiatrist met with our client and diagnosed her with schizophrenia, paranoid type. He administered 5 milligrams of Zyprexa just hours before I saw her. Upon my examination, she did not appear to have a history of any of the symptoms typically associated with schizophrenia. When queried further she indicated her husband had done something that shocked her and was antithetical to her religious beliefs. She was very conservative in her beliefs. The client described a scene in which she awakened at 3:00 a.m. to find her husband not in bed. After a few minutes she went looking for him downstairs and found him masturbating to pornographic videos. This behavior by her husband caused her such distress that it precipitated her suicide attempt. She indicated that if she were a "better wife" he never would have had to turn to pornography, and had thus not only disappointed her husband but God as well. She described her religious beliefs, and they led me to conclude that she espoused a very strong, fundamental religious faith.

Prior to her suicide attempt she indicated that she had spoken with her sister to ask for her guidance. At this point I was still unclear as to why she had been diagnosed with schizophrenia. After a few minutes she indicated that her sister had been dead for three years. Many readers might agree with the diagnosis because she may have experienced auditory and visual hallucinations. However, that did not appear to be the case when speaking with her. When asked further about her faith, she indicated that her church believed there are times when one can speak with the dead, and added some detail regarding the strict circumstances under which this can occur. She described it almost as a dream state, though awake. I then began to interview her about past psychiatric history, hallucinations, and delusions, and conducted a mental status exam, which was unremarkable. Nothing in the written evaluation completed by her husband indicated significant psychological symptoms either. My opinion was that she had not hallucinated in the traditional psychological sense but that it was an extension of her beliefs, and I did not diagnose her as a person with schizophrenia (or any psychotic disorder for that matter). I had considered, though, a brief psychotic break possibly precipitated by grief and distress, but did not diagnose her with a psychotic disorder. We then briefly discussed whether her sister would approve of the suicide attempt and other issues in which the sister was involved. After my interview I learned that the judge committed her to the state hospital.

Islam

Islam will be the second largest faith community in North America by 2010 (Haddad & Lummis, 1987), creating an urgency of therapists to increase their understanding of this rapidly growing faith tradition. The majority of African Americans in the United States consider themselves Christian, but 90 percent of American converts to Islam are African American, making Islam one of the fastest growing religious groups for African Americans in the United States. Approximately 42 percent of the U.S. Islamic community is comprised of African Americans, which is why Islam is covered in this chapter. It seems appropriate to discuss Islam here with regard to its beliefs about suicide.

Muslims believe in one God and that Muhammad was the last of the Prophets, after numerous others including Abraham, David, Moses, and Jesus. Islam (Arabic for "submission" to God) is the fastest growing religious faith in the world, with a growth rate of about 2.9 percent a year (www.religioustolerance.org/islam.htm), but it is considered the youngest of the major religions. Most Islamic followers believe that forty-year-old Muhammad received his first divine communication in a cave in Hira from the Angel Jibreel (Gabriel) in the year 610, and the communications continued over the next twenty-three years. The revelations eventually became the Quran (the holy scripture of Islam). Muhammed memorized the revelations and verbally handed them down to the new followers of Islam prior to converting them into the Quran, which is structured into 114 *suras* or chapters, with each chapter being called a *surat*. The text is not ordered chronologically, but structured so that the longest *surat* is the first and the shortest the last. The Quran is often spelled "Koran" in English but some Islamic followers find this spelling offensive and therefore the proper, respectful spelling will be used in this chapter.

To this day, Muslims adhere to memorizing various prayers and verses in part to continue the tradition handed down from Muhammad. Clinicians would be well served to be familiar with these prayers to show sensitivity and respect to the client. Islam is considered one of the three major monotheistic world religions (the other two being Judaism and Christianity). Followers of Islam also heed the *Hadith* or tradition, which are collections of Muhammad's declarations and a guide for living. It elaborates the verses of the Quran and offers examples of appropriate daily living. To discuss all of the beliefs of any religious faith is well beyond the scope of this chapter, and a full discussion of Islam is no exception. However, overarching beliefs will be discussed prior to a narrower examination specific to this book.

Islam follows the five pillars of faith, which are as follows:

1. To recite the *Shahadah* (*Laa ilaaha ill-Allah* [There is no God but Allah]). Most Muslims recite this daily as a declaration of their faith in the Oneness of God.
2. To offer prayers, *salat,* which are performed five times a day while facing Mecca. Less conservative Muslims pray less frequently. These prayer rituals are performed to strengthen belief in God, and to purify and cleanse the heart to strive toward attaining a higher moral ground.
3. To fast during the month of Ramadan, which changes based on the lunar calendar and is considered the month that Muhammad acquired the first revelation of the Quran from God. During this month, Muslims abstain from food, sex, and beverages from morning until evening as a means of cleansing the self. It is performed to learn patience and willpower, and to discourage evil.
4. To offer *Zakat,* a fixed donation to charity, which helps to distribute the wealth among the community.
5. To make a *hajj* or pilgrimage to Mecca at least once during one's lifetime if physically and economically able.

Islam and suicide. Muslims (the term "Muslim" refers to people whereas "Islam" refers to the faith) as a group have a low suicide rate, as most believe that people completing suicide are destined to reside in hell. Followers of Islam believe strongly in reward, punishment, perseverance, and forgiveness, all of which are intended to enhance feelings of hope and increase willpower. Two highly regarded fundamental values within Islam are endurance and patience (El Azayem & Hedayat-Diba, 1994). Similar to Christianity and Judaism, tô kill oneself is to take away the life given to you by Allah, thus committing sacrilege against him. To kill oneself is to negate the generosity of life given to you by Allah, as he is the only one who can grant life and death. Suicide, and other aggressions against humans, defies Allah, and is considered the second greatest sin after the denial of Allah himself. In the Islamic faith to even consider suicide is forbidden, as it is a reflection of the individual's lack of devotion and depth of religious despair, defined as *kufr* (disbelief). The Quran and Hadith are very clear on the topic of suicide, as the two examples in the following paragraphs demonstrate:

> And he who intentionally kills a believer, his reward is Hell. He shall abide therein forever, and the wrath and the curse of God are upon him. He has prepared for him a dreadful doom. (Sura 4:93)

> And take not life which Allah has made sacred, except by way of justice and law. (Al-An'am 6:151 and Bani Israel 17:33)

Both of these quotations have been interpreted to include killing oneself. Human life is considered one of the highest values within the Muslim faith and was decreed by Allah even prior to Moses, Abraham, Jesus, and Muhammad. Suicide is another means of killing all of humankind. Since life was not created by humans, a human cannot take his or her own life, and those who do are destined to spend eternity in hell. Numerous examples of hell after completing suicide are vividly described by God through Muhammad in the Hadith. For example:

> One who killed himself with iron would hold that instrument in his hands in the Hell and continue striking himself with it. And who killed himself by poisoning, would have that poison in his hands and would kill himself with it repeatedly. Whoever jumps off a mountain and kills himself will forever keep falling down in the depths of hell. (Hadith-Bukhari 2:445, 7:670)

Conversely, the saving of a life is equivalent to saving humankind. This belief is also consistent with teachings from Judaism's Torah.

> Anyone who has saved a life, it is as if he has saved the life of whole mankind. (Al-Ma'edah 5:32)

The justification of hastening death to avoid further discomfort or pain is not acceptable either. This becomes particularly difficult for some physicians when considering euthanasia. The idea of perseverance and willpower is seen throughout the Quran. Two brief examples, one from the Quran and one from the Hadith, are listed here:

> Be sure we shall test you with something of fear and hunger, some loss in goods and lives or the fruits (of your toil), but give glad tidings to those who patiently persevere, who say, when inflicted with a calamity: "To Allah we belong and to Him is our return." (Al-Baqarah 2:155-156)

> Say, "Oh My servants who believed, you shall reverance your Lord." For those who worked righteousness in this world, a good reward. Allah's earth is spacious, and those who steadfastly persevere will receive their recompense generously, without limits. (Al-Zumar 39:10)

There is an oft-told story in the Hadith (Qudsi 28) in which a man was inflicted with a wound and was in tremendous pain. He took a knife, cut his wrists, and died. Allah then said, "My servant has hastened his end, I deny him paradise." Similarly, during a military campaign, a Muslim was wounded after having killed many of the enemy. The Prophet mentioned, "His lot is Hell." Upon inquiry by his companions, they were informed that while wounded he fell on his sword to quicken death.

Islamic views of the afterlife. Like in some other religions, for the Muslim, life on earth is merely a testing ground for an eternal life. There is a belief in *quadar* (destiny), but this does not mean that people have no free will. Instead, it means that people can choose and determine their destiny based on these choices, similar to the Hindu view of karma. There is a strong philosophy of reward and punishment that undergirds not only views of the afterlife but Islamic culture itself. Rules within the Islamic community are followed closely because they are embedded in the Quran and the Hadith. Followers of Islam believe in the existence of heaven and hell, similar to what many Christians believe, and rewards in this life are dependent on adherence to the five pillars of faith (El Azayem & Hedayat-Diba, 1994). The word of God, through the Quran, illustrates heaven as a place that is close to nature (e.g., trees, fruits, rivers) and is a place of paradise. Conservative Muslims take these images literally whereas those less conservative may view these descriptions as metaphors, similar to the desciption of Christianity's heaven as being paved with gold (Smith, 1991). Examples follow:

> And give good news (O Muhammad) to those who believe and do good deeds, that they will have gardens (Paradise) in which rivers flow. (Sura 2:25)

> A space in Paradise equivalent to the size of a foot would be better than the world and what is in it. (Saheeh Al-Bukhari 6568)

Paradise awaits believers in Allah. Heaven is beyond human comprehension, and existed during the time of Adam and Eve who lived in paradise prior to their original sin. Many Muslims believe in two "high heavens" and two "lower heavens." Each level houses both human beings and *jinns* (spiritual beings created by Allah who are invisible to humans but walk the earth, though many Muslims believe jinns to be just folklore; see later). Humans and jinns who have developed a strong faith in Allah will be allowed into high heaven upon the Day of Resurrection. Those who have not developed their spiritual beliefs significantly will have a place in lower heaven. Both heavens are wonderful places of peace and comfort. In addition, those who die before the age of forty (age of responsibility) and have not fully come to peace with Allah automatically go to heaven (either high or low), regardless of their faith. This includes atheists and people who have committed evil acts. Differences in the heavens include the amount of joy and possibilities experienced. For example, in high heaven, there are all kinds of fruits and other benefits whereas in lower heaven there is a restriction in the variety of fruits (www.submission.org).

Purgatory is reserved for those who have not attained the faith necessary to reside in heaven, yet whose souls are not bad enough to reside in hell. They will appeal to Allah to allow them into lower heaven, upon which Allah will show mercy and integrate them into lower heaven. Finally, those whose souls are not developed and who do not believe in Allah will spend an eternity in hell. Upon death, they will be beaten by angels on their faces and backsides (Sura 8:50; 47:27; 79:1). According to the Hadith, the person experiencing the least severe punishment in hell will feel a burn so bad that it boils within his head.

Angels and jinns. Angels *(malak)* are spiritual beings who act as mediators between the known (earthly) and unknown (spiritual) worlds. The Quran explicitly states, "The Messenger believes in what was sent down to him from his Lord, and the believers: Each one believes in God, His angels, His Books, and His Messengers" (Sura Al-Baqarah 2:285). Angels clearly play a large role in the Islamic faith, as they are mentioned eighty times in the Quran. The relationship of humans to the world and the cosmos, to worship, spiritual life, prophecy, and death cannot be understood without an understanding of angels.

Jinns are spirits or demons on a lower level than angels, are good or evil, and assume human and animal form. They are often considered mischievous and they punish humans. Thus, many followers of Islam believe that when bad things happen they are the work of jinns. Some Muslims believe that suicide may be the result of the influence of jinns.

Case Example

Ahisma was a twenty-three-year-old African Muslim woman who had been married to her twenty-nine-year-old African Muslim husband for five years. She was repeatedly physically abused by her husband, and was brought to the United States because of her husband's academic and career opportunities. She was referred to a female counselor by her physician (because of cultural laws stating that a married woman should not be in the same room with a man who is not her husband) and indicated during the first session that she wished to get out of the relationship but could not because of her views on marriage. "A good Muslim woman doesn't leave her husband." She reported suicidal ideation and had a partial plan, though it became evident that she would not attempt suicide in the very near future. Aside from the abuse her issues included being taken from her family by her husband. She had no support system in the United States, including friends and family, while her husband's professional network kept him connected with numerous others. She had extreme difficulty acculturating, which increased her level of depression and hopelessness. Unfortunately, calling the local cleric was not possible because the town was small and he would be able to identify her. During the next session, discussions revolved around her views of the Quran and whether it was appropriate within the Islamic faith for her husband to beat her. Discussions also included her views of the afterlife and whether an eternity of hell was her only choice. Her anxiety about seeing a counselor was also discussed, as she feared her husband or the cleric would find out. Unfortunately, she failed to return for future counseling and her current whereabouts are unknown. There were no reports of suicide in the paper and follow-up contact was unsuccessful.

This example highlights the difficulty in counseling a traditional Muslim woman, particularly when she is considering suicide. Clerical assistance would have been optimal but not possible in this case. The Quran has formal, explicit restrictions against suicide, and her cultural beliefs also did not allow her to leave her marriage, though she had considered alternative Quranic perspectives.

African American Women

Fatal Suicides

African American women have the lowest rates of completed suicides of all of the ethnicity-by-gender groups (Alston & Anderson, 1995; Nisbet, 1996), and often have greater social support and are more religious than African American men, alleviating some cultural, personal, and social stressors (Marion & Range, 2003b; Watt & Sharp, 2002). Chance et al. (1998) argued that much of the literature on suicide behavior compares African Americans and European Americans, an unfair comparison because individual cultures should be taken into account. They recommend that suicidal behavior needs to be examined in its cultural context, thus increasing our understanding of cultural effects unique to the African American community. Others (e.g., Stack, 1996) found that determinants of European American suicide, such as marital status, are also determinants of African American suicide.

Consistent with Stack's (1996) thesis, many of the oft-reported diagnostic and interpersonal factors that are correlated with suicide (e.g., post-traumatic stress disorder [PTSD], abuse, hopelessness) appear in the literature with African American women. For example, Thompson, Kaslow, Lane, and Kingree (2000) found that African American women with a history of maltreatment and PTSD were at greater risk for nonfatal suicide attempts than women without maltreatment and PTSD. Overall though, there has been very little research on fatal suicides with African American women because of the low rates, though some studies have focused on positive suicide buffers within the African American female community. For example, previous investigations have identified sources of buffers such as religiosity, negative attitudes toward the acceptability of suicide, residence in rural, traditional locales, and positive social support (Marion & Range, 2003b). Many authors have argued that African American women have managed the burdens of slavery, child rearing, and building strong community ties, which has led to a cultural value of resiliency (Gibbs, 1997; Gibbs & Fuery, 1994; Marion & Range, 2003b; Paniagua, 2005).

Nonfatal Suicides

African American women have greater nonfatal suicide attempt rates than either African American men or European American men, but show no significant differences when compared with European American women. It is extremely difficult, if not impossible, to obtain accurate nonfatal suicide numbers, because of underreporting (Whitehead, Johnson, & Ferrence, 1973). However, Hickman (1984) found that African American women will engage in nonfatal suicidal acts at a ratio of 4:1 over African American men. Women in general, regardless of ethnicity, are more likely to participate in nonfatal than fatal behaviors. Both European American and African American women also report more thoughts of death and hopelessness and depressive feelings than do European American and African American men (Nisbet, 1996).

Buffers Against Suicide for African American Women

Social support is considered a buffer against suicidal behaviors and among African American women may actually be a more important determinant of decreased suicide than professional support (Nisbet, 1996). According to Dunston (1990), African American women rely on social support due to their being discriminated against for being ethnic minority women (also sometimes called a "double minority"). Social support among African American women has tended to focus on two areas: (1) extended family and (2) close female friendships. The importance and reliance on the extended family and female relationships has been well heralded in the research literature (e.g., Alston & Anderson, 1995). Brown and Gary (1985) found that a family member was rated as one of the African American woman's closest relationships, even though the family member was not a parent or sibling. Both unmarried and married women reported similar numbers of social support size and composition, mainly extended family and friends. African American women who utilized more extended family support reported fewer depressive symptoms than those who used less kin support, though age and economic status were better predictors. Specifically, low SES women were more likely to report depressive symptoms than women in a higher SES bracket. Nisbet found that social and family support systems kept suicide rates down, but the effect may actually be largest among European American men and weakest among African American women. This is not to suggest social support is not a critical factor but that the type and meaning of the support has yet to be fully examined. Regardless of the relative impact, social support and extended family are critical factors that help decrease suicidal behaviors, and clinicians should incorporate a wide range of social support systems into assessment and treatment.

According to the U.S. Census Bureau, African American women represent a greater proportion of single-headed households with children than European American women. It has been argued that the greater proportion of female-headed households actually contributes to lower suicide completion rates for African American women because they must rely on extended networks for child care. These economic, psychological, and emotional care and support systems lead to increased involvement in the community, which buffers completed suicide. Nisbet (1996) found that dependent children add more stress to African American women than to European American women, yet the relationship between suicide attempts and dependent children is almost double that for European American women than for African American women. Further, living in large households with multiple children has a less negative effect on African American women than European American men and women. Therefore, although the probability of a suicide attempt increases as the number of children in the house increases for all three groups, detrimental effects are moderated for African American women.

Marion and Range (2003b) found family support, a view of suicide unacceptability, and a collaborative religious problem-solving style as buffering suicide ideation. It should be noted that suicide attempt rates increase when African American women enter mental health treatment, although these rates are still lower than for European American women and men in treatment. The African American community is much less likely than the European American community to participate in professional mental health services, often choosing to seek out religious figures, friends, and family. Therefore, it is possible that African American clients who seek mental health services contemplate it only as a last resort and may be considered at greater risk for suicide.

The notion of resiliency is particularly prevalent among African American women given that they have been the primary caregivers of families and communities (Gibbs, 1997). Using the Reasons for Living Inventory, research on sanctions against suicide are reported by Ellis and Range (1991), who found that African Americans (both men and women) scored higher than European Americans on the Moral Objectivity and the Survival and Coping Skills subscales (including total score) of the instrument. No significant differences were noted between African American and European American women on Moral Objections, indicating that these groups had equivalent moral objections to suicide (though suicide rates for European American women are higher). Therefore, resiliency was considered an important factor within the African American, particularly female, community. In addition, Neeleman et al. (1998) found that African Americans were less accepting of suicide than European Americans. Interestingly, marriage, which is generally considered a form of social support, is viewed as a suicide buffer for European American women but the effects for African American women were weak (Marion & Range, 2003b; Nisbet, 1996; Stack, 1996). In essence, married African American women do not perceive marriage in the same manner as European American men and women and it is not seen as a strong protective factor against completed suicidal behaviors.

Overall, there is no one protective buffer that accounts for the low rate of African American women's suicidal behaviors. The best preventive characteristics for suicide thus far appear to be the availability of the social support, particularly family support, and a resilient disposition. These support systems may decrease the probability of a fatal suicide, but they do not appear to decrease the probability of nonfatal suicide. Consistent with other research on suicide attempts, perhaps these attempts are not supposed to be serious enough to be completed, but rather are a call for help to overwhelming life situations.

Case Examples

LaKeshia is a twenty-six-year-old, single, African American female with two children, six and eight years old. She earned a high school degree and works as a cosmetologist. She lives near her mother who cares for the children when she is at work. Recently, she has been feeling depressed because "I want to do more with my life but guess I won't be able to do anything about it until the kids get older. I just see myself in a dead-end job with no future." She has had a number of relationships but none described as serious. She admits to smoking marijuana three times a week and does not socialize much. She reported no hobbies or other interests, has few friends, and also reported signs of major depression (e.g., change in appetite, excessive sleep, lethargy). There have been no suicide attempts in her past but she has considered it recently. She has a partial plan ("I'd use the pills in my bathroom") but admitted, "I'm not sure if I could do it anyway." She does not have a date or time or other circumstances that may increase risk. As a counselor, what factors are in your favor? First, she is an African American female. Research shows that African American females have low rates of suicide. Second, she lives near her family, a source of support for herself and her children. It could be argued that because her family is taking care of her children and they are cared for she may be more likely to attempt suicide. However, research does not support this. Third, although she has a plan, it sounds as if she may also have some hopefulness, or at least a future orientation, because she indicated that "I won't be able to do anything until the kids are older." An issue to consider is her religious beliefs. Considered broadly, the African American community tends to have a stronger faith orientation than the European American community and may not consider suicide to be a viable option.

A thirty-two-year-old African American female saw a colleague of mine and entered counseling because of a history of multiple forms of abuse. She was the wife of a conservative Southern Baptist minister whom she reported as being very controlling. Due to her religious and philosophical worldviews discussions occurred around her having an inauthentic life. At one point, she indicated that she was considering suicide because "there is no other way out." A suicide assessment was initiated immediately and she reported that she would probably drive her car off the highway, which would be easy to do as she drove an hour each way for the appointment. The counselor responded with "There is no guarantee that it would work," which led to discussions of seriousness of suicide in general and the response from family and community members if she did and did not complete suicide. Other discussions surrounded her religious beliefs and the meaning attributed to suicide and that what God wanted from her was for her to be more authentic.

Elders

Older African Americans (over sixty-five) have the lowest rate of completed suicides of any major ethnic group in the United States (Baker, 1994). First, increased roles in the African American Church have been presented as a primary reason for continued low rates of suicide among the African American elderly, particularly for men. The church acts as a buffer and has been presented as a strong reason for the lower suicide rates in the South, where most African Americans reside and where the strength of the church among African Americans is considered high. In general, as people age they tend to become more committed to a religious faith or a belief system, regardless of ethnicity. It would be expected that the combination of age and commitment would lend itself to lower suicide rates, though this hypothesis has not been confirmed. Second, as discussed earlier, the majority of African Americans live in the South, and it has been suggested that the collective experience associated with high numbers of people perceived as similar to oneself may give rise to decreased suicide rates.

Third, within the African American community it is often the case where both older men and women are placed in positions as primary caretakers of their grandchildren (Gibbs, 1997). Although this can be perceived as increased stress, which could lead to suicidal behaviors (e.g., Davis, 1979), it can also be viewed as a positive, buffering indicator, as discussed earlier. Frequently, depressed African American grandparents who are caring for their grandchildren and whom I have seen at a local mental health center report that suicide is not an option because of their responsibilities toward raising the grandchildren. The research examining suicide among African American elders is paltry, though they seem to be less likely than other age groups to engage in fatal and nonfatal suicidal behaviors due to the previously mentioned factors.

Extended Family

Bush (1976) and Comer (1973) believed that the reason for lower suicide rates was due to increased cohesiveness within the African American community (e.g., extended family and kin networks, collective identity) when compared to the European American community, including greater reliance on the church and other community institutions. Positive reliance on the community and the church family belies suicide as an option by acting as a buffer. E. E. Griffith and Bell (1989), however, argued that if the African American community were as cohesive as has been proposed, then homicide rates, particularly in southern regions where the majority of African Americans live, should be low, which they are not. The question then becomes, why would the community protect against suicide but not homicide? These questions are currently left unanswered.

Another consideration is that the African American family is much closer emotionally than the European American family, thus reducing feelings of alienation, which acts as a suicide buffer within the African American community. Some research has suggested that African American suicide attempters were more likely to report greater feelings of alienation and less racial identification with the African American community than nonattempters (Kirk & Zucker, 1979), whereas others have indicated increased suicide rates due to decreased family and community support, leading to personal internalizations of failure (Davis, 1980). Shaffer, Gould, and Hicks (1994) suggested that movement away from the African American community led to increased rates of suicide. Feelings of alienation are considered within the realm of racial identity, which may influence suicidal behaviors.

African American (and black) racial identity models (e.g., Cross & Vandiver, 2001; Helms, 1995) describe a sequence of statuses that African Americans move through to help define themselves as African American individuals in a European American–dominated society. Racial identity assesses the degree to which one feels a connection with a particular ethnic group. People may move through various statuses that emphasize a collective identity. Essentially there is an initial unawareness of being African American, followed by moving toward pro-African American attitudes and beliefs about being part of a larger African American community (and oftentimes not trusting the European American community), and toward more of an integrative attitude in which identity is not defined primarily by ethnic makeup. Though it has never been studied it, would be presumed that African Americans who have a stronger connection to the past and hold current pro–African American attitudes are less likely to complete suicide than those with less historical and present community connections.

As a general rule, being a European American clinician, if an African American client enters the office I immediately begin to assess for racial identity status that provides clinical direction for treatment. For example, an African American client arrived for an initial session and was visibly upset, defensive, and angry. My clinical judgment was immediately determined by the meaning I gave to his emotional distress. Could it be that (1) he does not want to be there and does not think he needs treatment regardless of the ethnicity of the therapist,

(2) there is some characterological disorder that needs to be addressed, (3) he is just having bad day, (4) something happened in the waiting room that disturbed him, or (5) he is in the immersion status (e.g., Helms, 1995) and does not want to see me and does not trust me because I am European American? (For a review of African American racial identity, see Cross & Vandiver, 2001; Helms, 1995.) If the issue is the last of those mentioned, then the racial differences should be addressed in order to build trust with the client. If clinicians are wary of discussing racial issues, particularly with clients in the immersion status, it is unlikely that counseling will be effective. If the client does not appear to be in the immersion status then interventions may differ initially.

During the period of the Black Power movement in this country, Bush (1976) reported that a collective African American identity may act as a buffer against suicide. Others (e.g., E. E. Griffith & Bell, 1989) argued that decreased identity connections with the African American community may lead to increased identity confusion, which may result in suicide. Factors often considered to be integral within African American culture include those described earlier. However, only two empirical studies to date have investigated the role of racial identity in suicide ideation or nonfatal and fatal suicidal behaviors. Wells (1995) assessed adaptive functioning with high school students using racial identity as a component of adaptation. Using paper and pencil measures, racial identity was determined to be a strong predictor of suicide, with those holding stronger orientation to the African American community being less likely to consider suicide. Unfortunately, racial identity was not measured using standardized methods. Sanyika (1995) attempted to use racial identity as a means of separating fatal from nonfatal behaviors. People who had completed suicide were less likely to possess strong African American consciousness and used fewer available support systems than nonfatal people. Though the research is sparse, there is evidence to indicate that increasing African American consciousness and connections with the African American community may be beneficial influences against suicide.

Cohesion in Ethnic Neighborhoods

Completed suicide rates for African Americans are higher in the northern and western sections of the United States than in the southern section (Gibbs, 1997; Wingate et al., 2005). Almost 70 percent of

African Americans live in the South and retain the lowest suicide rates, whereas the highest rates occur in the West, which has the least proportional number of African Americans. Gibbs (1997) and Lester (1990-1991) indicated the reason for the differential rates may be due to issues of social cohesion. There are more small, rural communities in the South than elsewhere and African Americans may be more likely to use extended family networks, rely on social support systems, and have more intimate relationships with the church. However, as suggested earlier, the homicide rates do not appear to be consistent with this hypothesis. It must be noted though that completed suicide rates have increased in the South over the past fifteen years at a greater rate than in any other region of the country, probably because rates were low initially. Spaights and Simpson (1986) suggested that upward economic mobility may be associated with role confusion, thus contributing to suicide.

GAY/LESBIAN/BISEXUAL/TRANSGENDER ISSUES

Overview

Negy and Eisenman (2005) noted that little empirical evidence exists on the attitudes of African Americans toward homosexuality, and this paucity of research continues today. However, open expressions of homosexual behaviors within the African American community are generally less accepted than within the European American community, though there is some tolerance if kept behind closed doors. In fact, many African American social scientists have argued that homosexuality is virtually nonexistent within the African American community, and many clergy within historically African American churches have consistently voiced concerns about gay rights (Icard, 1996; Schulte & Battle, 2004). What often occurs within these communities is that GLBT desires must be kept hidden, particularly by adolescents. Consistent with features of the gay Hispanic community, it is not uncommon for gay African Americans to define themselves as straight if they take an active or dominant sexual role. Sexual orientation definitions are often based on the role one takes when engaged in sexual behaviors instead of the orientation itself.

Cultures define the acceptability of sexual orientation and sexual behaviors. The European American community may define two men engaging in sexual behaviors as being gay, for example, yet within the African American culture only one of the men may be considered gay because he takes a passive or submissive role. It is the submissiveness that is considered negative within the community and not the behavior of engaging in a same-sex act. Savin-Williams (1990) found that African American men were more likely than European American men to self-identify as bisexual. Defining oneself as bisexual can have multiple meanings within the self, from including possessing an expanded view of acceptable sexuality to means of not defining oneself as gay. Regardless of the differences in proportioned bisexual rates, some African Americans may have differing definitions of what constitutes gay behaviors when compared with the European American community. Counselors must be cautious not to jump to the conclusion that someone is GLBT simply because he or she engages in same-sex behaviors. If this mistake becomes an early clinical issue, then the client may be more likely to terminate early and not seek out future services.

Icard (1985-1986, 1996) and others have written about the identity stress of African American gay men and lesbians. There is the notion of a "double oppression" in society, which includes being African American and GLBT. For many African Americans it is difficult to find a community in which to belong. Being a gay man or a lesbian is not considered acceptable in carrying out socially defined gender roles in African American culture, yet identifying as African American does not often lead to acceptance in the overwhelmingly European American gay community. Many GLBT African Americans are implicitly ostracized from the European American gay community. Therefore, many gay African Americans may have difficulty, particularly during the coming out process, finding a way to positively reframe their gay identity (Icard, 1985-1986). In what group does the African American gay and lesbian person fit, and what identity struggles must occur? In the African American community, there is a lack of a GLBT reference or support group (Loiacano, 1993) to which one can adhere, and often African Americans believe that they must choose between being African American and being gay or lesbian, thus increasing feelings of internal conflict. It is possible for a dual identity to develop, yet it may be difficult given the cultural forces.

The racial identity models (e.g., Cross & Vandiver, 2001; Helms, 1990) implicitly stress heterosexuality, or no sexuality, whereas homosexual identity models (e.g., Cass, 1979; Troiden, 1979) were developed tacitly with European Americans in mind. M. Hall (1991) reported that African American lesbian attitudes toward their sexual development were not consistent with the Cass model because it was not applicable to them. Very few studies have combined the two types of models though, and many African American gay men or lesbians feel marginalized from both African American and GLBT communities. In fact, Croom (1998) found that the racial identity instruments used in her study failed to consider the concept of dual identities, and conflicts occurred between racial and sexual orientation allegiances. In another study though, D. A. Hall (1997) found a lot of variety regarding whether African American lesbians identified primarily with one group or another, or whether they were equally identified. Clearly the relationship of sexual and racial identity issues, and other multiple identity issues for that matter, need to be further clinically and empirically assessed.

Loiacano (1993) discussed general questions for counselors to consider when working with gay men and lesbian women:

1. Does the client perceive support for his or her dual identity in the community?
2. Are there groups organized specifically for the needs of African-American gay men and lesbian women in the area, or are there groups in which racial and sexual minorities find both acceptance and validation?
3. What assumptions does the counselor (or client) have about ways of expressing one's homosexuality that might not be realistic for an African American in his or her particular community? (pp. 372-373)

Issues for Counselor Consideration

There are a number of issues for therapists to consider when counseling elderly gay men and lesbian clients. These are not necessarily specific to suicide but may be contributing factors. Although some of the following information can be applied to this population regardless of ethnicity, it is nonetheless important to consider with elderly clients of color because of differing ethnic views of homosexuality. In other words, ethnic community views impact being GLBT, including elders. Kimmel (1993) offers an expansion of the following information that will be summarized here.

First, older gay men and lesbians are likely to be less visible than the younger ones because of the stigma that occurred during earlier portions of their lifetime. Most elder GLBT persons were required to stay "in the closet" and there was an even greater fear of arrest and abuse than today. It was not until the 1960s that the GLBT rights movement began to emerge, including uprisings and civil rights demonstrations. Hate crimes against GLBT persons are still greater in number than other hate crimes, so it is easy to understand the hesitancy of older people to "come out" to everyone.

Second, there are few support systems for GLBT persons after the death of a loved one. Hospital and other agencies place restrictions on visitation if one is not family, and blood family members can block visitation access for gay partners. Often there are legal issues to consider because many of the laws are written for heterosexual couples. Third, age itself becomes an issue because of our youth-oriented society. Kimmel (1993) indicated that older people become stigmatized, creating a barrier between older and younger generations. This barrier is particularly salient in the gay community. Therefore, support and other links are cut, leading to feelings of low self-worth and isolation. Being an African American may add to the complexity given that GLBT issues are not discussed as openly in the African American community in general, much less when considering older African American gay men and lesbians. The suicide literature among the African American gay men and lesbian community is extremely small. Thus, it is difficult to determine whether this community has similar issues, particularly given that older African Americans are generally more respected and accepted within their community than older people within the European American community. However, some of the issues discussed earlier could be addressed with any client. The addition of ethnicity adds another layer of potential prejudice and discrimination counselors should consider.

Suicide and African American GLBTs

Bell and Weinberg (1978) found that African American gay men were twelve times more likely to report suicidal ideation or to engage in nonfatal behaviors than straight men, primarily during adolescence and young adulthood. However, there is a dearth of literature discussing being African American, gay, and suicidal. As a result, to work with African American, homosexual, suicidal clients clinicians must work harder to raise their awareness of even the most basic racial and sexual orientation identity models. Clinicians must understand the relationship between the African American and European American gay communities and how homosexual African Americans may feel ostracized from both communities. They may also benefit from extrapolating some of the GLBT information presented in the Hispanic American and Asian American chapters of this book, given the paucity of African American suicide and sexual identity literature. It is not difficult to see that a poor sense of community or identity can lead to depression, substance abuse, family disruption, or a host of other concomitant factors associated with suicide.

Islam and Homosexuality

It should be noted that homosexuality within the Muslim community means male homosexuality. In short, homosexual behavior is considered shameful and an abhorrence, and there is no distinction in Islam between homosexual orientation and behaviors, as will be discussed later. Lesbianism *(musahaqa)* is rarely discussed and is viewed as sex outside of marriage. Therefore, lesbian sexual behaviors are seen in a similar fashion as adultery and carry the same penalties. Some scholars believe that lesbianism is not discussed because there is no penetration, and Islam distinguishes between male penetration and the one who is being penetrated (Schild, 1992). Bouhdiba (1985), as found in Halstead and Lewicka (1998), argued that because of the diversity found within individual Islamic communities, one must consider the combination of the "invariant" (unalterable and fixed Islamic teachings) and "variables" (what individual communities are willing to permit). This section will primarily focus on Islam as a religious faith and not as individual communities, because religion is what is shared, regardless of geography.

Homosexuality from a Christian perspective is considered differently than homosexuality from an Islamic perspective. In fact, the majority of the world's religions define homosexuality in terms of behaviors and not orientation or preference. The notion of orientation is a relatively new term and was not considered in historical religious texts. Christianity, however, has a broad range of definitions and beliefs, ranging from conservative attitudes condemning homosexual behaviors to Christian denominations that believe that the New Testament acknowledges a GLBT sexual orientation and therefore are open to greater acceptance of homosexuality. Within Christianity (though not the Bible), as discussed in Chapter 2, there is often (1) a distinction between homosexual orientation and homosexual behaviors and (2) much within-group variability regarding how various Christian faiths and denominations view homosexuality. The Islamic faith also does not distinguish between orientation and behaviors and is less variable in its stance on homosexuality than Christianity.

Based on the Quran, there is no separation between sexual orientation and sexual behaviors, be they heterosexual, homosexual, or bisexual. Evidence for this view stems from the story of Lot in Sodom and neighboring Gomorrah (see Chapter 2). The term *liwat* (the doing of Lot's people) is mentioned in the Quran about a dozen times (e.g., Sura 7:80-84, 15:59-77; Halstead & Lewicka, 1998). However, the accepted interpretation of the Quran is that *liwat* refers to homosexual behaviors. In particular, Quranic scholars believe that the term *liwat* refers to a specific sexual behavior—sodomy—and therefore does not offer any information about sexual orientation. There is no distinction according to Islam. Homosexuality is considered the cause of the downfall of Sodom and Gomorrah; therefore, it is strictly forbidden. In many countries, Muslims found guilty of sodomy (usually by four witnesses) receive severe penalties, even death. As dictated by Islamic beliefs, homosexuals are doomed to hell. According to Halstead and Lewicka (1998), "No attempt has ever been made, as far as we are aware, to encourage discussion of these issues between Muslims and homosexuals. Indeed, there appears to be no room for genuine discussion" (p. 50). Since that time, the first gay conference for Muslims occurred in early 1999, albeit with a very small number of participants. Many gay Muslims find that they have to choose between their faith and being gay, consistent with those in the LDS tradition. Combine this choice with the idea that homosexuality is generally not openly discussed in the African American community and there becomes a possible formidable barrier within the client. The practice of converting to Islam if one is GLBT is extremely rare.

SUICIDE PREVENTION AND INTERVENTION

Given the small amount of research on African American suicide, it is difficult to discuss culture-specific prevention and intervention efforts. The overwhelming majority of suicide prevention efforts have been aimed at the majority population, considering the number of suicides in this population when compared with ethnic minority groups. Some ideas, though, will be presented here.

Primary Prevention Efforts

Since the majority of suicide deaths occur among African American youths, prevention efforts should be directed there. It has been well documented (e.g., Paniagua, 2005; Sue & Sue, 2003) that the African American community is often mistrustful of (generally white) mental health clinicians, with fewer African American appropriate services, increased drop-out rates, and more severe diagnoses made when compared with the European American community. In addition, there is a greater stigma associated with receiving mental health services within the African American community than within the European American community. Social, political, and community initiatives need to occur to lessen the mistrust and stigma of the mental health field. Portions of current suicide prevention efforts aimed at youths can then be better received by African American youths, as many of these programs include seeking mental health services, especially school counseling services. Counselors can discuss the role of guns and accident prevention, and the relationship between firearms, depression, and suicide. The majority of schools and community agencies are reluctant to discuss suicide awareness for a multitude of social and political reasons. Other primary prevention efforts include depression, anger, and interpersonal problem-solving skills, school enhancement programs, surrogate role model programs (e.g., Big Brothers, Big Sisters), and help-seeking skills (Berman & Jobes, 1995). Of course, the majority of these programs do not utilize culture-specific approaches and thus their ecological validity has yet to be confirmed.

Increased efforts need to occur regarding social connectedness and ethnic identification, including pride and historical connections. Prevention efforts in the schools might focus on how Afrocentric values include community, fairness, and giving back to the community. Although some efforts can be made through the schools, much of the prevention may have to come from community organizations such as the Boys and Girls Club, churches, and juvenile justice systems (Joe & Kaplan, 2001). Various community organizations have been helpful with the maturing and guiding of youth, and these efforts should continue. After-school events and activities may decrease the chances of suicide by increasing positive mental health and interpersonal relationships. Historically, churches have not been receptive to discussing topics such as suicide, but more awareness of this concern and related topics such as depression, drug use, and firearms needs to occur. Males, particularly adolescents and young adults, are at greatest risk for completed suicide, and special attention may need to be directed toward them, though ideation and attempts are prominent for females also.

Secondary Prevention Efforts

Secondary prevention efforts are aimed at early intervention for at-risk populations. These include tutoring, peer counseling, and hotline programs, and limiting gun accessibility. Counselors should be aware of whether their local programs include culture-specific interventions when appropriate. For example, peer counseling may be most effective with similar ethnic, gender, or sexual orientation groups. Mental health counselors should also receive training in suicidology because very few clinicians actually receive this training (Berman & Jobes, 1995; Bonger, 1991). Equally, most graduate training programs do not include significant suicide risk evaluation and treatment approaches. Suicide is often enveloped into other courses, such as alcohol and drug or assessment and diagnosis courses.

Tertiary Prevention Efforts

There are no culturally sensitive behavior interventions aimed at suicide that have been validated with African American women and men. Alston and Anderson (1995) discussed the idea that African American women are under increased strains due to decreased social support and the changing role of the African American church. Therefore, the myth of the strong African American woman who would not kill herself may be in need of modification in the future. As indicated earlier, nonfatal suicidal behaviors are fairly high and thus the counselor should not get lulled into believing that suicide is not an option. The likelihood of completed suicide may be lower than other ethnic groups, but that fact alone, or any fact alone, is not sufficient for clinicians when faced with a suicidal African American client.

Heron, Twomey, Jacobs, and Kaslow (1997) discussed a therapeutic model when working with suicidal African American women who were domestic-abuse survivors. In their treatments they include the Transtheoretical Stages of Change Model (Prochaska & DiClemente, 1992) as a framework to understand the woman's meaning system or her worldview, and focus on positive coping strategies and social support. As many clinicians are aware, the model describes four stages that clients may journey through on their way through the therapeutic process. In the first stage, *precontemplation,* clients have not considered the idea that change may be needed and are often unaware that a problem exists. The second stage, *contemplation,* is defined by clients who admit a problem but have not committed to change. In the third stage, *preparation,* action is initiated through making a plan or attempting changes. The fourth stage, *action,* is defined by clients actually making specific changes. Suicide attempts were viewed as emotion-focused coping strategies in the first two stages, meaning that the clients were rather impulsive and did not include much consideration prior to their nonfatal suicidal behaviors. In the third stage, clients used either emotion-focused or problem-focused attempts, with the latter being a more deliberate act. Clients who attempted suicide and were in the fourth stage did so using problem-solving strategies as a means of controlling their environment. Thus, using the model to theoretically drive their interventions the authors began to gain a greater understanding of the impulsivity and motivations of different types of clients (i.e., emotion focused or problem-solving focused). Heron et al. (1997) discussed some specific treatment issues associated with low-income African American abused women, such as promoting culturally sensitive coping strategies and relationships. While not a treatment for suicidal, African American, female clients specifically devoid of abuse issues, it is a step in the direction of promoting culturally sensitive interventions.

African Americans may feel more guilt or shame than European Americans due to their beliefs that suicidal ideation should never be experienced. For example, multiple African American female clients I have interviewed because of depression and suicidal ideation have expressed remorse for their suicidal thoughts for numerous reasons, including taking care of their own and others' children, and their family generational history. Specifically, a number of clients have indicated that "generations in my family were slaves and had it a lot worse than I do so I shouldn't be feeling this way." The opinion is that depression and suicide ideation are inappropriate because others in previous generations have had to overcome more strenuous and dangerous situations. As clinicians it may be helpful to address this issue by focusing on this information. The connection with previous generations may act as a buffer in order not to let down the legacy. The shame needs to be addressed carefully, indicating that although they are feeling bad and having these thoughts presently, their connection to the past shows strength and is a foundation from which to build.

SUMMARY

The majority of empirical suicide research including persons of color involves African Americans, but it is still small when compared to the suicide literature within the European American community. This chapter was intended to summarize many of the issues involved in suicide among African Americans. The women have had consistently low rates of completed suicide, though the noncompleted and ideation rates are much higher. African American men have rates lower than European Americans, but the completion rates appear to be increasing, especially among young adults. This increase has become alarming, and it is imperative that suicidologists, other researchers, and clinicians continue to examine within-group variables in their studies. For example, the role of racial identity and feelings of connection to the African American community may offer greater insight into the increasing rates, above and beyond well-studied issues such as substance abuse, hopelessness, and sexual abuse. Other issues that affect suicidal behaviors include the seemingly decreasing role of religion and elders in the African American community and GLBT issues. Strengths and buffers need to be assessed continually; these include the increasing median income of African Americans and the increase in the number of young African Americans opting for higher education. Studies can focus on suicide prevention and intervention programs that target African American youths, particularly the inclusion of increased community connections and church attendance.

Chapter 4

Asian Americans

Asian Americans comprise just over 2 percent of the U.S. population, but there is tremendous variation in cultures, history, views of mental illness, and suicide. It has been estimated that there are at least fifty different Asian American groups residing in the United States, speaking thirty languages. In the psychological literature these groups are often categorized into four groups: East Asian (e.g., Chinese, Japanese, Korean), Southeast Asian (e.g., Laotian, Thai, Vietnamese), South Asian (e.g., Indian, Pakistani), and Pacific Islander (e.g., Hawaiian, Samoan) (Baruth & Manning, 2003). Due to differential birth and immigration rates, Asian subgroup populations are increasing in the United States at different rates from both each other and the majority group. The three largest ethnic groups in the United States include the Chinese, Filipino, and Japanese, each contributing to 20 percent of the Asian cultures (Paniagua, 2005). The Chinese and Filipino populations, along with the Korean population, have the highest growth rates, and the majority of Asian Americans are foreign-born and speak their native languages and dialects in their homes.

When considering Asian Americans one cannot discuss mental health issues without discussing generational differences, implying some acculturative differences. For example, some Chinese families have been residents of the United States for five generations, whereas others such as the Hmong and Laotians are fairly recent immigrants. In addition, members from both these and other ethnic groups, primarily from Southeast Asia, have histories of significant traumas due to various governmental regimes. Wherever possible, this chapter will delineate both ethnic group and acculturative differences when discussing Asian Americans, their religions and philosophies, death customs, and suicide.

Cultural Diversity and Suicide
© 2006 by The Haworth Press, Inc. All rights reserved.
doi:10.1300/5680_04

DATA AND GENDER

Overall, Asian American males complete suicide at lower rates than Native Americans, European Americans, African Americans, and Hispanic Americans at 9.1 per 100,000, though there are large ethnic variations (Chang, 1998; National Strategy for Suicide Prevention, retrieved January 6, 2005, from http://www.mentalhealth.samhsa.gov/suicideprevention/diverse.asp). Female completion rates are 3.3 per 100,000, placing them at a rate lower than Native American and European American women, but greater than African American and Hispanic American women. Liu and Yu (1985) indicated that health rates in general for Asian Americans are fragmented and unsystematic; hence, it is difficult to report valid nonfatal and fatal suicide numbers. Limited specific suicide rates are available primarily for only three of the groups, Chinese, Japanese, and Filipinos, and only a very few data give us a glimpse into suicide among other Asian American ethnic groups.

When considering ethnic differences, studies over the past thirty-five years indicate that Japanese Americans complete suicide at slightly higher rates (approximately 9.1 per 100,000) than Chinese Americans (8.3 per 100,000), whereas Filipinos were significantly lower than either of these two groups, especially for men (3.5 per 100,000; Kalish, 1968; Lester, 1994b). Liu and Yu (1985) found that, on average, Chinese Americans and Japanese Americans completed suicide at about the same rate per 100,000 (almost 8.0), whereas the Filipino American rate was much lower at under 4.0. In a study including Vietnamese Americans among the three ethnic groups mentioned earlier, Diego, Yamamoto, Nguyen, and Hifumi (1994) found that each had rates lower than European Americans. When comparing Asian Americans with Asians in their country of origin, rates are generally lower in the United States, though the rank order of rates are consistent across nations (Lester, 1994a). As Lester noted, cultural influences impact suicide rates.

AGE

In the older women category (over age sixty-five), East Asian women occupy the highest completed female rates of suicide among all ethnic groups in the United States (McKenzie, Serfaty, & Crawford, 2003). Shiang et al. (1997) found that suicide rates of Chinese in

San Francisco for the years 1988 to 1994 have changed little over forty years, with the highest rates being within the older age groups for both men and women. This finding differs from Hispanic, Native American, and African American groups, where rates decrease with age. Baker (1996) found similar results, with high rates among those over age fifty-five. Baker partially attributed the high elderly rates to decreasing respect among elders. Their cultural identity and status in the community changes over the years, possibly contributing to suicide.

Kachur et al. (1995) and Shiang et al. (1997), using Asian and European American samples, found the highest rate was among fifteen- to twenty-four-year-olds (consistent with other ethnic group rates) and seventy-five years and older males, and among fifty-five- to sixty-four-year-olds and seventy-five years and older females. The method of suicide differed among Asians and European Americans. European Americans favored gunshots and both alcohol and drugs, whereas Asians typically preferred hanging (reasons for hanging will be discussed later) and drugs only. When measuring suicide ideation among Chinese in China and U.S. students in the United States, Zhang and Jin (1996) found females in both countries reporting greater levels than males. Suicide ideation is greater for women than men among all major U.S. ethnic groups and is a worldwide phenomenon.

Though data with adolescent populations are sketchy, Liu, Yu, Chang, and Fernandez (1990) found that the age-adjusted rates for fifteen- to twenty-four-year-old Chinese more than doubled from 1970 to 1980, placing adolescents and young adults in a high-risk category. Therefore, Chinese adolescents and young adults are at greater risk for suicide than other Asian age groups (except perhaps over the age of seventy-five), but consistent with adolescents and young adults in other ethnic groups. Again, high adolescent rates are consistent with data globally.

RELIGIOUS AND SPIRITUAL ISSUES

Buddhism and Suicide

Suicide is discouraged among Buddhists. There are no known empirical studies that have investigated suicide in the context of Buddhism specifically, with suicidologists typically discussing various

Asian ethnic groups instead. In Buddhist culture, suicide, unexpected deaths, and deaths of small children are viewed as particularly difficult because the person did not have time to prepare for death. Specifically in the case of suicide, the person did not have the correct mind-set to enter the next realm. If a suicide occurs, relatives will consult with religious figures in order to compensate for the negative manner in which the person died. Historically, custom has dictated that additional rituals must be performed when a family member dies in such a manner, because to deviate from tradition may add disapproving influences to the deceased's next journey (Truitner & Truitner, 1993).

Braun and Nichols (1997) interviewed Hawaiian representatives of Chinese, Filipino, Japanese, and Vietnamese cultures, including spiritual leaders, regarding death and dying issues. Although only a small sample, responses covered a range of Buddhist beliefs. The Chinese Americans considered suicide to be wrong except under certain specified extreme circumstances. The Japanese Americans interviewed indicated that Buddha would show compassion, and a nonjudgmental attitude should be shown the person who completed suicide and the remaining family. Suicide is still considered wrong according to Buddhist philosophy, since it is an affront to ancestors and involves hurting someone, including oneself. However, they also indicated that suicide can, at times, be perceived as "the only way out of a bad situation" (p. 348). The Vietnamese Americans indicated children are taught at a young age that suicide is wrong because Buddhism equates suicide with killing, and one's karma is disturbed. The majority of Filipino Americans interviewed were Catholic and therefore admonished suicide as an affront to the sixth commandment of the Bible.

Hindus and Suicide

Hindus maintain a fairly high rate of fatal suicide, with males attempting suicide more than females, opposite to patterns typically seen with Christians. Also inconsistent with Christians is that the majority of Hindus who complete suicide are not under the influence of alcohol or drugs. Further, the majority of people completing suicide use household poisons. Counselors would serve their clients well to ask about poisons along with other suicide methods.

Suicide is not specifically considered wrong by the Hindu faith, but completing suicide to escape suffering is not condoned. Suicide is condoned, however, by some elderly and holy men on religious grounds (Richards & Bergin, 2000). Hindus distinguish between a "good death" and a "bad death." A good death is one in which the person is in the proper frame of mind, has all of his or her faculties, has made appropriate good-bye gestures to family and friends, and retains solace. A person who dies after having lived a long, prosperous life can be considered to have had a good death; death becomes welcomed instead of something to be avoided. Bad deaths, conversely, involve an inadequate amount of time for the person to get his or her affairs in order. Fatal heart attacks and car accidents, for example, are considered examples of bad deaths, as is the death of a child. Suicide would fall into this category, and community members may view suicide with trepidation. Some Hindus believe that the spirit of a person who has completed suicide will return as a ghost to haunt the living, whereas others believe that the person will be reincarnated to a lower animal form, or at least suffer in the next life. Family members of persons who complete suicide often enlist the aid of numerous religious figures and fortune-tellers in order to help the deceased receive the best conceivable next life.

SPECIFIC ETHNIC GROUPS

Chinese Americans

Chinese philosophies and worldviews are influenced by a confluence of Confucianism, Buddhism, and Taoism; hence, distinguishing which rituals are associated with which philosophy is a daunting, if not an impossible, task. In fact, consistent with Chinese culture, each of the religions have melded together to form an interrelational approach that guides living. Conversely, in the West one generally cannot be a Muslim and a Hindu and a Christian, as they have different philosophical underpinnings. "Traditionally, every Chinese was Confucian in ethics and public life, Taoist in private life and hygiene, and Buddhist at the time of death, with a healthy dose of shamanistic folk religion thrown in along the way" (H. Smith, 1991, p. 189). That said, as with all clients, it is more significant to understand the meaning associated with the client's philosophies, religions, and rituals than the importance of their origin.

Method and Cultural Meaning

Numerous studies of suicide have found that Asians, particularly the Chinese, are more likely to hang themselves than to use any other means (e.g., Lester, 1994b; Shiang, 1998; Shiang et al., 1997). Comparatively, European Americans, Native Americans, and African Americans, particularly males, are more likely to use handguns. Hanging has meaning within Chinese culture and must be considered within the context of how suicide itself is viewed. In Western culture, suicide is viewed as an individual act in which the person must have had a concomitant psychological or psychiatric disturbance. Our theories of suicide are largely based on an individual model in which the person completing suicide is responsible for his or her actions. Even sociocultural explanations of suicide eventually lend themselves to an individual, selfish choice, though the motivation may have had social implications.

Traditionally, the Chinese have viewed suicide from a much more contextualist perspective than their Western counterparts. The individual is understood as secondary to the needs of the group, and suicide is viewed as an interpersonal, familial act. In fact, most Asian cultures view suicide as an interpersonal, community act, largely because of the influences of Buddhism, Confucianism, and Taoism (Farberow, 1975). Suicide is often associated with shame, as in the failure of a son to achieve the expectations of the family, and attitudes toward suicide are associated with saving face, indicating that the person takes responsibility for actions and has saved the family or community from further shame. Therefore, suicide is often perceived as honorable (Ryan, 1985). Questions may arise pertaining to who was responsible for the person's death instead of asking why the death occurred.

Because of the interpersonal nature of the act of suicide, it is sometimes the intention of the deceased to "send a message" to the living as an act of revenge, and hanging is a means of sending that message. The individual who "caused" the suicidal person to act can then be shamed by the community. Traditional Chinese culture held that when a person completes suicide, his or her troubled spirit can return and plague the living. By hanging oneself, the implication is the victim was angry, particularly for those who had little voice in the Chinese community such as women. No one really knows how this intergenerational tradition came to become common. As Bourne (1973; as cited in Shiang et al., 1997) stated, "While this method is probably rarely, if ever consciously considered by the victims, it has perhaps established a cultural precedence for selecting hanging as a method for suicide which is unknowingly passed on from one generation to another" (p. 89).

Suicide and Age

In Chinese society, female adolescents complete suicide at a higher rate than males, contrary to U.S. data. The data on suicide ideation, however, are less clear, with some U.S. studies indicating higher rates for Chinese females and others indicating no differences in ideation between males and females. Research does tend to indicate that greater adherence to a personal religious system has traditionally resulted in lower rates of suicide, but the majority of these data is limited by college student samples. In a study examining the relationship between family cohesion, religiosity, and suicide among Chinese and U.S. college students, Zhang and Jin (1996) found interesting differences in attitudes toward these variables. Chinese students reported significantly lower suicidal ideation than the U.S. sample, with females reporting more ideation, but more Chinese males attempted suicide than females. There was consistency regarding family cohesion; the greater the decrease in family cohesion the more likely that both samples had increased suicide ideation and considered suicide as an acceptable option. Depression was not a strong factor in the Chinese sample considering ideation, except when religion was involved. Contrary to numerous studies, the more religious the Chinese sample the more likely they were to consider suicide and feel more depressed. The reader should keep in mind that many future Chinese students will choose U.S. colleges and universities and will bring their cultural beliefs with them. Lester (1994b) found that suicide rates were higher in country-of-origin Asian samples than U.S. samples, thus increasing the odds that an international student may hold greater suicidal beliefs and pro-suicide attitudes if more religious. Regardless, counselors should be aware of the cultural influences surrounding suicide for their clients (e.g., international students) and should not assume the same factors (e.g., depression) are primary factors.

There has been a plethora of information written about Asian American problem-solving abilities and attitudes of perfectionism. Some European American data indicate that perfectionism and self-criticism may be considerable suicide factors (e.g., Blatt, 1995; Blatt, Quinlan, & Pilkonis, 1995), as consistently striving for and often failing at perfection leads to low self-esteem, anger, shame, and depression. Comparing Asian American and European American college students, Chang (1998) investigated the relationship between social problem solving, perfectionism, and suicide potential (including hopelessness). He found European American negative problem solving connected to self-schemas, or the whole person, whereas Asian American problem solving was attributed to bad individual decisions. Asian Americans were also more perfectionistic and concerned about external, often parental, criticisms, and also reported higher hopelessness scores than European Americans. However, Asian American suicide rates as a whole are still lower than that for European Americans. In sum, this research may indicate that negative self-evaluation on specific tasks may be less likely to translate to the whole self for Asian Americans than European Americans, and thus less likely to contribute to suicide. Therapists may want to consider the use of differing problem-solving abilities and Asian American clients' views of these abilities in treatment, if suicide ideation is suspected.

Japanese Americans

Japanese views on suicide appear to be more flexible than those of the Chinese, at least according to the interviews conducted by Braun and Nichols (1997). They found that while suicide is not condoned, it can be considered an honorable (or only) way out of a bad situation. A Buddhist minister interviewed iterated that Buddha is compassionate and does not differentiate based on the manner of one's death. The extent to which his belief is merely his and how much it represents Japanese Buddhism itself is unknown. However, it does show some variance in thinking about suicide from a Buddhist perspective. Hirayama (1990) discussed the greater Japanese leniency of suicide from an historical perspective. *Seppuku* or *hara-kari* (an honorable and ritualistic form of suicide) was founded within Buddhism approximately 400 years ago but officially ended about 150 years ago. However, the influence of honorable suicide has been maintained in the collective Japanese culture. As a developed country, Japan has one of the highest rates of suicide in the world, and Japanese Americans in the United States have one of the highest rates of suicide among the broader Asian American population.

Vietnamese Americans

Vietnamese Americans may hold a more conservative stance on suicide, indicating that Buddhism does not condone it. According to some Vietnamese Buddhists, someone who kills himself or herself will live in Suicide Land until the day that they were supposed to leave this earth, in order to fulfill their karma. For example, if someone completes suicide at the age of twenty but they were supposed to live until the age of seventy-seven, they will stay in Suicide Land for fifty-seven years. Consistent with Chinese doctrine, the ghost of the person who completes suicide will return to haunt the living, indicating that suicide may be a means of accomplishing a measure of revenge. Funeral ceremonies are consistent for the person who completed suicide and who dies of natural causes, and hence, no special ceremonies or rituals are performed because of the manner of death (Braun & Nichols, 1997).

Filipino Americans

Of the Asian groups with known empirical data, Filipino Americans have low rates of suicide. Lester (1994b) reported rates two to three times lower than that of both Japanese and Chinese Americans, and about half that of African Americans. Erdman et al. (1998) found that though Filipino American and European American adolescents had similar rates of depression, few Filipino Americans reported previous suicide attempts. As a result of over three centuries of Spanish rule, the vast majority of Filipinos (and thus Filipino Americans) are Roman Catholic, and generally follow the traditions and customs of other Catholics globally. Suicide is viewed as breaking the sixth commandment, "Thou shall not kill." However, there are culture-specific beliefs in the Philippines that may differ from those in other Catholic countries. Death is seen as a natural part of life and is viewed with happiness in many cases. For example, when an elderly person dies and enters heaven there is cause for joy. This does not mean that there is no sadness from family and friends, but that sadness is only one emotion that embodies Filipino views of death. Filipino clients may express a range of positive and negative emotions upon learning of a death, which should not be considered atypical within their cultural group.

Traditionally, most Catholic priests would not perform ceremonies for persons who completed suicide and they could not be buried in a Catholic cemetery. However, these values have changed a bit, with many priests now offering their services. Many Catholic priests now believe that anyone who completed suicide must have been mentally ill, thus absolving the person of responsibility for his or her death. Community members may have a different, less-forgiving perspective, at least initially. Often when a suicide occurs, the person is blamed for not taking responsibility and for being cowardly, but it is followed by compassion for the individual and the family. Euthanasia is also, at least in part, based on Catholicism. Active euthanasia (e.g., "pulling the plug") is condemned, but some Filipinos favor passive euthanasia (allowing the person to die naturally without extensive life-saving measures).

Younger generations of Filipino Americans may be more afraid of death than the older generation because the latter hold the deceased in high esteem. Filipino people in general are considered to be more open when discussing death compared with other Asian American ethnic groups—an openness that makes the clinician's job a bit easier. Discussion is considered a means of coping, and the more they can share with others, particularly family members, the better. Due to the expectation of openness, counselors, especially non-Asian Americans, may be more likely to have an easier time working with Filipino Americans surrounding grief and loss issues initially than with other Asian American groups.

Case Example

A seventeen-year-old bicultural Filipino American female was recommended for counseling after having been sexually abused by a "counselor" at a national after-school program and was told by a program staff member that it was "no big deal." She was willing, after some typical hesitation during the rapport-building phases, to discuss the abuse that she reported to the local authorities. After the abuse became public the director of the after-school program supported the abusing male, causing significant depression, fear, and anger for the client. During one early counseling session, she said, "I just want to see the face of God." At this point it was unclear whether suicide was a serious option for her, and the counselor responded with, "What is it that you want God to say or do when you see God?" Discussion of God's response led to which needs were not being met (i.e., security, power) and treatment quickly moved toward empowering the client. Treatment included journaling, anger expression, problem solving, and cognitive restructuring. These approaches were couched within a cultural lens in which views of abuse, future relationship possibilities given social roles, emotional expression, power, and her role within God's plan were presented.

Korean Americans

Korean religiosity is a conglomeration of shamanistic, Buddhist, Confucian, Taoist, and Christian philosophies. In Korea though, it should be noted that while shamanism is the oldest of the religious faiths, it is primarily accepted only by the economically disadvantaged. People from the upper economic strata often dismiss it. Shamanism emphasizes harmonious relationships among all human and animal beings, plants, and spirits. In essence, all things are related and have life, and a shamanistic philosophy focuses on the interrelationships of all beings. In the United States, shamanism is generally not consciously accepted, yet features such as ancestor worship (consistent with Confucian customs) are still practiced in some Korean American communities.

In one of the few studies on Korean suicidal behaviors, Juon, Nam, and Ensminger (1994) found depression to be the strongest predictor among adolescents, whereas other factors included substance use, male gender, academic concerns, and hostility. The extent to which the results can be translated to Korean Americans is not known, but many of the critical factors described in this study are typical of factors found among numerous U.S. suicide and adolescence studies. Obviously, research studies are greatly needed to gain a better understanding of the cultural nuances associated with suicide among Korean Americans.

Cambodian Americans

Very little research has been conducted in understanding the relationship of death, suicide, and grieving issues with Cambodian

Americans. However, some nuances will be profiled later. The overwhelming majority of Cambodian Americans observe Buddhism, and their culture closely follows many of the philosophies of that faith. Traditional Cambodian Americans believe strongly in spirit possession *(Khmoch),* which influences their daily lives. In essence, ancestral spirits can return and influence the living (Lang, 1990). Because of their strong belief in *Khmoch,* it is important to please ancestors and follow proper traditions of death and dying.

Consistent with Buddhist teachings, suffering is part of the human condition. Therefore, Cambodian Americans may be less likely to acknowledge illness, including psychological illness, until it becomes almost unbearable. Family members are likely not to discuss mental illness with other members, and it is unlikely that they would feel comfortable speaking with a therapist about these issues (unless assimilated into mainstream U.S. culture). In addition, counselors should recall that the Khmer Rouge regime dominated Cambodia for decades and the effects are still felt. Many people were punished or killed for speaking out against the government, and this was often translated into speaking about any negative issue, including personal problems. Thus, speaking to counselors may not be perceived as acceptable to many Cambodian Americans. Also, many Cambodians took their own lives during the Khmer Rouge regime and it was considered acceptable during those times. Interviews with refugee survivors indicate that many saw family members or others kill themselves rather than fall into the hands of the oppressive regime (e.g., Paniagua, 2005). Thus, suicide was considered acceptable under these extremely difficult circumstances. We can only speculate as to whether suicide has become more acceptable in today's mainstream Cambodian American culture.

GAY/LESBIAN/BISEXUAL/TRANSGENDER ISSUES

The overwhelming majority of information about general GLBT issues is derived from the European American, middle-class population. There is an exceptionally small amount of professional literature regarding gay Asian populations, and what little is available will be summarized here. Virtually no professional information exists regarding the relationship between being Asian, gay, and suicidal, with the preponderance being anecdotal and conjectural.

Asian countries vary on the acceptance of gay men and lesbians with Thailand, Vietnam, and the Philippines being much more accepting, or at least tolerant, than other countries such as Korea, China, Japan, and India. In these and most other Asian countries, sexuality is not discussed openly, even among family members. In some countries such as Korea, being gay is almost synonymous with being invisible (Hahn, 1989; Nakajima, Chan, & Lee, 1996; Sohng & Icard, 1996). There is a long, documented history of GLBT behavior in Asian cultures from India to China to Japan (Hinsch, 1990; Nakajima et al., 1996). Why then is it that GLBT behavior is considered a taboo topic and generally not accepted? Let us first begin with a discussion of GLBT issues in traditionally Confucian and Hindu cultures. From there I will move to two other Asian cultures considered to be more accepting in their views, largely because sexuality itself is defined differently than in the United States. These different definitions have direct relevance for clinicians.

Confucianism and Hinduism say nothing specifically about homosexuality either as an identity or as a behavior (Richards & Bergin, 2000), though early Buddhist teachings considered homosexual behavior unwholesome and thus forbidden. Unlike in many Asian countries, in the United States many Buddhists accept GLBTs both in orientation and behavior. Because of its central importance in many Asian cultures though, both Buddhist and Confucian religions, nevertheless, influence the Asian American family, through expectations of filial piety, conformity to societal norms, and the clear delineation of gender role expectations. Men are considered of greater importance in Asian American families and are expected to marry and carry on the family name. Women are supposed to fulfill their roles as daughters, wives, and mothers. "Coming out" to society, particularly to the family, is considered as a threat to the family lineage and may even bring shame to the family (S. Chan, 1989, 1992; Greene, 1994, 1997). Although these issues may be consistent with other ethnic (including European American) families, they appear more relevant in Asian American families because of the threat to Confucian and Hindu beliefs about family and social customs. For example, Korean Americans rarely, if ever, talk about homosexuality, seeing it as something very odd and something to ignore (Sohng & Icard, 1996). Indian Americans view it as an aberration and in opposition to the family. Y. B. Chung and Katayama (1998) acknowledged that historical economic influences also contribute to the lack of acceptance of gays and lesbians. Asian communities grew from agricultural societies where it was critically important that families become large for economic purposes. The greater the labor force, the greater the potential wealth.

Considerations for Counselors

There are multiple identity issues that may need to be addressed by clinicians. First, being GLBT alone has social and personal acceptance implications in the United States, regardless of ethnic background. Compared with many Asian countries, the United States is considered to be much more accepting, or at least tolerant, of GLBT concerns and "lifestyles." However, one does not have to look far to realize that GLBT persons do not have equal societal status with heterosexuals. Numerous issues such as coming out, social acceptance, identity formation, and legal restrictions all impact GLBTs more than the straight community. These issues are compounded by the fact that in the United States, the gay and lesbian community of color is visibly small and often nonaccepting. Gay and lesbian persons of color are often shunned by their own ethnic community and by the (predominantly European American) GLBT community, leaving such people without a fixed community with which to identify. Wooden, Kawasaki, and Mayeda (1983) found that the Japanese American gay men were not likely to be political activists and had difficulty fully synthesizing being gay into their personal and cultural identities. They did not believe that they would be accepted in the mainstream Japanese American community. S. Chan (1992) reported that her Asian American lesbian and gay male participants felt the need to choose between their Asian American and their GLBT identities. Most respondents identified more strongly with their gay or lesbian identity than with their Asian identity, though situational factors such as community identification and term selection (e.g., Asian American gay man versus gay Asian American) were important factors.

Second, being Asian American often leads to identity confusion, discriminatory practices, and stereotypes. S. Chan (1989) found that most Asian American gay men and lesbians identified as gay first and Asian American second because of the general lack of Asian American community support. Once in counseling though, client views often changed depending on the specific ethnic identity and sexual orientation developmental status of the client. There are very few specific GLBT Asian American support systems and services in the United States, often leading to a sense of alienation from both the GLBT and Asian communities. Further, Asian–Asian gay relationships are uncommon, leading to an increased lack of role models to identify with and befriend. Community support for gay male, lesbian, and bisexual individuals differs depending on the part of the country one is located in and local norms and attitudes. In many areas, general support is virtually nonexistent for GLBT persons, much less those who identify as Asian American. Counselors should determine the extent to which the Asian client's family is accepting of GLBTs. Research indicates only half of Japanese male gay adolescents come out to their families (Wooden et al., 1983, as reported in Y. B. Chung & Katayama, 1998). It becomes apparent that the counselor needs to gain a realistic perspective of support systems for this population and understand the variety of cultural attitudes toward Asian American GLBTs.

Third, in the United States we generally label people as gay, lesbian, or bisexual (and perhaps transgendered) because Western thought tends to trichotomize sexuality, and place people into discreet categories. These views are contrary to most of the sexuality research that suggests few people can actually be categorized so easily. In fact, commonly used sexuality indices repeatedly show that the majority of people do not fall neatly into these categories. In Asian and Asian American cultures also, sexuality cannot be as easily delineated into these categories. There is greater flexibility in views of sexual behavior, sexual identity, and gender identity (Nakajima et al., 1996). For example, in some Asian cultures, cross-dressing is seen as fairly common and has even been included in Japanese (i.e., Kabuki) and Greek theater. In the United States, if someone cross-dresses he or she is often quickly perceived as gay, transgendered, or transsexual, although this may not be the case in Asian American cultures.

In some Asian American cultures, sexual orientation and identity are defined not by the object of the sex act but by the feelings that the person has for others and the role within the sex act itself. There are traditional male–male and female–female relationships, which are considered a form of egalitarian homosexuality. However, there are other forms of homosexuality that do not easily fit into a

Western category. For instance, an Asian American man can have sexual relations with other men involving penetration but still maintain heterosexuality because he is the dominant figure. Many Asian men have wives and families also but still maintain an active same-sex relationship(s), and can still be considered "men" (and therefore "straight") because they are not in the subservient position. The role defines the man, not the object of the sex act. Oral sex is included also; the man who gives oral sex may be considered gay, whereas the man receiving the oral sex may consider himself heterosexual. These attitudes are similar to attitudes often held in some Hispanic and Hispanic American cultures. The differences in sexuality definitions are critically important for therapists in order to understand cultural differences and not categorize someone either incorrectly or needlessly. Sexuality is defined by cultures, and thus it is important for counselors to check their own preconceived ideas about sexuality, especially when counseling Asian American clients.

The Filipino role described by the *bakla* has been recently discussed in the Asian American male sexuality literature (e.g., Rodriguez, 1996; Tan, 1995). *Bakla* have been considered a "third sex" in that they are not considered gay or straight by Western definitions. They are men who either give (orally) or receive (anally) sex from straight men, often cross-dress, and are effeminate. They might be considered transgendered in the United States, as it "refers to men having assuming the gender of a woman" (Rodriguez, 1996, p. 94), and have been described as a man with the heart of a female (Manalansan, 1990; Rodriguez, 1996; Tan, 1995). The men who have sexual relations with a *bakla* still consider themselves straight and a "real man." In fact, it is often seen as a sign of masculinity to have sex with a *bakla,* which increases the dominant partner's virility. To be on the receiving end of sex makes one become a *bakla*. In fact, two *bakla* having sex is considered to be a lesbian relationship (Tan, 1995). Often, straight men will be married with families yet still maintain a relationship with a *bakla* in the form of a boyfriend. Usually there is a material benefit for the *bakla,* either through gifts, alcohol, or money (Tan, 1995).

In addition to Filipino culture, other Asian and Asian American cultures have other terms for the same concept, as do many other cultures globally. In addition, many share similar problems. Even though some societies may be tolerant of *bakla* (both U.S. *bakla* and non-

U.S. *bakla*) and other same-sex behaviors, it does not mean that they are not victimized. Most Filipinos and Filipino Americans have mixed views toward *bakla*, and negative views stem from the Catholic Church, which condemns same-sex relationships. Gay Filipino men often arrive in the United States with a strong Western identity due to U.S. media and Western governmental histories. They arrive with the belief that the United States is more tolerant of homosexuality than their home country, and this belief applies to other Asian American cultural groups as well (see Sohng & Icard, 1996). However, these new immigrants are still often viewed as outsiders to other U.S.–born Asians and by the European American majority. There is increased chance of identity confusion and stress, and it becomes difficult to seek out appropriate Asian American partners. In many Asian American cultures, *bakla* find it difficult to approach another male whom he is interested in because of social norms around masculinity. Therefore, he may not seek out the opportunity to become involved with another Asian American male and instead connect with a European American man, for example, who may be more assertive (Sohng & Icard, 1996).

Counseling Factors

There has been no research examining the relationship between being gay, Asian, and suicidal. However, we can speculate on factors counselors should consider to decrease the likelihood of suicidal ideation or behaviors. The counselor must consider the fact that Asian American support systems (e.g., counseling groups and networks) for gay men and lesbians are extremely rare and if they exist at all are typically located in large cities. Even when they exist they are sometimes not helpful as a means of support. Culturally sensitive authors have discussed the fact that Asian Americans are less likely to join a counseling group or verbally interact much when in group due to cultural norms about keeping personal matters within the family unit (Sue & Sue, 2003). Further, the Asian American gay community does not appear to be as organized as the European American gay community. Asian gays often believe that they have to choose between attempting to become more involved with the European American gay pride movement and the Asian community (Chan, 1993).

Thus, gay Asians often have difficulty with identity issues, and this is where counselors can help integrate both ethnic and sexual identity.

Any time identity issues (regardless of type) become diffuse or not defined an increased chance of depression and suicide may occur. Some authors indicate that identity and role confusion contributes to the high suicide ideation and/or completion rate among teenagers and among some with DSM Axis II disorders. Another area of concern involves partner choice and its social implications. Asian gay men are often concerned with initiating relationships with European American men but are also concerned that the latter will not initiate a relationship with them. Within the Asian American gay literature, the fact that many gay European American men will not approach an Asian American man is viewed as a form of racism. There have been a number of articles describing perceived discrimination, prejudice, and stereotyping from European Americans with the Asian gay community (e.g., S. Chan, 1989; Wooden et al., 1983). It is also difficult for gay Asians to find others of the same ethnicity (e.g., Vietnamese American with a Vietnamese American partner), thus increasing the likelihood of alienation and depression.

Sohng and Icard (1996) and Rodriguez (1996) discussed other areas that counselors should consider, particularly when working with Korean Americans and Filipino Americans, respectively. Counselors must understand the confluence of history, cultural-religious influences, sociocultural mores, U.S.–based attitudes, racial influences, and individual conflicts that may arise as a result of being a gay Asian American. They must understand the conflict often felt by clients to remain Chinese, for example, but also to have same-sex relationships. With many clients a belief arises that a choice needs to be made between one's national identity and sexual orientation. It is important to consider more flexible ways of considering sex roles, and that if a man has been dominant in a same-sex relationship, he may not consider himself gay. It does not preclude discussion of that possibility during treatment. If a Filipino man is fairly acculturated into mainstream U.S. culture, then counseling may include more of a gay-affirming and gay-activist position. As always, it is useful to assess the level of acculturation of the client and/or family members early in treatment.

Nakajima et al. (1996) discussed counseling and support system recommendations, both what may and may not be helpful. For example, if one resides in a large city then either mixed-race or all-Asian-

American organizations may be beneficial to reduce anxiety and alienation. However, the author also mentioned that Parents and Friends of Lesbians and Gays (PFLAG) rarely have Asian members. Smaller organizations are often formed, and it would be beneficial for counselors to keep socially connected in order to maintain their knowledge of these groups. A social, interracial group discussed by the authors, "Asians and Friends," often has a fairly good following, but they indicated that it is often a means for non–Asian Americans to meet Asian Americans. However, they are a potential resource for discussions of interracial relationships.

BUDDHIST VIEWS OF DEATH AND DYING

In Buddhism there is a well-known true story in the *Pali Canon* (the collection of Pali language books that makes up the doctrinal basis of Theravada Buddhism), in which the son of a woman named Kisa Gotami (or Gotamis) died, and she carried his body through the town looking for medicine to bring him back to life. This grief-stricken woman eventually took the body to the Buddha and pleaded with him to help her son. After listening to her the Buddha said, "Go enter the city, make the entire rounds of the entire city, beginning at the beginning, and in whatever home no one has ever died, from that house fetch tiny grains of mustard seed" (Burtt, 1982, p. 45, as referenced in Goss and Klass, 1997, pp. 378-379). After going from house to house she recognized the futility of the exercise, as every home had been affected by death. Death is a natural part of life, and one does not exist without the other.

Buddha recommended his followers contemplate death in order to understand the impermanence of life. By viewing death as natural and merely part of a larger cycle, Buddhists with strong beliefs should not fear death. However, most Buddhists still fear death because like most religious persons, their faith is not strong enough to ward off fear. From these teachings we can begin to understand the meaning behind rituals surrounding death from a Buddhist perspective. Many of the rituals described later are not specific to suicide, but readers can gain an appreciation of the ceremonies should they lose a client to suicide or work with the family of a person who completed suicide.

Traditional Rituals at the Moment of Death

The rebirth process is partially determined by the state of mind just prior to death, which makes the time before death crucial. Monks often chant *sutras* (teachings) that drive away evil spirits, calm the dying person, and prepare them for the transition from death to rebirth. According to Tibetan Buddhism, there is a transitional period called *Bardo* that separates death from the next life. Often these preparations take the form of instructions from the *Bardo Thodol* (Tibetan Book of the Dead) to make the transition easier and alleviate fear (Goss & Klass, 1997; Truitner & Truitner, 1993). Traditionally, family members are available at the time of death, and most dying persons want to die at home in the presence of family. The Vietnamese believe that it is bad luck not to die at home.

The person's spirit (*bla,* or consciousness or soul) is released from the body over a period of twelve hours after death, meaning that no one can touch or alter the body in any way. Doing so may cause the spirit to enter into a suboptimal next life. Many U.S. Buddhists have not followed this tradition, according to Yeung, Kong, and Lee (2000), because either hospitals do not allow for this practice or many people are interested in donating their organs, a relatively new, and controversial, phenomenon to Buddhist practices. There are numerous rituals performed after the body's death, all designed to assist the person into their next birthing. These rituals will differ depending on the culture in which they are performed, and counselors can become familiar with local customs and norms to gain a better understanding of what is considered appropriate. For example, some traditional Tibetan Buddhists will perform such rituals as setting up shrines with pictures of the Buddha, rolling the body on the right side because that is the death posture of the Buddha, burning incense, and making offerings.

Traditional Funeral and Burial Practices

Traditionally, *sutras* are performed by monks, nuns, and family members during the funeral ceremony. A brief recitation of the life of the deceased follows, presented by the head monk. Burial practices differ depending on culture, as some cultures prefer burial, some cremation as followed from the Buddha, and some having no preference.

There is a forty-nine-day time period between the time of death and the transition into the next life. This period dictates that certain rituals be performed during that time to assist the person into the best possible life, though some U.S. Buddhists have modified these rituals. Traditionally, decisions on the next life are decided every seventh day after death up to the forty-ninth day, and day one hundred. Therefore, mourners should perform a funeral ceremony and recite *sutras* every seventh day in the presence of the body. However, due to time constraints and movement toward a U.S. way of life, many mourners in the United States typically only recite the *sutras* on the seventh and forty-ninth day, though a few of the more traditional mourners will also perform a ceremony on the one-hundredth day.

U.S. Modifications

There are some death traditions that have to be modified because of health and legal mandates in the United States. In addition, death practice customs are typically modified once immigrants arrive into the United States from Asian countries, usually due to acculturative changes. For example, funerals can occur in a funeral home, though most funeral homes still do not make the accommodations needed to maintain traditional Buddhist funeral practices. However, some funeral homes in areas with high concentrations of Buddhists, typically in California, have made accommodations such as allowing the chanting of *sutras,* permitting burning incense, and not allowing the embalming process. Monks are not always deemed mandatory in the funeral process, with family members carrying on traditions and reciting the *sutras*. The more sincere the chants, the more effective they will be to enable the deceased to move into the next life. The primary purpose of the funeral is to assist the person in being reborn.

During the funeral, mourners wear white. In Buddhist cultures internationally the mourners wear all-white, whereas in the United States they often wear a white armband or a white headband. Buddhists employ burial, cremation, and other means depending on the wishes of the family and the cultural traditions. For example, the Chinese bury their dead whereas persons with a Thai background practice cremation. Buddhist traditions typically allow for the outward expression of grief at the funeral, but grief is not encouraged, because death is a natural part of the life cycle. If mourners do grieve, other mourners may attempt to persuade the griever to chant *sutras* more heartily (Truitner & Truitner, 1993).

Buddhism, Euthanasia, and Organ Donation

Buddhism does not take a position on euthanasia specifically, though it is accepted in some Buddhist communities that passive euthanasia may be acceptable. For example, in their interviews, Braun and Nichols (1997) found that Japanese American Buddhists supported the family's decision on passive euthanasia (allowing the person to die without significant means) but condemned active euthanasia (assisting the person with death). Vietnamese Americans shared similar views. Both active and passive euthanasia are viewed as killing, but passive euthanasia may be more acceptable, particularly if finances become burdensome. The Chinese Americans interviewed believed that ending suffering would be acceptable only after extensive discussion with both the family and the medical staff.

Historically, many Buddhists were unwilling to make organ donations because the body is considered to be a gift from one's ancestors and to give one's organs upon death would be to disfigure and maim the body, thus showing disrespect for the ancestors. Donating organs also has direct influence over the body in the next life. Some Asian American cultural groups, regardless of religious beliefs, believe that donating eyes in this life means that one will not have eyes in the next life. Some non–U.S. Buddhist monks now take a pro–organ donation stance, which has allowed other, primarily U.S., Buddhists to consider donation seriously. The position is based on the belief that the Buddha was giving and concerned with the welfare of others, and thus organ donation may be considered honorable. Some Buddhists also believe that only the soul is reborn and not the actual body from this life.

HINDU VIEWS OF DEATH AND DYING

Karma and Reincarnation

Souls *(jivas)* are brought into the world through God and do not disappear upon death. In the Hindu faith, as with other religions, the soul does not need the body, as it exists and will continue to exist when the body dies. This is known as reincarnation or "in Sanskrit, samsara, a word that signifies endless passage through cycles of life, death, and rebirth" (H. Smith, 1991, p. 63). In Hinduism, human beings are considered the highest life form on earth as a result of a series of cycles from lower forms through higher forms of life. The "glue" tying all of these cycles together is called karma. Karma is concerned with moral cause and effect in which humans are punished because of morally corrupt previous decisions and can receive positive effects because of good morality and good decisions. As with Buddhism (which some say was born in India), some Hindus believe karma can be influenced within this lifetime whereas others believe that it influences future lifetimes. Hinduism is not fatalistic in the sense that people have no control over their destiny, but can, instead, influence the future (Almeida, 1996). Some recent Western writers have misinterpreted karma as equated with fatalism and helplessness, which is inaccurate. Each act and thought affects future experiences. Therefore, Hindus have full responsibility for their lives, but as H. Smith indicates, most Hindus are not willing to admit fault. Instead, many project blame onto others (including God as in God's will) and have misinterpreted Hinduism themselves. Through the paths discussed earlier, the individual cycles through multiple incarnations until it reaches the final passage called nirvana. Achieving nirvana is the ultimate spiritual goal of Hindus, and is, in part, influenced by their preparation for death.

Traditional Hindu Funeral Rituals in India

Hindu rituals surrounding death are often based on the caste system that is, in part, an economic system. The caste system itself is an ancient stratification system based on purity beliefs. I realize that Hindus who live outside of India (e.g., Great Britain, South Africa, United States) may not follow a caste system in the same manner as in India, but this system does influence how some death rituals are performed in the United States (and counselors may be counseling families who hold on to traditions). For example, in a high-caste family, traditional Hindu beliefs dictate that the sons of a father who dies should have the majority of their head shaven by a barber as part of the twelve-day funeral ceremony. In India, barbers are traditionally of a low caste and thus, because of purity beliefs, are not allowed into the house to cut the hair (for an excellent review of rituals involving a high-caste family, see Laungani, 1997). There is tremendous variation in Hindu practices depending on their caste, region, and financial resources. In fact, because of the historical confluence among Hindu, Islamic, and Sikh faiths, funerals are, in reality, a mix of these traditions and practices, even in the United States. Unfortunately, it is beyond the scope of this chapter to discuss all practices. It is not the actual practices themselves that are of extreme importance for the therapist. More important are the client's beliefs and that the practices are followed according to their traditions. Many practices have had to be modified or negated altogether in Western countries because of local health and safety laws and ignorance or apathy concerning traditional customs. Therefore, discussion of a Western perspective is presented later. A few of the more consistent traditional practices will be discussed in order for the therapist to grasp some of the cultural nuances surround funeral proceedings.

If pending death is not due to suicide, little or no discussion occurs about the death and there is often denial that death is pending, particularly among the wives. Traditionally, wives were expected, and hoped, to die before their husbands because society did not treat widows well, particularly if they had children. Prayers are offered, and families may call upon astrologers, family members, and Brahman priests (if upper caste) to please the gods so the sick individual can be restored to health. Readings from the Bhagavad Gita (a Hindu religious text) may be offered by local priests, or in some cases elderly, respected family members or clergy from another faith (e.g., Sikhism) may offer prayers from their respective holy books. When it becomes evident that the person is nearing death, he or she will be placed close to the ground, as the Hindu faith believes this will help the person be absorbed by the earth. The point of these and other rituals, consistent with other religions, is to assist the person into the next life (Laungani, 1997).

Regardless of the type of death, including a suicide, at the time of death the eldest male becomes the family decision maker, and it is appropriate for the women to wail loudly. The body is then washed by relatives or close friends and wrapped in white cloth. There are numerous specific ceremonies over the twelve days that the funeral occurs. For example, the widow will wipe off her *sindoor* (wedding mark), and food may or may not be served from the house during those days depending on local custom. During the next twelve days, the body is taken to the crematorium by the men as women are not allowed to go there. In India, it is often customary for the eldest son to first light the funeral pyre, followed by other sons, as a sign of respect, particularly if the deceased was an elderly male member of the family (Laungani,1997). In the United States, this is often not permitted due to various laws. Female relatives close to the deceased may wear white saris for at least a year after the death (Almeida, 1996).

Hindu Funeral Rituals in Western Countries

Funeral rituals are modified from ancient customs belonging to the country of origin when immigrants arrive in the United States or other Western countries. Laungani (1997) makes a number of poignant points regarding changes that have occurred in Western countries, and how Western systems involved in funerals could make some easy modifications to allow immigrants to retain at least some traditional cultural customs. For example, it is customary for the Hindu family members to touch the lips of a dying or deceased person with a basil leaf dipped into water from the Ganges. Companies now sell water from the Ganges and, as Laungani points out, it would be a wonderful, culturally sensitive gesture by a hospital to keep some of this water on hand. If the person is pronounced dead at a hospital, staff can leave the family alone with the deceased for an extended period of time and allow them to prepare the body if they choose.

Funeral directors can wear white instead of black, can carry the body to the crematorium in an Indian *bier* instead of a coffin, and do not have to be confined to a very narrow window of time often accepted in the United States. However, views of death in the West would have to change in that, even though Western systems may not always fully comprehend the rituals, culturally sensitive hospitals and funeral directors can learn to understand some of them and the need for them. It is unfortunate, but changing from a financial perspective to a person-centered position may be very difficult if not impossible to attain, particularly with the seemingly innumerable laws that the United States (and other Western countries) have surrounding hospitals and death-related businesses. Counselors should be willing to discuss the loss of traditional rituals and the potential anger, fear, and disappointment that may accompany relatives of the deceased.

Given the importance of funeral and other death ceremonies within Hindu and other cultures, it is critical that counselors be sensitive to these cultural losses. Perhaps the most realistic option expressed by Laungani (1997) is for Hindus to operate their own funeral homes. If these modifications are not made, then cultural customs die, and as Laungani indicates, "The death of a culture is the death of a civilization" (p. 71).

Hindu Views of Mourning

It is appropriate in the Hindu faith for expressions of mourning to occur, particularly for women. In India and in traditional U.S. Hindu families, rituals during the twelve days of the funeral process may include daily crying times for the women, and professional mourners may be hired to lead the ceremonies. These professional mourners will lead the group by talking fondly of the deceased, whereupon someone will begin to sob and then others will join in. Traditionally, wailing in what some Westerners may call an uncontrollable manner is appropriate. Western approaches may be more controlled. However, mourning the loss is still expected. If called upon later in a therapeutic role, therapists can expect crying in a manner often expected in mainstream U.S. culture. Crying is not perceived as a weakness among women and is an indicator of the person's relationship with the deceased.

SPECIFIC CULTURAL GROUPS

Some traditional and contemporary rituals surrounding death and dying in Asian cultures are profiled earlier, specifically when considering these rituals from a religious perspective. However, there are some rituals discussed in the literature that are somewhat specific to particular cultures, and this section will outline these. In addition to the authors listed in the following paragraphs, Braun and Nichols (1997) offer a helpful overview of death and dying rituals for Chinese American, Japanese Americans, Vietnamese Americans, and Filipino Americans. Counselors may want to consider this and other authors who have written on the topic.

Chinese Americans

Chinese rituals are a mixture of Confucian, Buddhist, and Taoist beliefs. During the mourning period, happy occasions such as weddings and birthdays are postponed. As with many cultural groups, the amount of grief expressed is often proportional to how close the deceased was to the mourner, with close relatives mourning the longest. Men are allowed to cry openly during a family gathering soon after the death. During the funeral ceremonies, women are allowed to express their grief but the men remain stoic. In fact, women can often be seen wailing. It is less likely though that this type of expression of grief would occur in the counselor's office because of Chinese (and Asian in general) beliefs that one does not express oneself substantially outside of the family. Mourners wear white robes and burn incense, and blue and white flowers are placed around the coffin at the mortuary (Watson & Rawski, 1988). Traditionally, the funeral procession is loud and ends with the family placing dirt on the coffin. After three days, the family may have a picnic at the graveside and burn food and fake money as an offering for the afterlife. The burning of money has been incorporated somehow into Chinese culture over the centuries, though no one knows for sure its significance. Nonetheless, it is still considered an important ritual in the United States.

The Chinese prefer burial to cremation, and traditionally it has been critically important for the proper burial spot to be found. The belief is that burial location influences the deceased's spirit's peacefulness and future generations. With finite cemeteries in the United States and many laws surrounding burials, this burial location choice necessarily becomes less of an issue. Chinese culture indicates that the person should not be buried for at least three days, and open casket funerals are expected. In traditional Chinese religion, if one is not buried with the appropriate amount of respect and tradition, living relatives and friends can be haunted by the deceased's soul.

Sutras are chanted every seven days for seven weeks, which help to raise the soul from hell. There are daily offerings to the recently deceased, including burning incense in the home and bowing to a portrait or other remembrance of the individual. There are a number of days during the year (e.g., holiday of Ching-Ming) when rituals such as offering food and drink are expected in order to show respect for returning ancestral spirits (Braun & Nichols, 1997). Some Chinese

Americans have indicated that the furniture in the house of the deceased should be rearranged in order to ward off bad luck. It should be reiterated that the amount of influence U.S. culture has on these ceremonies is, in part, related to the client. However, these rituals were discussed briefly here in order to give the reader an introductory sense of how death is viewed, where some of the worldviews of their clients are derived from, and rituals that might be discussed in therapeutic treatment (Braun & Nichols, 1997).

It is highly likely that older immigrants and other adults retain some of their Chinese spiritual heritage, whereas third, fourth, and fifth generation Chinese Americans may have given up their traditional spiritual roots, with some converting to Christianity. Therefore, their views of suicide and death are probably consistent with both Asian and non-Asian Christians. However, as with most clients, it is a good idea to ask Chinese American clients about their religious beliefs and influences. In their interviews surrounding funeral rituals, Braun and Nichols (1997) found that the Chinese were more interested in simplicity and convenience than tradition. For example, they tended to believe less in karma and spend less time in official mourning. The Chinese Christian minister interviewed noted that he was as likely to preside over a Taoist ceremony as over a Christian ceremony for younger constituents, indicating the blending of the ceremonies. The family of someone who completes suicide may feel shame and attempt to hide it, thus mourning in private. It is likely that normal funeral arrangements would be made.

Considerations for Counselors

Chinese American and European American cultures differ in ways too numerous to mention here. Many texts are available discussing these differences in greater detail, such as those by Baruth and Manning (2003), Paniagua (2005), G. Hall and Barongan (2002), and Sue and Sue (2003). Historically, European American culture has relied on individualism and autonomy, two seemingly diametric values to Chinese American values of collectivism and allocentrism. These values influence counseling and attitudes toward mental health.

If a counselor is working with a Chinese client who identifies as Buddhist, he or she should have a basic understanding of the relationship between Buddhism and mental health. In many ways, Buddhist mental health has similar philosophies to Western cognitive-behavioral approaches, though Buddhist "treatment" is probably more far-reaching. Buddhism does not separate mental and spiritual health, and many of the recommendations for treatment are spiritual in nature. In Western thought, the "self" is made up of the ego, personality, and similar constructs. Buddhist philosophy, however, indicates that these constructs are merely illusions in that they are not forms of truth because they are transient. In fact, constructs such as happiness and depression are also transient and are not central to Buddhist thought. We are depressed or happy because of faulty attachments with others that we believe we need. From these relationships with others we get a sense of our identity. Unfortunately, depression is based on unfulfilled desires, for example, and desire is not something that humans should strive toward. Buddhism has what are called the five hindrances: lust, anger, torpor, worry, and skepticism (Groth-Marnat, 1992). As counselors, we can see how any of these hindrances can lead to depression and possibly suicide.

A Buddhist therapeutic approach would involve understanding the cause of the concern (*dukkha* or "suffering" in Buddhist vernacular), meditation, and stories. Understanding the cause of the concern is similar to cognitive-behavioral philosophy. The endpoint is for the person to gain a deeper understanding of self-statements and assumptions, where they were derived from and the meaning gained from this newfound understanding, and letting go of dysfunctional beliefs. Though the majority of this understanding is through meditation, often impractical or resisted by many U.S. clients, the philosophy is similar. Understand that you are responsible for your own condition and that others cannot influence you significantly if you do not allow them to. Through self-examination, either through a counselor or through meditation, one eventually relinquishes the idea that one must achieve various goals or be dependent on someone else to be happy (though, as mentioned earlier, happiness is also a transient state in Buddhist thought). Both cognitive-behaviorists (and other theoretical approaches) and Buddhists share the belief that freedom comes through achieving self-sufficiency. Buddhism also emphasizes the significance of community. The aim is to achieve "enlightenment" or perhaps what Western therapists might call "self-actualization." Through these common principles, and consistent with Buddhist philosophy, death can be better understood as a natural part of life. Often, family members and friends of someone who has completed suicide feel responsible for the death. For survivors, according to Buddhist philosophy, by taking responsibility for one's own condition, one can give up ultimate responsibility.

For example, a client of mine, described elsewhere, had a brother-in-law who killed himself by gunshot near a lake they had frequented. We worked on existential death issues. The client had thoughts that he "should have seen it coming and done something." These discussions grew largely out of issues of responsibility that were initiated within cognitive-behavioral and existential frameworks, though they are typically not considered consistent philosophically. Although the client did not identify as a spiritual man, he was a deeply reflective man who, through cognitive-behavioral therapy, was taught to question the origin of his beliefs. He was also taught to rate the strength of these beliefs, which led into discussions of his own death anxiety. A better understanding of his own anxiety forced him to consider his place in the world as well as that of his brother-in-law, and he began to construct a healthier meaning surrounding the concept of death itself. In conclusion, given that many Asian cultures tend to de-emphasize outward emoting, particularly around non–family members such as a counselor, it may profit counselors to become familiar with the principles of Buddhism and their relationship to cognitive-behavioral principles.

Japanese Americans

Most Japanese and Japanese Americans are followers of Buddhism, Shintoism (similar to Taoism), or Christianity. Therefore, their beliefs surrounding suicide, bereavement, and traditional burial customs generally follow one or a mixture of these religions. It is difficult to discern the origin of the beliefs in that some beliefs may have originated from a particular religion and others may simply be "just Japanese."

At the time of death, surrounded by family members, a minister recites a *sutra*. Unlike suicide, if the person is dying slowly then the *sutra* is designed to allow him or her some comfort and peace. The idea is for the person's final thoughts to be peaceful, important because a Buddhist belief is that the final thoughts of a person prior to death influence the next life. This is another reason for concern from the Japanese American (or other Buddhist) family when a family member kills himself or herself. Generally, the suicidal person has mixture of depression, shame, guilt, or hopelessness, none of which offer hope for a better next life.

Funeral ceremonies involve very precise, ritualistic procedures. A ceremony not following protocol decreases the chances of the individual attaining the next life, thus tormenting the survivors (Hirayama, 1990). They are generally held in the evening. If it is a Buddhist ceremony in the United States, the body is laid on an altar from north to south, incense is burned (in the Shinto faith, strips of European American paper are burned; in the Christian faith, flowers are offered instead of burning anything), and family members sit on the right side, while friends sit on the left side. After a ceremony, a vegetarian dinner is served to participants (though in the United States, meat is often included). In Japan, each attendee offers money to the family, the amount being determined by the level of relationship with the deceased. Christian funeral services follow typical Christian customs. However, outward expressions of grief are not expected, particularly among the men. On rare occasions among the women, a few tears may be shed in public, but it is likely that grieving will occur in private. It is highly unlikely that the men would ever cry outwardly. As part of Japanese Buddhist culture, suffering and pain are to be endured and expected. Historically, numerous rulers spoke about endurance and overcoming adversity (Hirayama, 1990), thus embedding them in Japanese cultural worldviews.

Consistent with Chinese American funerals, white is worn. Unlike Chinese American funerals though, cremation is preferred over burial. Many traditional Japanese Americans still prefer to have their ashes returned to Japan for burial in the family plot. Traditionally, memorial services are held every seventh day for seven weeks, and sometimes on day one hundred, though these services have decreased in the United States. Memorial services are held on the one-, three-, seven-, thirteen-, seventeen-, twenty-five-, thirty-three-, and fifty-year anniversaries of the death. Many Japanese Buddhists also observe the religious and secular ceremonial season of *Obon* (or Bon) (August) to celebrate those who have died (Braun & Nichols, 1997).

Vietnamese Americans

The majority of Vietnamese Americans follow Buddhism, followed by Taoism, Confucianism, or perhaps Catholicism, or some combination of the four. Vietnamese Americans may take a more conservative stance on suicide, indicating that Buddhism does not condone it. According to some Vietnamese Buddhists, a person who completes suicide will live in Suicide Land until the day they were intended to leave this earth since they have not fulfilled their karma. Consistent with Chinese doctrine, ghosts of the person will return to haunt the living, indicating that suicide may be a means of accomplishing a measure of revenge. Funeral ceremonies for a person who completed suicide and for a person who died of natural causes are consistent (Braun & Nichols, 1997). Again, depending on the deceased person's faith and the faith of the family, death rituals will vary. The Vietnamese language includes terms such as *qual dof* (to move to another life) to connote movement to another existence instead of the physical qualities of death (C. H. Chung, 1990).

Death Rituals

As in traditional Buddhist doctrine, a monk or priest determines the correct time for the burial. Items are placed in the casket along with the individual. For example, Braun and Nichols (1997) indicated that both gold and rice are placed in the mouth of the deceased, whereas other items such as tea are placed in the coffin. Typical Buddhist rituals during the funeral proceedings are followed, such as comforting the family and offering financial assistance. In the United States, cremation is becoming more common, though burial is still the predominant means of interment. Depending on the level of cultural assimilation, altars may be placed at home with a picture of the deceased, and ceremonies are held around the altar, regardless of religious affiliation. These practices are associated with "ancestor worship" but are not considered consistent with the meaning of "worship" often found in U.S. culture. In Vietnamese and other Asian cultures, worship means to commemorate instead of placing an individual on a status consistent with God (C. H. Chung, 1990). The practices maintain Asian values of filial piety. According to Braun and Nichols's (1997) interviews, in traditional Vietnamese American culture, ceremonies remembering ancestors are performed during the third (Thanh Minh) and seventh (Vu Lan) lunar months. Counselors should consider discussion of the ceremonies and the relationship of the altar to the surviving family members. Ancestor worship is often a foreign concept and has negative meanings for many U.S. therapists; hence, it is important to understand the meanings associated with this tradition and its relationship to the continuation and respect of previous family members.

Considerations for Counselors

It is recommended at the time of the death of a loved one that Vietnamese Americans not show significant emotion because it might prohibit the soul from entering the next life. There is grief, yet it may not be forthcoming and would probably be a mistake for therapists to attempt to help the client emote without considering the cultural impact of emotional expression to an "outsider." The belief that emotional expressiveness is helpful stems from Western therapeutic approaches to grief and may not be fitting when working with Vietnamese Americans, particularly men. Some Vietnamese women are expected to cry uncontrollably at funerals, but this behavior is often based on religion, culture, and assimilation levels. Grief among Vietnamese Americans should often be approached by therapists as helping the mourner return to a normal routine as quickly as possible, and mourning the loss over time (C. H. Chung, 1990). Unlike white middle-class Western thought that one should control feelings, Vietnamese Americans are often raised to believe that one must live with feelings. Therefore "coping" with feelings may not be considered a culturally consistent concept. Doing something therapeutic may be more important than talking "therapeutically" (C. H. Chung, 1990). Therapists should inform traditional clients to consult with the family patriarch to determine the appropriate rituals, thus showing respect for both the living patriarch and the deceased. If the ceremony does not follow the appropriate steps, there is a chance that the deceased person will not enter into the next life, and this shows disrespect to the individual. Of course, the more assimilated the individual is to mainstream U.S. culture, the more likely it is that the person will not follow the patterns of behavior noted earlier.

Filipino Americans

Upon death, family members and friends will say novenas (prayers) for the first nine nights. In the Philippines, the body stays at the house for the nine days and is never left alone by family members. Because of a variety of laws and cultural differences in the United States, the body stays at the mortuary, typically less than nine days. A feast *(atang)* of the deceased's favorite foods is prepared on the final resting day, and a place set at the table so that the spirit of the deceased can also eat. Often, items are placed in the coffin and women wear black to the funeral (Braun & Nichols, 1997). Traditionally, the men wear black pants and a white shirt. Pictures taken of the deceased with family members are not uncommon. After the ceremony, a wake *(lamay)* is conducted, with food, music, and other festivities. These rituals are similar to those found within other Christian religious groups such as Southern Baptists and Presbyterians. Cremation is becoming more popular within the Filipino community, but burial is still the preferred approach to interment. Traditionally, after forty days another memorial service is held, and widows are supposed to wear black for a year. In the United States, the tradition of wearing all black may be limited to only a few days because of work schedules and cultural nuances; however, the person will often continue to wear something black (e.g., a ribbon) for a period of time (Braun & Nichols, 1997).

Korean Americans

Korean religiosity is a conglomeration of shamanistic, Buddhist, Confucian, Taoist, and Christian philosophies. In the United States, shamanism is generally not consciously accepted, yet features such as ancestor worship are still practiced in some Korean American communities. Many Korean Americans consider themselves Christian, though they often also display some beliefs from other spiritual systems such as Confucianism and Buddhism. For example, ancestor worship is still recognized and is connected with filial piety and respect. The practice maintains a tie with deceased family members and contributes to the collectivism of Asian American communities. There is a connection with family and the community through the centuries instead of the immediate family and the immediate time and place. Two annual festivals *Ch'usuk* (autumn) and *Tano* (spring) are observed to show respect for the ancestors.

Funeral Rituals

Traditionally, when a person dies a chief mourner announces the death to the community. The display of grief is expected, particularly among the women. During this time there is silence, if possible, in order to show respect for the deceased. In the United States, it is often difficult to respect the dead through silence because of other responsibilities, but the mourners are expected to do their best. Burial is common and cremation of the body is rare. There are chants and family gatherings, which occur over the three days prior to burial, and the family is expected to offer a meal to the deceased on the first and fifteenth days of the following months, for a year. The mourning period lasts between three months and three years, depending on tradition and local culture. Recent changes to funeral rituals have made them more practical and simple, and many families incorporate both traditional and less-conventional rituals. This new perspective is also displayed in the United States. Some funeral homes sensitive to Korean American culture do help follow cultural traditions, but many of the historical practices are bypassed due to time and economic constraints.

Cambodian Americans

Consistent with Buddhist ritual described earlier, the family is usually available to the deceased. Rituals are sung and Buddhist stories are told. A Buddhist monk recites prayers in order for the deceased's soul to join the next world. At the time of death, Cambodians also believe that the eyelids should be shut, or else the spirit of the person is still connected to this world and will not be able to make the next spiritual journey. It is generally not expected that crying and other emotional displays will occur in public, particularly for the men. During the Khmer Rouge period, dictator Pol Pot outlawed mourning (Lang, 1990).

Hmong Americans

The Hmong are a seemingly unknown group living in the United States, and it has been only in recent years that researchers and other writers have begun to discuss their culture, beliefs, and customs. The

Hmong are primarily from China, Burma, Vietnam, Thailand, and Laos, and are a people who have endured numerous hardships due to cultural changes and oppressive political regimes. Their history extends almost five thousand years, beginning in China, and many families emigrated to the other countries in the eighteenth century. The majority of Hmong refugees live in Minneapolis, central California, and Wisconsin. Much of the following information is taken from a chapter by Bliatout (1993) and from an article by Hayes and Kalish (1987-1988), both of which serve as good overviews of the Hmong people and their death customs. The Bliatout chapter is well detailed, and the following information is merely to be used as a brief guide to understanding the death rituals of the Hmong people.

Hmong Religious Beliefs

Traditionally, the Hmong have believed strongly in spirits, including spirits that interact constantly with the living. Ancestor spirits (particularly from the male side of the family) influence the living, house spirits inhabit the house, nature spirits live in all natural things (e.g., mountains, streams), and evil spirits cause intermittent disruption for people. Many of their religious rituals pertain to their pleasing the spirits. Since immigrating to the United States, many Hmong have converted to Christianity and follow the beliefs consistent with Christianity.

As with other Asian American cultures, appropriate burial procedures are necessary to increase the benefits of the family in the future, as karma plays an important role in their beliefs. There are at least three major souls, though some Hmong believe there may be as many as thirty-two major and minor souls. Upon death and proper burial proceedings, one of the souls enters heaven and then returns to watch the family (house spirit), the second soul enters heaven thirteen days after death occurs and then returns as a human or another existence based on karma, and the third soul stays at the burial site (Bliatout, 1993).

It is considered acceptable to express grief openly upon death. The body is dressed by the family if possible and is laid out for a number of days. It is not to be altered in any way. Funerals will last multiple days, and the body is not buried for three days following death. Traditionally, only certain types of wood were used for coffins, and each clan had its own wood type. Along with the wood is the belief that if a particular wood is not used, then the person will be reborn into another clan, though in the United States this requirement is difficult to fulfill.

During the funeral, which occurs in the afternoon (because the souls leave the person at sundown), there are three critical officials: the spirit world guide, the descendant counselor, and the reed pipe player. These three officials, among others, are to ensure the deceased person's spirit journeys into the next world. The soul is in an orientation period from the fourth to the thirteenth day. During the Thirteenth Day End ceremony, a family member revisits the burial site in order to request that the soul of the person return to the home.

Bliatout (1993) discussed a number of concerns that the non-Christian Hmong have come across when someone dies in the United States. For example, custom dictates that the body should not be altered in any way and is to remain whole. However, U.S. laws often require autopsies (especially in the case of suicides). As with other religions beliefs, which include karma and reincarnation, the body needs to be kept whole or the person will not be whole in the next life. The act of embalming prevents the souls from entering heaven or would deform the body in the next life. There are numerous beliefs specific to the Hmong with which therapists should be familiar should they work with Hmong clients. Due to U.S. laws and customs differing from their cultural traditions (given that they are a recent immigrant group), survivors may have acculturation concerns surrounding death, particularly with being forced to behave in a new manner. These laws have direct implications on Hmong views of death and their ancestors.

SUICIDE PREVENTION AND INTERVENTION

There are no specified, empirically validated prevention efforts directed toward Asian American ethnic groups. However, we can extrapolate from the general Asian American counseling literature. Takahashi (1989) discussed prevention and intervention issues unique to working with Asian American clients, particularly since mental illness carries a significant social and familial stigma. First, counselors need to demonstrate patience due to potential English-language difficulties of the client (assuming, of course, that the counselor does not speak the specific Asian language). Patience becomes particularly salient during crisis intervention. Typically, during crisis intervention, counselors often ask a series of quick questions in the first fifteen minutes in order to elicit information and determine suicide risk. With many Asian clients the session may take longer than expected due to cultural norms. Counselors should show willingness to be respectful by being patient and not asking very personal questions too early. In addition, counselors should expect the client to be fairly reserved. Traditional Asian clients are not likely to immediately answer questions because suicide is difficult to discuss. This should not be perceived as resistance, or showing restricted affect or nonexpressiveness on the mental status exam. Often, cultural shame accompanies suicidal ideation and behaviors. Thus, building rapport over an extended time frame would be welcomed. In many Asian American cultures direct communication is not welcome; instead they rely on passive approaches.

Second, Paniagua (2005) and others (e.g., Sue & Sue, 2003) have repeatedly discussed that Asian American symptoms may be manifested differently from those based on white middle-class norms, and should be attended to appropriately. For example, many Asian Americans are more likely to display somatic symptoms rather than immediately discussing mental health issues. Even perceptions and discussions of depression may differ based on cultural expectations and norms (for an expanded discussion, see Sue & Sue, 2003; Paniagua, 2005). Of course, these generalizations differ based on the acculturation level of the client.

Third, Asian American cultures are interdependent and collectivistic, concerned about community beliefs and behaving accordingly. Takahashi (1989) recommended asking the client how others have reacted to their suicide ideation or attempt. Again, this demonstrates respect for the client and indicates that the counselor has an understanding of the client's culture. Finally, the client may present with atypical depressive symptoms (e.g., longstanding sensitivity to interpersonal rejection, leaden paralysis, hypersomnia), which may also include introverted aggression overlooked by counselors, though it increases suicide risk.

SUMMARY

It is clear that suicide is poorly understood among various Asian American groups and more research is needed. It is also clear that counselors should become familiar with the rituals and beliefs surrounding suicide within individual ethnic groups. Many texts discuss Asian American culture as monolithic, or give only lip service to individual ethnic differences. Even an abbreviated understanding of religious beliefs and the ceremonies associated with them, along with appropriate mourning rituals, can help with the counseling process. For example, it would be inappropriate for counselors to expect Japanese Americans to show significant emotion in session until trust is established and a bond is reached, while Filipino Americans are more likely to express themselves. Concepts surrounding death and suicide are often novel for counselors, particularly for clients who may believe in Suicide Land or other concepts not typically found in mainstream U.S. culture. Of course, it is never easy for surviving family members, regardless of ethnic background, to grasp and accept the fact that someone they cared deeply about has completed suicide. However, understanding cultural nuances surrounding death, suicide, and bereavement can help the counselor establish a trusting relationship and help ease the pain of the survivors.

The professional literature is replete with articles attesting that Asian Americans are reluctant to seek professional counseling services because of stigma, shame, and a desire to keep personal matters private. Recent research, albeit small, suggests that Asian Americans may seek mental health counseling if treatment is culturally sensitive. For culturally sensitive counselors then, it may not be unusual to see clients with some of the issues described in this section, particularly in highly populated Asian American areas.

Chapter 5

Hispanic Americans

By the year 2020, approximately fifty million Hispanic Americans will be living in the United States (Dana, 1993), continuing as the largest minority ethnic group in the United States. One of the difficulties estimating ethnic suicide rates in general is that U.S. classification systems are inherently flawed, as people self-identify differently (e.g., Hispanic, Latino/Latina, Chicano/Chicana, Mexican American, Cuban American). Heacock (1990) found that Hispanic suicide data are particularly flawed since they are based on supposed representative comparisons or derived from extrapolated numbers. Multiple groups in the United States identify as Hispanic, with heritages from Mexico, Central and South America, Spain, and the Caribbean. Although many may share language and common ancestry, they also possess unique identities that distinguish the groups. No present term fits every person's ethnic identity, and, as with all terms, there are problems with using categories such as Hispanic, Latino, and Chicano. Hispanics are not a homogenous group. Since the majority of the research literature discusses suicide with respect to "Hispanics" I will use this term, though I understand that it is not all-inclusive. Specific groups (e.g., Puerto Rican) will be highlighted in the chapter when the data allow. Regardless of specific identity, it is important for counselors to be able to understand the unique and overlapping features of these groups, particularly when considering nonlethal and lethal suicides.

DATA AND GENDER

There is a small but ever-increasing amount of empirical research regarding Hispanic suicide rates and completions, and the study of specific factors accounting for Hispanic suicide is small. It is only

Cultural Diversity and Suicide
© 2006 by The Haworth Press, Inc. All rights reserved.
doi:10.1300/5680_05

over the past two decades that the Hispanic population has been recognized as a significant risk group. Collectively, Hispanic Americans have lower relative rates of suicide than non-Hispanic whites (Oquendo et al., 2001; Rasmussen et al., 1997; Sorenson & Golding, 1988a, 1988b). In a study of five southwestern states, Smith and colleagues (J. C. Smith, Mercy, & Rosenberg, 1986; J. C. Smith, Mercy, & Warren, 1985) found Hispanic suicide completion rates to be much lower than European American rates, except for adolescents and young adults (ages fifteen to twenty-four). In fact, European American completion, attempt, and ideation rates are approximately two to four times the rates for Hispanic Americans, depending on geographic region and identified ethnic group (e.g., Mexican Americans, Puerto Rican Americans). Becker, Samet, Wiggins, and Key (1990) examined suicide and homicide completion rates among New Mexico's Hispanic, Native American, and non-Hispanic European Americans over a thirty-year period. The authors found that among injury-related deaths suicide ranked third among Hispanics, and male rates surpassed female rates by a 5:1 margin. Completion rates from 1996 to 1998 were 10.5 and 1.9 per 100,000 for males and females, respectively. Male completion rates are less than Native American, white non-Hispanic, and African American rates, whereas female rates are less than Native American, white non-Hispanic, and Asian American rates. African American and Hispanic women both have the lowest gender-by-ethnic-group rates (National Strategy for Suicide Prevention, retrieved January 6, 2005, from http://www.mentalhealth.samhsa .gov/suicideprevention/diverse.asp).

As indicated earlier, there is a dearth of suicide research information that includes the numerous ethnic groups that comprise Hispanic Americans, instead relying on general research rates under the heading of "Hispanic." Because of the small amount of Hispanic American data, perhaps inferences can be drawn from international statistics. There is always a danger of overgeneralizing results when using suicide rates from other countries, but the following figures may give clinicians some initial, brief insight into the acceptability of suicide among different ethnic groups based on country of origin. However, it is purely speculative given the influence of acculturation and the generation of a Hispanic American client (perhaps more applicable to first- and second-generation clients). Cuba, Spain, Puerto Rico, El Salvador, and Portugal report the highest suicide rates within the global Hispanic community, while Peru, Nicaragua, Guatemala, Brazil, and Colombia have the lowest (Canetto & Lester, 1995b). Though we cannot draw firm conclusions, these rate differences do strongly suggest that culture may have a significant influence on Hispanic suicide. We know that Asian Americans and Native Americans show significant rate differences depending on country of origin or tribal affiliation, and it is expected that clients' ethnic backgrounds may be equally important.

Acculturation

Some researchers (Griffith & Villavicencio, 1985; Ng, 1996; Range et al., 1999; Swanson, Linskey, Quinter-Salinas, Pumariega, & Holzer, 1992; Vega, Gil, Warheit, Apospori, & Zimmerman, 1993) have argued that acculturative stress may account for the significant increases in Hispanic suicides across recent generations. Acculturative stress is the stress that occurs during the acculturation process, with associated feelings of marginality, depression, anxiety, and identity confusion (Hovey & King, 1997). The belief is that acculturative stress contributes to increases in suicide rates, such that it is a cultural stressor that may be fairly unique to ethnic minority groups. This hypothesis makes intuitive sense given that stress itself increases suicide, and the theory is consistent with Berry's (1990, 1995) acculturative stress framework from which cultural stress and adaptation can be identified. Berry's model distinguishes the relationship of cultural and psychological variables between mental health and acculturation, and is comprised of the constructs of assimilation, biculturalism, tradition, and marginalization. People who are assimilated hold values and attitudes consistent with the dominant culture, whereas bicultural people hold beliefs consistent with two or more cultures and can move fluidly from one to another. Those who espouse traditional beliefs maintain values consistent with their earliest culture, and marginalized people feel ostracized and have difficulty feeling at ease in any culture. Clients entering a counselor's office should initially be assessed for their level of acculturation, and it is highly recommended that counselors assess for acculturative stress, particularly if the client feels marginalized. Primitive but quick acculturation assessment methods may include determining familiarity with the English language, asking about family role structure, discovering generation status, and assessing willingness to see a non-Hispanic counselor.

The degree to which acculturation is a significant independent contributor, or even a cause of suicide, has been debated. Using a low SES adolescent sample, Rasmussen et al. (1997) tested the model that acculturative stress causes an increase in suicide ideation and found that it may need modification. The researchers found that although acculturative stress explained a considerable portion of the variance in suicide ideation scores, it did so only when combined with other predictor variables (i.e., depression, self-worth, gender). Therefore, acculturation *by itself* did not appear to contribute significantly to suicide ideation in Hispanic adolescents but was important when combined with other, more commonly considered suicide variables. Of course, clinicians should not negate the importance of considering acculturative stress but should view it in combination with other, frequently implicated suicide variables such as depression and self-worth. It seems that the *additive* effect may be the critical feature when considering acculturation and suicide. It is easy to take into account depression and other variables in suicide assessments because of training and experience, but many clinicians fail to consider acculturative stress as a significant variable with suicidal clients.

Following the work of Padilla, Wagatsuma, and Lindholm (1985), who found that self-esteem predicted stress among Japanese and Japanese American students, Padilla, Alvarez, and Lindholm (1986) found that Hispanic students who immigrated after age fourteen and who experienced high acculturative stress scored low on self-esteem. However, work on coping strategies related to acculturative stress with Hispanic students was never discussed. This study did not assess suicide directly, but it does attest to the idea that immigration and stress are related and should be considered by clinicians conducting suicide assessments.

Mena, Padilla, and Maldonado (1987) assessed coping strategies of Hispanic college students with varying degrees of acculturation. They reported that students who arrived into the United States after age twelve (considered late immigrants) experienced more acculturative stress than students who arrived before that age (considered early immigrants), or than second- and third-generation Hispanics. In other words, Hispanic children who arrived after age twelve had more difficulty adjusting to mainstream U.S. culture, often torn between maintaining their home culture and being pulled into mainstream culture. In addition, late immigrants used more individualistic approaches to cope with stress, whereas second- and third-generation groups utilized social networks as a coping mechanism. First-generation students used both methods. By examining the individual items rated most stressful on an acculturation scale, the authors concluded that the late immigrants felt most stressed when they had to reevaluate their societal role and considered their feelings of societal alienation. Further, the authors concluded that the late immigrants who attempted to stringently hold on to their ethnic identity experienced more stress and lower self-esteem than those who more willingly acculturated to their host culture.

A concern with these studies is that they exclusively include college students, who typically are more acculturated than some other citizens within the population. What about individuals whose first language is not English, or who are not as educated as college students? In a study using a mental health catchment area in Southern California, J. E. Griffith (1985) assessed emotional support networks of Spanish-speaking Mexican Americans, English-speaking Mexican Americans, and European Americans. He found that English-speaking Mexican Americans and European Americans utilized a larger support system comprised of friends and neighbors than Spanish-speaking Mexican Americans, who utilized a smaller, extended family network. None of the groups utilized professional caregivers to a significant extent. Many culturalists (e.g., Bernal & Guitierrez, 1988; Paniagua, 2005; Sue & Sue, 2003) have indicated that when individuals from communities historically suspicious of counseling arrive for counseling they may be considered at high risk for dangerous (including to self) behaviors. In other words, the mental health system is often a last resort and the counselor would do well to consider the first session a crisis management and assessment session. Of course, a suicide assessment may be a critical component.

The majority of studies involving a specific ethnic group from the Hispanic population have focused on Mexican Americans. Mexican Americans make up about 60 percent of the Hispanic American population in the United States, and some authors have compared suicide rates of Mexican Americans born in the United States, Mexican Americans born in Mexico but immigrated to the United States, and Mexicans. Noting differences can attest to cultural differences and the influence of acculturation on suicide. Sorenson and Golding (1988a) found Mexican Americans born in Mexico reported significantly fewer suicide ideations (lower acculturation) than Mexican Americans born in the United States. In essence, the greater the identification with mainstream U.S. culture, the greater the likelihood of suicidal behaviors. The reader must be mindful that both of these group rates were still significantly lower than non-Hispanic European Americans. In a second study of suicide ideation and nonfatal attempts using catchment area data, Sorenson and Golding (1988b) found much lower rates of both ideation and attempts among Hispanics when compared to non-Hispanic European Americans. Both Hispanic and European American women reported greater nonfatal suicide attempt rates than men, and educated Hispanics reported higher rates of suicide ideation and nonfatal attempts than less educated respondents. Depression was the most prevalent psychiatric diagnosis, but it should be noted that 20 percent of those reporting a suicide attempt were not diagnosed with a disorder. It appears that the acculturation process does increase the risk of nonfatal and fatal suicidal behaviors overall, particularly when considering concomitant psychiatric concerns.

AGE

Adolescents

Very few studies have considered ethnic differences in nonfatal suicidal behaviors among Hispanic American youths. Overall, the data seem inconsistent, though it appears that Hispanic adolescents (particularly those of Mexican American, Dominican, and Puerto Rican origin) are more likely than European Americans and African Americans to engage in suicide ideation and attempts, but are not more likely to complete suicide (for a review, see Canino & Roberts, 2001). Nonfatal rates of 12.8 percent (6.7 percent African Americans and 7.3 percent European Americans) and higher suicide ideation (19.9 percent; 15.3 percent African Americans and 17.6 percent European Americans; Youth Risk Behavior Surveillance System, 1999, as reported in Canino & Roberts, 2001) indicate that being a Hispanic American adolescent is related to high nonfatal suicide rates. Adolescent Hispanic females are twice as likely to attempt suicide, especially when requiring medical attention, than African American and European American adolescent females (Rew, Thomas, Horner, Resnick, & Beuhring, 2001; Zayas, Kaplan, Turner, Romano, & Gonzalez-Ramos, 2000). In addition, the completion rate for twenty- to twenty-four-year-old Hispanics is 17.8, well above the national average (Kachur et al., 1995). Hispanic Americans over the age of sixty-five have the highest suicide rates within this ethnic group.

Consistent with general U.S. national data, Mexican American female adolescents reported lower self-esteem, greater depression, and greater suicide ideation than Mexican American male adolescents. Many of the factors often associated with suicide have been found with both Hispanic males and females. Issues of alcohol and drug use, family abuse and neglect, and pathology are consistent with increased risk for suicidal behaviors. For example, D. S. Lipschitz, Bernstein, and Winegar (1999) found that in an inpatient sample, adolescents most likely to attempt suicide were abused Latinas, and over a third of both the males and females had been either sexually or physically abused. The need within the suicide literature is of more studies of familial cultural variables and their interaction with traditional suicide correlates. For example, sexual and physical abuse may increase the chances that an individual attempts suicide, but what role does acculturation play on the willingness to disclose both the abuse and suicide ideation, the method used, the age of first attempt, and the rate of potentially concurrent psychiatric symptoms? What are the unique characteristics of family makeup that may or may not lead to suicidal behaviors? For researchers interested in the area of suicide and culture, studying the leading factors and buffers within the Hispanic American community offers fertile research potential.

Zayas and colleagues (Zayas & Dyche, 1995; Zayas et al., 2000; Zimmerman & Zayas, 1995) have presented well some of the cultural factors that appear to be important determinants of suicidal behaviors within the Hispanic community. Zayas et al. (2000) and Zayas (1989) offered a useful, succinct model of Latina suicide, which includes sociocultural, familial (especially mother–daughter relationships), developmental, and psychological domains. They appropriately indicated that one domain may not have more influence than others but stressed important cultural issues to consider when counseling Latina adolescents. Generational standing and acculturation, SES, cultural identity, gender role socialization, and other cultural factors were presented as important determinants of nonfatal suicide. For example, the fact that suicide rates increase for U.S. Hispanics when compared with rates from the country of origin (e.g., Mexico; Swanson et al., 1992) lends credence to the idea that acculturation may affect the suicide spectrum. In fact, the rate of suicide ideation for adolescents in the Swanson et al. study for Mexican Americans was almost twice that of Mexicans. The United States has higher rates of suicide among older teenagers than most other countries in general though.

Zimmerman and Zayas (1995) outlined therapeutic characteristics of the Puerto Rican and Dominican Latina adolescents they have counseled who engaged in nonfatal suicidal behaviors. As with other ethnic groups acculturation becomes a factor in families, especially when acculturation levels differ between parents and children. Issues such as child rearing (i.e., traditional gender roles lead to authoritarian parenting) and its relationship to daughter dating preferences (more likely to engage in nonfatal suicidal behaviors after conflicts involving a boyfriend) are significant contributing factors among suicidal Latina adolescents (Zayas et al., 2000). Often, these acculturation issues lead to confusion of ethnic identity and sense of self above and beyond identity confusion typically expected in adolescence. The transition or process of moving toward acculturation is stressful and can cause strife within families, leading to suicidal ideation and behaviors. Saleem (2002) reported that Hispanic identification, along with gender, anxiety, depression, and physical abuse, were strong predictors of suicide ideation among adolescents, though none of these variables were good predictors of future attempts. However, consistent with suicide among many ethnic groups, acculturation difficulties increased the chances of suicide attempts when associated with cocaine, PCP, and tranquilizer use (Vega et al., 1993). In other words, drug use increased the risk of suicide attempts, but stress due to acculturation further increased the rate.

Although acculturative issues are not unique to Hispanic American families, it must be highlighted here given the increasing numbers of Hispanic Americans and the amount of research including this important variable. First-generation parents often maintain values consistent with their country of origin, whereas the second-generation adolescents are conflicted between maintaining traditional ways while concurrently seeking their own identity based on the new culture. Identity is manifested in numerous ways, such as socialization, autonomy, sexuality, and family relationships, all of which pose issues to be addressed therapeutically. Conflicts in these and other areas often lead to clients holding no firm ethnic identity and resulting in a sense of disconnection and confusion. With no perceived solid cultural connection, the risk of suicide increases. As with all intergenerational counseling, it becomes imperative that both the parents and adolescents understand the often conflicting value systems involved and work toward a middle-ground agreement. With acculturation these value differences can become extremely salient and must be handled with care. However, counseling must involve mutual understanding of the others' positions before future counseling can occur. Zimmerman and Zayas (1995) reported that nonfatal suicides among many Latinas were actually a way to reconnect with their mothers empathically. "Cries for help" are not new for clinicians who have worked with suicidal clients, and many adolescents regardless of ethnicity have struggles with identity, which often lead to suicidal acts. However, many Latinas seem to be "crying" because of the unique cultural characteristic of acculturation in addition to common developmental concerns. Overall, the literature presently indicates that acculturation itself does not appear to be a significant factor in nonfatal and fatal suicides, but it does exacerbate concomitant problems such as depression and low self-esteem, or drug use among adolescents (Rasmussen et al., 1997).

Case Example

Selena, a thirteen-year-old biracial adolescent (mother European American and biological father Mexican American), moved from Texas to Mississippi due to her stepfather's (European American) job placement. She was placed in a private Catholic school with a mix of Mexican Americans, African Americans, and European Americans. She was referred to counseling after a series of verbal and physical altercations with her Mexican American classmates at school. During counseling her anger and blatant prejudice toward Mexican Americans was easy to detect. She identified with the European American adolescents and, at thirteen, reported that she wanted various surgeries "to look more like the (European American) models on TV." Selena was early pubescent and had no physical flaws. She reported suicide ideation and treatment revolved around her anger toward her father for abandoning her mother and how she wanted to distance herself from her Mexican American heritage. She essentially wanted to kill part of herself. Her parents eventually became involved in the treatment and she began to understand the relationship between her anger toward her father and her anger toward her classmates. Counseling also included discussions of positive traits of herself, her father, and her Mexican American ethnic identity. After eight months of counseling, her stepfather received another transfer back to Texas and follow-up reports indicated that she had joined various Hispanic organizations at the school and had reconciled her identity. She contacted her biological father according to the last report from her mother.

Adults

There is evidence that acculturative stress may lead to increased psychiatric disorders and suicide ideation and completion among adults. Vega et al. (1998) found that recent Mexican immigrants had comparable rates of suicide ideation and psychiatric concerns with Mexicans but lower than Mexican Americans born in the United States. In a sample of lower SES Puerto Ricans who had attempted suicide, Marrero (1998) found many of the usual factors associated with suicide—poor living conditions, substance abuse with the men, unemployment, hopelessness, psychopathology, and family history of suicide. However, depression itself was not a strong correlate, perhaps consistent with other authors who found that the role of depression in suicide functions differently depending on the ethnic group being discussed (Gutierrez, Rodriguez, & Garcia, 2001). In one of the few studies of suicide rates among elderly Hispanics, Llorente, Eisdorfer, Loewenstein, and Zarate (1996) reported that Cuban American males were over one-and-one-half times more likely to kill themselves than other older American males, and Cuban American females were also more likely than other females. The reasons for these rates are currently unclear, but what is clear is that researchers and clinicians should consider cultural factors that influence suicidal ideation and behaviors. Perhaps societal acceptance differs with older Cuban Americans and suicide acceptability is greater within that community, or perhaps other issues such as retirement and medication compliance differ. These are purely speculative, but counselors would do well to understand that older Cuban Americans may be at particular risk for suicidal thoughts and behaviors when compared with other older Hispanic and non-Hispanic groups.

CULTURAL BUFFERS

Why are suicide completion rates among the Hispanic population lower than European American and Native American ethnic groups? A clinician discussing cultural buffers of suicide with clients can help reduce the chance of future attempts or completions. Nonfatal suicidal behaviors (particularly among Hispanic youths) are higher than in other ethnic groups, but there do not appear to be high fatal completion rates within the Hispanic community. Offering counseling from a position of strength and positives often decreases the chances that clients will consider and follow through with suicidal impulses. The following is a discussion of cultural factors that have been found to buffer suicide completion for Hispanic Americans.

Religion and Spirituality

Christianity

The majority of Hispanic Americans espouse Catholicism, a religious faith that has made clear its views on suicide (Barry, 1999; Maris, 1981). Some authors (e.g., Durkheim, 1897/1951; Kennedy & Tanenbaum, 2000) concluded that Catholicism plays a role in the reduction of suicide, whereas others (Stack, 1980; I. Wasserman & Stack, 1993) found no relationship between Christian religious denomination and suicide. Still others, when examining suicide globally, have concluded that in some cultures the rate of suicide among Catholics is higher than that in other cultures (Kelleher, Chambers, Corcoran, Williamson, & Keeley, 1998). Regardless, as an ethnic group Hispanic Americans tend to be more intimately committed to their faith (similar to African Americans) than European Americans.

Hovey and King (1997) pointed out that Catholicism generally acts as a protective agent within the Hispanic community through its influence on social and cultural norms. These authors noted that many Mexican Americans participated in cultural activities influenced by the church, such as the Day of the Dead ceremony, communion, baptisms, and confirmation. Through these activities and rituals, family and community members show support for one another and offer social connections that may not be found as readily in other communities. This form of religion may only be a part of the picture though, as it is not just Catholic faith within the Hispanic American community that influences suicide attempts. In a sample of both male and female adolescent Hispanic Seventh Day Adventists, many of the often-cited factors contributed to attempted suicide, including family dysfunction and abuse. However, a warm church climate was a significant factor in reducing suicide attempts (Trivino, 2000). Consistent with the African American community, which includes a strong religious tradition, Hispanic culture may consider suicide to be simply unacceptable (Domino, 1981).

There appears to be evidence that church attendance and the degree of religious conservatism may help predict suicide ideation, regardless of faith. Both church attendance and degree of religiosity, not simply denomination itself, help predict suicidal behaviors and various psychiatric and social problems. Bagley and Ramsay (1989) found that being born-again Christians and high church attenders (e.g., some Roman Catholics, Fundamental Protestants, and Mormons) predicted an absence of suicidal ideation. With the recent revival of the study of religious issues in psychology and more empirically sound ways of measuring religiosity, numerous authors have determined that within-group variation of religiosity may be a more effective means of studying pathology, suicide, and various psychological constructs than between groups (for a review, see Spilka et al., 2003). For example, simply stating that someone is Catholic tells the clinician little about the strength, type, and behaviors associated with their religious and spiritual beliefs. It is more beneficial to understand *how* a person is religious and not *whether* he or she is religious. Questions such as "How does your faith influence your life?" and "What do you do for others or yourself that is faith-based?" may help determine how an individual is religious or spiritual.

Numerous psycho-religious constructs have been developed to determine how integrated religion is within the individual and what that means for behaviors. I have counseled numerous clients with suicidal ideation who exhibit strong religious beliefs. To such clients, I offer open discussions about how suicide is viewed within their faith, their views of afterlife, and other religious and spiritual issues. Numerous clients have indicated that they have frequent suicidal ideation but "I'd never do it because of my religion." The majority of clinicians reading this book have probably had similar experiences and can recall multiple clients who claim similar attitudes. The research tends to indicate that most clients are willing to discuss their faith as one piece of their treatment if counselors initiate the discussion, yet most clinicians are either wary or unable to do so.

Case Example

A colleague counseled the wife of a Hispanic man who, after ten years of marriage, attempted nonfatal suicide using prescribed medication. According to her, he had numerous bouts with depression, and they had discussed that she and his faith system were the only reasons keeping him from killing himself. When my colleague saw the client, her husband had been involuntarily committed to a state hospital after this attempt. Months later the counselor met the client's husband, who had been released and was mandated for counseling, and asked him about the attempt. The husband indicated that his religious faith may have kept him from using more lethal methods, and that, perhaps, he unconsciously wanted to stay alive. He also indicated that in his culture one just does not kill himself.

The Catholic Church believes that suicide is an unpardonable sin and, in some cases, that the family of a suicide completer will be shamed (Barry, 1999; Kalish, 1980). Further, Catholic beliefs of the afterlife may act as a deterrent for suicide attempts, as many believe it to be an unpardonable sin resulting in everlasting hell. There has been modification by some Catholic priests over the past few years regarding whether suicide is an unpardonable sin. These priests believe that there are circumstances where suicide is justified, but they are unlikely to speak publicly on their views for fear of retribution. Also, as with many religious faiths, an individual who completes suicide is often considered mentally ill and not responsible for his or her actions. Because of the view that mental illness and suicide are linked, many Catholics can forgive the deceased and believe that the individual can still go to heaven. For counselors working with Catholic families of a person who has completed suicide, it may be comforting to offer that not all priests and parishioners believe that the soul of their loved one is residing in hell. If the counselor is in contact with a local priest who is less conservative in doctrine, he may be included in the counseling situation.

Case Example

A colleague referred a Latina client to her priest after the death of her husband from a one-car automobile accident. Though ruled an accident by the police and coroner's office, the client wondered whether her husband had intentionally run off the road because of recent bouts of depression and a failing business. Through the expected grief she was concerned that her husband was damned to hell because of her beliefs of suicide as an unpardonable sin. Her priest, whom the therapist had talked with first after being granted permission by the client, spoke with her about alternative beliefs about suicide.

As most clinicians are aware, it is critically important for counselors to talk with specific religious figures first in order to assess theological beliefs before referring a client to do the same. Priests who are very conservative theologically may not help the clinician's chances of working successfully with the client.

Curanderismo

Some Mexican American families value *curanderismo,* a philosophy that includes folk medicine. It has been incorporated into cultures in a multitude of Central and South American countries, and this section will briefly focus on *curanderismo* within the Mexican American culture. *Curanderismo* has been discussed extensively in the literature (e.g., Castro, Furth, & Karlow, 1984; Cervantes & Ramirez, 1992; de la Cancela & Martinez, 1983) and includes a variety of ceremonies, beliefs, and customs that address psychological, spiritual, and cultural needs of Mexican American people. It is a philosophy of holism and spiritual connectedness. A *curandero(a)* is a healer who incorporates spirituality and transcendence into treatment. He or she helps the person in need through the use of the supernatural. Some Mexican American families rely solely on *curanderismo,* others put their faith in Catholicism, whereas still others maintain a combination of the two. Although there has been no data on the relationship between belief in *curanderismo* and suicide, the wise practitioner would benefit from understanding some of the cultural beliefs that surround the *curanderismo* (see Harris, Velasquez, White, & Renteria, 2004). Readers interested in brief case illustrations of *curanderismo* and its relationship to family therapy are reffered to Cervantes and Ramirez (1992).

Fatalismo

Another factor that may contribute to lower levels of suicide within the Hispanic community is an emphasis on *fatalismo* (fatalism). Viewed superficially (and incorrectly) this emphasis could be interpreted as helping increase suicide rates because of its (false) association with depression and hopelessness. *Fatalismo* is associated with Catholicism and is defined as "believing that a divine providence governs the world and that an individual cannot control or prevent adversity" (Paniagua, 2005, p. 43). The closest variable within U.S. psychology culture is external locus of control. It maintains an adaptive response to uncontrollable life events and is thus considered healthy. Mirowsky and Ross (1984) contended that while European Americans attempt to control, Hispanic Americans seek to accept, attributing situations to fate or luck. Hispanic cultures vary in their allegiance to *fatalismo*. For example, Mexican Americans are more fatalistic than some other Hispanic ethnic groups and are more likely to accept the psychological anxiety associated with powerlessness over environmental control. Mirowsky and Ross found that although fatalism led to increased depression, it did not lead to increased anxiety.

The role of fatalism in suicide has not been empirically validated, yet therapists should note that having a fatalistic worldview does not necessarily lead to suicidal behaviors and can be considered a natural (and perhaps healthier) part of life. Passive coping styles in general are often associated with more depression and anxiety, but fewer negative consequences are expected if the coping style is part of a cultural worldview. Cuban American culture retains a fatalistic quality, but also possess a seemingly inconsistent component of perseverance and activity (Queralt, 1984). Individual differences do occur, as fatalism can become detrimental and mimic the definition found in mainstream U.S. culture. When fatalism leads to depression and hopelessness, increased suicidal ideation, attempts, and behaviors are likely. Counselors should not immediately conclude that a fatalistic worldview is always considered negative, and a close assessment of this worldview and its relationship to Catholicism and community should be conducted.

Whereas the majority of scientists accept that *fatalismo* is an intrinsic part of Mexican American culture, others offer evidence that it is simply connected to economics. For example, Buriel and Rivera

(1980) found that when family income was controlled, ethnic differences in locus of control was not a significant factor. However, some evidence (e.g., C. R. Chandler, 1979) found that even when economic factors were regulated external locus of control played a significant role in Mexican American culture. As a follow-up, C. R. Chandler, Tsai, and Wharton (1999) found increased convergence on modernity scales over the past twenty years. Although the data are inconclusive, most studies tend to indicate that the Mexican American population relies on fate and other external factors to a greater degree than do middle-class European Americans. Much more research is required comparing ethnic group differences with this variable, and its relationship to suicidal behaviors.

Social Support Systems

Hispanic American families tend to be closer emotionally than European American families on average, offering greater support during difficult times (Valle, 1986). Both family and social support may act as buffers against acculturative stress and negative fatalism, as Hispanic families are more likely than European American families to be intact (Canino & Roberts, 2001; Earls, Escobar, & Manson, 1990). This hypothesis is consistent with research with African American women indicating that their increased support systems may decrease suicide completion. Social support often differs depending on the ethnic group considered. Cuban Americans place a large emphasis on extended family and are also likely to include friends frequently encountered through social activities. For a clinician to concentrate on the family without including friends as a support system would be an error. In essence, a broader social-system approach increases the odds of a successful therapeutic outcome. Social support helps alleviate negative symptoms and psychological outcomes in a number of areas, including schizophrenia and depression. It would be expected that among Hispanic populations the greater the social support the less likely it is that one may consider suicide.

GAY/LESBIAN/BISEXUAL/TRANSGENDER ISSUES

The empirical literature on adult Hispanic gay men and lesbians is extremely limited, and literature on suicide is virtually nonexistent for this group. The overwhelming majority of studies involving gay Hispanic Americans focuses on the effects of HIV/AIDS almost to the exclusion of other important social and psychological variables. The little research that has been accomplished will be summarized here.

There are wide variations regarding the acceptance of homosexual behaviors within the Hispanic community, and it may be based largely on degree of acculturation. When accounting for acculturation levels (though defined differently depending on the research study), Zamora-Hernandez and Patterson (1996) reported that the research literature is contradictory. Some research indicates that the Hispanic community is less tolerant toward gays than either the European American or African American communities, whereas others find that Hispanic Americans are more tolerant than the other two groups. Counselors may be placed in the delicate position of discussing views of homosexuality with a variety of different-minded family members of a suicidal client, particularly when the client is concerned about sexual identity. Assessing the level of acculturation and the acceptance of homosexuality within the family and community becomes an essential component of treatment. Family issues are similar when working with other ethnic groups around this issue, but the counselor should keep in mind cultural influences within the Hispanic community such as gender roles and Catholicism.

Guarnero (2001) found that Latino gay men in the San Francisco Bay area had significant difficulties with their families, culture, and culture of their country of origin. More specifically, these men were often ostracized from their families, were denied family and social acceptance of their homosexuality, had maintained sexual silence, experienced cultural machismo, racism, and oppression, and felt marginalized and rejected. The marginalization led to increased vulnerability for depression, thus placing this group at greater risk for engaging in unsafe sexual behaviors and suicide. Thus, being Latino and gay increased the risk of suicide.

Using predominantly African American and Hispanic American samples, Comstock (1989) found that gay men and lesbians of color were more likely than European Americans to be physically assaulted and chased. Further, von Schulthess (1992) found that European American lesbian women were recipients of verbal assault more than lesbians of color, but the latter were more likely to experience vandalism, rape, physical violence, and verbal threats. Herek and

Berrill (1992) indicated that victimization among these persons of color may have more to do with higher victimization rates in general for persons of color than for European Americans. The research clearly indicates that gay men and lesbians, regardless of ethnic background, are more likely than heterosexuals to be victims of verbal and physical assault because of their sexual orientation. Further, due to racism, it is possible that gay persons of color, including Hispanics, may be more likely than their European American counterparts to experience threats and assaults. In other words, add persons of color as an additional variable and the rate of victimization appears to increase. More research is needed to delineate some of these factors, and clinicians should be aware that many gay men and lesbians consider the double-minority status to be legitimate. In other words, both GLBT persons and Hispanics are minority cultural groups individually but when one is GLBT and Hispanic, he or she often feels doubly marginalized. Being marginalized does lead to increased depression and suicide rates, especially when combined with a number of psychiatric and substance abuse disorders.

Considerations for Counselors

Much has been written about the concept of Hispanic machismo. Gay men are perceived as feminine and weak and are subjected to ridicule, prejudice, and shame. Because of this stigma, it is difficult to determine the rates of gay men within the Hispanic community. However, the term "gay" needs to be clarified when discussing the Hispanic community. Similar to the Filipino term *bakla* the Hispanic American community does not as rigidly perceive heterosexual or homosexual (or even bisexual) labels as necessarily discrete categories like the overwhelmingly European American straight and GLBT communities tend to do within the United States. Typically, mainstream U.S. culture considers an individual as either heterosexual, homosexual, or bisexual, though the recent emergence of transgendered sexuality has gained more acceptance. These separate groupings are not always applicable in the Hispanic community. Self-definitions of sexual behavior are more role-based (i.e., dominant or nondominant) within the relationship than the biological sex of the partner, consistent with Filipino culture. Therefore, it is often considered acceptable, and sometimes it can even be macho, for a man to have sex with another man if he is sexually dominant (Green, 1997; Zamora-Hernandez & Patterson, 1996). In other words, sexual identity is often derived from the role one takes during sexual relations rather than the sex of the partner. Many Hispanic males who have sex with other men are also married to women but still consider themselves heterosexual and not bisexual (Carrier, 1989), though there are men who consider themselves bisexual by mainstream U.S. standards. Having a same-sex partner does not mean that some clients do not experience dissonance, but that the Hispanic community does not have as clearly defined categories simply based on the sex of the partner. Being labeled as gay is usually reserved for someone who has sexual relations exclusivly with same-sex partners and, in the case of men, is the passive recipient in those relationships.

A concern arises when individual Latinos and Latinas come into contact with the dominant (i.e., European American mainstream) GLBT views and definitions, which can create identity dissonance. For example, if a Latino identifies as "just gay," he may be perceived by family members and the Latino community as "selling out" both the family and the community, resulting in decreased family and social support. Thus, support through the gay community becomes increasingly important. However, resources to meet other Hispanic American gay men are limited nationally, and given the numbers of European Americans in the United States, it is likely that the person will come into contact with gay European Americans. Very few resources exist for GLBT persons of color, as most of the GLBT organizations nationally are predominantly European American. Many persons of color do not feel welcomed into these organizations or local hangouts, thus increasing identity confusion and decreasing comfort.

Identifying oneself is a way of validating the self. Some Latinos refer to themselves as Latino gay or gay Latino (instead of one or the other) in order to maintain connections with both their ethnic heritage and their sexual orientation (Zamora-Hernandez & Patterson, 1996). As mentioned earlier, it would be an error for a counselor to maintain restricted definitions of a gay sexual orientation simply on the basis of the sex of the partner. It would be equally egregious to make assumptions about this individual from these definitions, particularly if the client is discussing suicidal ideation or plans. Counselors should be very aware of allowing the client to discuss his or her sexual orientation and what that means to him or her before making the mental and therapeutic leap that the client is suicidal because of confusion over sexual orientation.

Hispanic lesbian rates are even less understood because of well-defined rules often placed on Latinas. These roles include being connected with the family, submissive, deferent to men, and respectful. Lesbian Latinas are often recognized if they violate these roles by dressing and acting "butch," for example (Espin, 1984; Tremble, Schneider, & Appathurai, 1989). De Monteflores (1993) reported that personal and social boundaries become increasingly difficult to juggle during the acculturative process. There is often a pull from both the lesbian European American and Hispanic American communities, causing potential distress for the individual.

Many lesbian Latinas hide their sexual orientation because their ethnic communities may not be very supportive of them (Espin, 1987). Consistent with males, the lesbian Latina community must reduce the dissonance that can occur due to others attempting to place them in a discrete category. Often clients will present information in which they are trying to decide whether to identify with being lesbian, with all of the political and social overtones, or to identify as Latina. They are often perceived as separate entities. Resolving this issue is not easy, but culturally sensitive counselors can assist the client in melding these two identities. One place to begin might be to assess the client's level of acculturation, as same-sex behaviors have different meanings to the Hispanic community based on level of acculturation (Zamora-Hernandez & Patterson, 1996). Second, it may be beneficial to discuss these definitional differences between Hispanic and European American cultures and help the client understand that one can maintain a culturally consistent view while understanding the more strict categories of the dominant culture. Unfortunately, it is a rare event when a Hispanic gay man or lesbian woman (or any other member of these communities) is accepted by all communities. This nonacceptance often leads to identity issues, particularly when they are also the victims of racism, sexism, and homophobia. Many Hispanic gays and lesbians can be considered marginalized from being fully accepted by either the larger gay community or their ethnic community; the merging of the two identities becomes necessary to help buffer suicidal ideation and behaviors.

Hispanic Gay and Lesbian Youths

Hispanic adolescents become victims of violent crime at a rate significantly greater than European American adolescents, often due to discrimination. This discrimination, combined with feelings of alienation, contributes to higher high school dropout rates among Hispanic adolescents than their European American counterparts (Davison-Aviles, Guerrero, Borajas, & Thomas, 1999). With the addition of acknowledging one's GLBT sexual orientation the increase in discrimination becomes perceptible.

The type and frequency of discriminatory behavior experienced by these students has received little attention in the professional literature. In a sample that included about half Hispanic gay male adolescents and lesbians, Hunter and colleagues (Hunter, 1990, 1992; Rotheram-Borus et al., 1994) found that 40 percent had experienced some form of physical assault, with half of those being gay-related. It is important to note that over half of those attacks were perpetrated by family members. Well above the national average, it was found that over 40 percent of those adolescents who experienced physical assault experienced suicidal ideation and between 30 and 40 percent had attempted suicide. The authors cautioned that this rate of suicide may be consistent for all adolescents who are victims of violence. Regardless, being gay, Hispanic, and adolescent tends to increase the likelihood of victimization, suicide ideation, and nonfatal and fatal suicidal behaviors.

Other research indicates that gay Hispanic American adolescents reported a higher frequency of illicit drug use than gay European Americans, though heterosexual Hispanic youths use recreational drugs at no greater degree than European American youths (Bachman, Wallace, & O'Malley 1991, as reported in Zamora-Hernandez & Patterson, 1996). As with other ethnic groups, both suicide attempts and drug use often mask underlying concerns associated with being gay. Not only do gay Hispanic youths have to deal with racism, sexism, and homophobia but they are also embroiled in normal adolescent development and may need counseling assistance in dealing with issues such as confusion, anger, impulsivity, and marginalization. However, so little research has been conducted with the gay Hispanic American population, particularly the adolescent population, that for now the best we can do is speculate as to some of the underlying issues and treatment approaches.

Therapists should let the client lead discussions about his or her definitions of self. By doing so the clinician shows respect for both the client and the client's culture instead of quickly concluding that the client is gay simply because he fits the clinician's cultural definition. As with other issues, the label is not as important as the meaning associated with the label. Clinicians can follow the client's lead to build him or her in areas that he or she believes is lacking, by helping to create a broader, more inclusive self-identity with previously underappreciated characteristics and abilities.

Case Example

Juan is a sixteen-year-old Hispanic male who recently transferred from a high school that was predominantly Hispanic to one that is 55 percent European American and 40 percent black. He has struggled with his feelings of attraction toward other males and has dated females briefly. He wonders if he is bisexual. Juan is having difficulty fitting in and making friends, fearing that others may find out about his sexual-identity struggle. He is also in the racial minority, finding few other Hispanics in the school. He is struggling with his grades, but that has occurred since elementary school. Juan's home life is stable, with two working-class parents who are home nightly. He has an older brother and younger sister and gets along with each of them. He has never attempted suicide before but has considered it.

What are some of the risk factors of suicide to consider and what might increase the risk in this scenario? First, the risk factors: students of color in general are assaulted at a higher rate than European American students. He is an adolescent, struggling with his sexuality and has moved to a new environment, both high risk factors. In addition, almost half of all GLBT students have seriously considered or previously attempted suicide. Second, what are the other issues to be considered? Given the high rates of alcohol in high schools, it may be beneficial to determine Juan's alcohol consumption since alcohol is associated with a majority of all suicide deaths. Counselors may also want to consider his religious faith, including his religion's views on both gays and suicide.

SUICIDE PREVENTION AND INTERVENTION

Unfortunately, no systematic suicide prevention strategies designed for the Hispanic population, including Hispanic youths, exist. Canino and Roberts (2001) indicated that Hispanic youths share similar risk factors with other ethnic groups, including substance abuse, stress, and depression, but no prevention strategies have been formally developed specifically for that culture. They did indicate that focusing on family and social support buffers acculturative stress, but much more research focusing on ethnic-specific prevention and intervention programs is needed. O'Donnell, Stueve, Wardlaw, and O'Donnell (2003) found that about half of the economically disadvantaged African American and Latino adolescents would not approach a family member during difficult emotional times. In addition, those who failed to approach their parents were more likely to attempt suicide than those who did talk. In an intervention study of incarcerated youths, Sanchez-Barker (2003) found that connecting with Hispanic culture increases emotional development. She suggested that counselors should focus on helping the adolescents increase ethnic identity development, the role of religion on their lives, awareness of their specific environmental influences and their reactions to these influences, and their role within society and the family.

Earls et al. (1990) suggested that counselors should include five areas when considering intervention strategies: religion, social supports, birthplace, acculturation, and somatization. The majority of the Hispanic population is Catholic, with strong reservations about suicide. Though the relationship between Catholicism and suicide is conflicting internationally, any religious component may likely be helpful. Implementing views of God and the afterlife can prove very useful once the counselor initiates discussion. The role of social support systems is common with all prevention and intervention strategies, and also useful with the Hispanic population given the cohesion of family systems discussed earlier. As mentioned earlier, groups differ depending on within-cultural group variations. Since the majority of Hispanics in the United States are Mexican Americans, the majority of suicide research has been utilized with this ethnic group. In general, the greater the acculturation level, the greater is the suicide risk. Assessing acculturation helps the counselor determine suicide risk in addition to the usual multitude of other factors associated with suicide. Finally, Earls et al. discuss the role of somatization in Hispanic culture. Often, physical symptoms will be presented as a way to approach a physician or mental health professional (Escobar, 1987). Because mental illness has negative familial connotations within the community and may include guilt, traditional Hispanic clients are likely to present with somatic concerns. These are not associated with somatic hallucinations and can be considered an entrance to the health system. Counselors should carefully assess the motivation behind the physical complaint during the course of treatment.

SUMMARY

The level of acculturation has been determined to be a critical factor in the assessment and treatment of suicidal Hispanic clients. Generally, the greater the assimilation into mainstream culture, the greater is the likelihood of suicide. Of course, acculturation level by itself is not the sole factor contributing to suicide, as suicide is multifaceted. Acculturation level in addition to depression, substance abuse, dysfunctional families, and a host of other issues are significant variables that should be included in any suicide assessment or research project. Language issues can also be particularly salient, especially if staff members do not speak Spanish and the client's English- language skills are limited. Paniagua (2005) discussed the need to treat clients of some cultural groups as emergencies because of an unwillingness to seek counseling. If these clients arrive at a counselor's office, it is often because other avenues (e.g., seeking help from family, priests) have been exhausted. This is especially true if there are language barriers because clients with limited English-language skills are less likely to seek mental health services.

As with other youths, teenagers and young adults are most likely to complete suicide. Issues such as substance abuse, dysfunctional families, and impulsivity are common in many teenage homes, and the Hispanic population is no exception. Buffers include the Catholic faith and social support systems, though the extent to which Catholicism is a protector against suicide is unknown with Hispanics. Larger support systems on average reduce the likelihood of suicide, and Hispanics tend to rely on extended family networks. As with other ethnic, religious, GLBT, age, gender, and country-of-origin groups, more research is needed to determine the effects of the interaction of culture and suicide. It is hoped that this chapter has included variables not often considered among clinicians, who may then consider them when conducting suicide assessments and ongoing treatments.

Chapter 6

Native Americans

Native Americans account for more than 2 million people within the United States and the population is increasing. History teaches us that Native Americans were viewed as one, generally homogenous group of people, but that is far from the truth. There are over 550 tribal groups representing over 250 languages, not including dialects (M. T. Garrett & Wilbur, 1999). There are a number of ways to be considered Native American, but essentially if someone is on the roll of a federally recognized Indian group, then they are considered Native American. The U.S. federal government recognizes at least one-quarter Indian blood, though it really does not have the legal authority to define who can be considered Native American, and allows for definitions to be determined through the sovereign status of each tribe, as specific tribal groups allow for differing levels of blood quantum. The Bureau of Indian Affairs (BIA) though recognizes at least one-fourth blood quantum, whereas the U.S. Bureau of the Census accepts self-identification (Paniagua, 2005). For the purposes of this chapter, it is not important to determine how someone identifies as Native American but that they do. There is wide variability in acculturation levels, living situations, familial backgrounds, customs, and beliefs among Native Americans. Approximately one-third of Native Americans live in urban areas, one-third on reservations, and one-third live either in other rural areas or move between urban and reservation areas.

HISTORY

Paniagua (2005) discussed four main historical time periods that have influenced, and continue to influence, Native American cultures—the Precontact, Manifest Destiny, Assimilation, and Self-

Cultural Diversity and Suicide
© 2006 by The Haworth Press, Inc. All rights reserved.
doi:10.1300/5680_06

191

Determination periods. Briefly, the Precontact period occurred prior to the arrival of the Europeans and it was during this period that traditional customs, values, and beliefs grew and matured. This period is considered to be the time before outside influences appeared and modified or changed traditional Native American thinking. Manifest Destiny occurred between 1492 and 1890 and is the period during which Christianity, European diseases, and the origin of reservations made their way into the Native American community. It became known as a period in which European Americans could not be trusted, a view that is still maintained by many Native Americans today. During the Assimilation period, which was maintained until 1970, European Americans continued to force Native Americans to assimilate into mainstream U.S. culture, thus reinforcing the notion that European Americans could not be trusted. Assimilation often occurred through Native Americans moving into urban areas, with previous governmental agreements about reservation lands being negated. For example, the U.S. federal government made one-way ticket payment offers to Native Americans to move from their reservation to major cities such as Chicago and Los Angeles. Many people took them up on their offer and moved, thus losing contact with tribal traditions. In addition, before the Indian Child Welfare Act of 1978, it has been estimated that about one-quarter of all Native American children were either reared by European American families through adoption or were placed in foster homes. Again, tribal customs and traditions were often lost (Tafoya & Wirth, 1996), and identity issues became paramount due to government relocation programs and adoptions. The present period, Self-Determination, is defined as the time when Native Americans are more involved in the political process and a number of federal acts have been implemented to give them more autonomy and tribal independence.

As with other ethnic groups living in the United States, Native Americans fall within Berry's (1990) framework of acculturation. Berry (1990) reported that when a culture intersects with a dominant culture, changes in economics, politics, religion, social relationships, and other areas occur, primarily for the nondominant culture. There is a melding between both cultures, but the nondominant culture generally makes the majority of changes. Some tribal members live in cities whereas others live in rural areas, small towns, or reservations. Berry's framework has been applied to Native Americans to help describe the social and psychological ills that impact various tribal groups. He discusses four types of acculturative levels:

1. assimilation, losing traditional cultural identity and accepting the dominant culture identity;
2. integration, maintaining both the traditional and dominant cultural identities;
3. separation, maintaining traditional cultural identity but not accepting the dominant culture identity; and
4. marginalization, not identifying with either the traditional or the dominant group.

Some tribes can be categorized based on the level of acculturation, and individuals within each tribal group can be categorized as such. Of course, there are numerous differences and clients cannot often be easily categorized based on some sterile system. However, the reader can keep these four acculturation types in mind when considering the rest of this chapter. Much has been written about the suicide rates among Native Americans, but surprisingly little research examining within-group differences is noted. This will be discussed in the following pages, beginning with suicide rates.

DATA

It has been well documented that Native Americans have the highest rates of suicide of all major ethnic groups in the United States, which are approximately one-and-a-half to three times greater than the national average. The rates do not apply across the age spectrum though, as elders typically possess lower rates. In addition, rates differ significantly by tribal affiliation and acculturation level. Early researchers either studied individual tribes or clustered tribes to gather aggregate data, leading to misinterpreted results and phrases designed to denigrate Native Americans. Fortunately, contemporary researchers became more scientific in their research methods and examined a number of tribal groups and variables instead of presenting aggregate data (e.g., May et al., 2002; Van Winkle & May, 1993). The high rates of suicide are highly variable, probably more than any other U.S. ethnic group, and dependent on a number of factors such as tribal affiliation, acculturation level, year of study, and age cohort. For example, some tribes have very high rates of suicide whereas others have rates close to zero. In the mid-1980s the suicide rate for Alaska Natives was over 60 per 100,000, over four times that of the national rate (Kettl & Bixler, 1993) and well above the European American suicide rate in that state. Forbes and Van der Hyde (1988) reported a 38 percent increase in Alaskan suicides in general between the years 1978 and 1985, with Alaska Natives accounting for well over two-thirds of these deaths. Other tribal groups such as the Blackfeet show high rates (130 per 100,000) whereas the Chippewa tribe has a rate of about 6 per 100,000 (Group for the Advancement of Psychiatry [GAP] as cited in A. Lipschitz, 1995). The problem with analyzing suicide rates among Native American groups is that there is such diversity among tribal groups that it is difficult to discuss suicide rates among "Native Americans."

Adolescents

Approximately one-half of all Native Americans are younger than eighteen (Nelson, McCoy, Stetter, & Vanderwagen, 1992), and the median age is between eighteen and twenty-six. Therefore, there are a large number of adolescents and young adults in the population, and these age groups also have the highest proportion of suicides. The median age of a completed suicide in the United States is sixty-four years, whereas it is twenty-five years in the Native American community. Overall, suicide rates among Native Americans are two to four times that of the national average, with men under thirty-five being at highest risk (EchoHawk, 1997; Johnson, 1994; Nelson et al., 1992; Range et al., 1999). Suicide rates among Native American groups overall are rising faster than the average rate of increase in the United States, particularly among male adolescent and young adult groups; female adolescent and young adult rates are consistently greater than female rates from other ethnic groups. A number of studies have found that nonfatal suicide rates among Native American adolescents range from 15 to 30 percent (Grossman, Milligan, & Deyo, 1991; Howard-Pitney, LaFromboise, Basil, September, & Johnson, 1992).

Elderly

Within the Native American community, the rates of suicide significantly decrease the older an individual grows. In fact, Kettl and Bixler (1991) found suicide rates to be nonexistent among Alaska Natives over the age of fifty-five between 1979 and 1984. The low rate of suicide for elderly Native Americans is often attributed to the fact that they hold positions of honor and influence within the community (Baker, 1994, 1996; Kettl & Bixler, 1991). Baker (1994) discussed factors contributing to suicide among ethnic elders, including Native Americans. Though the average rates of suicide among elders are relatively low, especially when compared with European Americans, there are contributing factors that increase risk. These included a disruption of traditional roles and family composition, cultural disturbances, alcoholism, unemployment, and events that show the elder as not being powerful.

Factors Influencing Suicide Rates

As indicated earlier, the rates of suicide differ based on state and/or tribal affiliation, but overall the rates for all but the elderly are high when compared with the general population. A number of factors have been postulated to be related to suicides in Native American populations and are consistent with any other ethnic group, including unresolved grief, multiple home placements, criminal justice encounters, family history of psychiatric illness, and depression. I will focus on a few that are frequently mentioned in the literature in order to highlight significant factors.

First, alcohol is often a major factor with any suicidal person but plays a greater role within the Native American community than other ethnic communities as alcoholism rates in general are high. Multiple studies indicate that alcohol is involved in Native American suicides at a rate greater than other ethnic groups. For example, Johnson (1994) found that alcohol was involved in 90 percent of the suicides, whereas May et al. (2002) and Van Winkle and May (1993) found alcohol to be a contributing factor in over 69 percent of the completed suicides. Although alcohol was a significant factor leading to suicide among European American Alaskans (48 percent) in 1983 and 1984, the rate was almost 80 percent for Alaskan Natives (Hlady & Middaugh, 1988).

More recently, Clark (2006) discusses the plight of substance abuse in many Native American communities, which often leads to suicide. The reader must keep in mind that the overwhelming majority of Native American completed suicides consist of males under the age of thirty-five, and alcohol use may be more prevalent in that age group than in any other. The critical feature is the significant increase in concomitant alcohol use with completed suicides among Native American when compared with other ethnic group populations.

By a four to one margin, fetal alcohol syndrome is more prevalent in Native American populations than in any other ethnic group in the United States, and infant mortality on some reservations is higher than in any third-world country (Johnson, 1994). Kettl and Bixler (1993) found that only about one-quarter of Native American suicide victims had a diagnosed psychiatric disorder, with 50 percent of these being a depressive disorder. Therefore, the rates of suicides due to diagnosed depressive disorder among Alaska Natives are lower than that among the general population, where they range between 45 and 65 percent. Kettl and Bixler suggested that other factors such as alcoholism, rather than a psychiatric disturbance, may play a greater role in suicides among Alaska Natives. Regardless of the specific percentages of suicides found in the professional literature, it is evident that alcohol is considered to be one of the most significant factors contributing to suicides among Native Americans and Alaska Natives.

Second, adolescents tend to be more impulsive than mature adults, and half of the Native American population is younger than eighteen years of age. The highest rates of suicide within the Native American community are by persons under the age of thirty-five. Suicide rates are also highest among Alaska Natives under the age of thirty (Forbes & Van der Hyde, 1988). As with other ethnic groups, within this age bracket many Native American suicides appear to be the result of impulsive acts, such as the breakup of a romantic relationship. This is especially true when combined with alcohol and drug use. The relationship between age and alcohol is less than clear though, since many tribal groups have very low levels of suicide or alcohol abuse. It would be interesting to see an increased number of research studies involving the relationship between tribal group alcohol consumption and suicide. The adolescent years are also associated with high rates of accidents and homicide across all ethnic groups in the United States, and the Native American community is not immune (Berlin,

1987). These social and personal ills often demoralize a community, leading to increased risk of depression, alcohol abuse, and suicide.

There is also evidence of suicide clusters within the United States as a whole, and there are numerous anecdotal accounts of young Native Americans from the same tribe completing suicide within a small window of time. When communities are small and clustered, as in the case of some reservations, there is an increased likelihood that multiple suicides can occur within a brief time period. LaFromboise and Bigfoot (1988) discussed how social responsibility and reciprocity values within Native American culture may increase the likelihood of suicidal behaviors after the death of a loved one, including imitating the deceased after viewing ceremonies in which the deceased is honored.

Third, unemployment and poverty are concerns often associated with the high suicide rates. Native American poverty rates are 2.3 times that of the U.S. average, whereas unemployment rates are almost twice the national average (Range et al., 1999). Travis (1984) postulated that differences in suicide rates between two geographically close Alaskan regions were due to employment rate differences. Lester (2001) found poverty to be a significant correlate with Native American suicide rates across the United States, including higher rates in economically less advantaged and more rural states. He partially attributed these rates to the larger number of reservations, which have higher suicide rates among Native Americans than in urban areas of these states. Also, impoverished communities often have concomitant concerns such as physical health problems, hopelessness, family disruption and violence, depression, and alcohol abuse. The noted psychiatrist William Menninger once said that "there is no better therapy than a job and a paycheck," and this saying seems to be particularly applicable to the Native American community.

Fourth, not all Native Americans are directly affected by prejudice and racism, but the effects of years of political and economic oppression cannot be overstated. Johnson (1994) pointed out that unresolved anger and grief over multiple losses often lead to negative internalized thoughts, which can cause depression, guilt, and emotional numbing. The most prevalent reasons for Native Americans initiating counseling are depression, anxiety, and alcohol issues, similar to those found in the country at large. However, the inclusion of years of oppression may add another variable to the therapeutic mix. In addition, the therapeutic literature is replete with research espousing the need for dominant-group counselors to consider the cultural mistrust that may occur with persons of color. For example, Paniagua (2005) highlighted the historical context of Native Americans and their relationship to European Americans. It is expected that some Native Americans may be initially mistrusting of European American counselors by assuming inherent racism or other forms of prejudice due to centuries of oppression by European Americans.

Fifth, as noted earlier, acculturation is a major factor with the Native American community, as with other ethnic communities. It is difficult to determine the extent to which acculturation itself is a suicide factor, but when combined with other personal, social, political, and economic factors, it becomes important nonetheless. It is likely that acculturation adjustment difficulties lead to depression or other psychiatric ills, but more research is needed. Many Native Americans are forced to look outside their local cultures for work or other schooling. If there is poor adjustment incorporating another culture into an existing worldview, dissonance occurs, which significantly increases the chances of suicidal behavior.

The influx of mainstream media also plays a role in adjusting to the incorporation of new ideas while questioning traditions. Dissonance causes stress and if not handled in a healthy manner can lead to significant levels of depression, anxiety, hopelessness, and eventually suicide. In his study analyzing state rates of suicide, Lester (2001) found that only 26 percent of the variance could be explained in Native American suicide rates, well below the 76 percent found for European American suicide rates. Therefore, it appears that suicide is extremely complex in Native American communities and researchers have yet to tap important variables contributing to high rates, particularly among young people. Few researchers systematically analyze reasons for the high rates of suicide, and it is imperative that they begin to delve deeper into cultural, social, acculturative, political, economic, and tribal factors that affect suicide. Counselors need to become well aware of local Native American cultures and begin to "think outside the box" when assessing for suicide. Even if Lester's (2001) finding that only 26 percent of the variance in Native American suicide is partially accurate, the typical questions and hypotheses associated with suicide assessments may need to be expanded. Assessing for depression and alcohol use should be conducted, but assessing for acculturation, spiritual practices, and future goals given poverty rates, and other factors, may be especially critical components of a good evaluation.

GENDER

The status integration hypothesis states that as the number of women enter the workforce, the number of suicides will increase, particularly for men. Young and French (1995) wanted to determine whether this hypothesis is true among the Native American community. Using suicide rates for the period 1979 to 1981 from the twelve Indian Health Service (IHS) areas under the U.S. Department of Health, Education, and Welfare, they concluded that as the number of Native American women in the workforce increased, rate of suicides increased for the women and not for the men. This was explained, in part, as a result of acculturative changes in the family in which Native American women are less likely to have kinship and economic support than in previous generations, thus causing increased distress. Collapsing age groups the male to female ratio of suicide completers is 12:1, almost four times higher than the national average of 3.3:1 (Range et al., 1999). There is also some evidence that Native American females complete suicide at a slightly lower rate than European American females, though higher than African American females (Young & French, 1993).

TRIBAL AFFILIATION AND ACCULTURATION

Suicide rates vary tremendously depending on tribal affiliation, state in the country, and acculturative differences. In studying social integration theory, Lester (2001) analyzed state-by-state data of Native American suicide for the year 1980 and compared these rates to European Americans in those states. Suicide rates ranged from zero to sixty-five per one hundred thousand depending on the state, showing wide variability. As mentioned previously, rates vary tremendously based on tribal affiliation, as tribal groups vary in their acculturation levels. Lester (1994c) also concluded that rates were higher in states with greater numbers of Native Americans. However, acculturation level and other variables were not studied, though acculturation was discussed in Lester (2001).

Van Winkle and May (1986) studied acculturation levels and suicide rates of the New Mexico Apache, Navajo, and Pueblo peoples from 1957 to 1979. The research is important because it offers data over an extended time period, unlike the majority of studies presenting data over a period of one or few years. Further, most studies tend to examine only one tribal group, thus limiting generalizability. The primary purpose for the inclusion of these specific tribes was because of their varying levels of acculturation and interaction with the European American community. The researchers found that acculturation level predicted suicide rates, with the high acculturation Apache group exhibiting the highest rate of suicide, the moderate acculturation Pueblo group revealing a moderate rate of suicide, and the low acculturation Navajo group exhibiting the lowest rate of suicide. The rate of suicide over the twenty-two-year time span fluctuated greatly depending on the individual year. On average, among younger people, the greater the acculturation level (toward mainstream U.S. culture), the greater is the suicide rate.

Two issues must be considered. First, counselors must consider whether acculturation changes are considered positive by the client, as negative acculturation is detrimental. Therefore, to talk about acculturation changes without considering the effects of acculturation on Native American suicide is useless. Second, there is evidence that completed suicides on reservations are greater than completed suicides in urban or other rural areas, but other evidence indicates that this is not so. Bachman (1992; see Lester, 1997a) found that economic deprivation was more of a critical indicator of Native American suicides than acculturation level. The overwhelming majority of completed suicides within this study were men (90 percent), consistent with many other studies indicating that males are researched to a greater degree than females and are much more likely than females to complete suicide. In a more recent article determining rates in the same New Mexico tribes, Van Winkle and May (1993) found suicide rates to be actually stabilizing or declining. Individuals in the fifteen to twenty-four and twenty-four to thirty-four age ranges still had the highest rates, and age groups under fifty-five were still above the nation's average.

METHODS AND CONCOMITANT FACTORS

Native Americans, particularly males, are more likely than any other ethnic group to use firearms (55 percent) and hanging (40 percent) as the primary means of suicide. Females have traditionally used household poisons or overdoses (43 percent), though many more are now using firearms and hanging as preferred methods (May, 1990; Range et al., 1999). Native Alaskans in general are more likely to use firearms (between 75 and 85 percent) than the average U.S. population (57 percent; Forbes & Van der Hyde, 1988). The firearms-versus-other-methods poses some dilemma for the counselor. Often during a suicide assessment, there is a contract with either the client or a close family member to remove firearms from the home. Firearms are also more difficult to buy than other items. This reduces the odds that an impulsive act will occur if a gun is presently unavailable. However, it is much more difficult to remove rope or household cleaning items, and these items are easier to access and purchase than firearms. Therefore, the counselor may need to become more creative and aware of typically nontraditional means of engaging in suicidal behaviors when considering no-suicide contracts or involuntary commitment decisions. If possible, interventions would include close monitoring by family members.

SPIRITUALITY AND RELIGION

Native American spirituality and religion have been misunderstood among non-Native counselors, but commitment to cultural spirituality has been associated with reduced suicide attempts (Garroutte, Goldberg, Beals, Herrell, & Manson, 2003). Many traditional Native Americans are often viewed as being nonreligious, or counselors with good intentions often do not understand the interwoven relationship between spirituality and daily Native American life. Therefore, these counselors may attempt traditional Native American treatment interventions but fail miserably. Many Native American languages do not have a specific word for religion or spirituality and this section of the chapter will focus on concepts that Westerners might call religion or spirituality. Further, the terms *religion* and *spirituality* will be used interchangeably in order to reduce redundancy.

However, know that these terms are not equivalent, with religion sometimes thought of as the rituals and spirituality sometimes considered the intrinsic relationship with the sacred.

Spirituality within Native American communities has a varied history that has been affected by two major factors. First, many Christian groups attempted to and succeeded in converting many Native American individuals and groups from traditional beliefs to a "Western" religious philosophy. These occurred through missionary schools and other church-related means. Choney, Berryhill-Paapke, and Robbins (1995) indicated that christianizing Native Americans probably had the biggest impact on their assimilation into a mainstream culture than any other means. Today, many Native Americans follow the traditions, beliefs, ceremonies, and values held within the Christian Church, and the majority of Native Americans are either Christian or hold an amalgamation of traditional and Christian beliefs. A minority hold on solely to traditional spiritual ways. The counselor should not be surprised that an individual's spiritual doctrines involve a mixing of tenets, which may not be consistent with mainstream Christianity.

Second, the U.S. government outlawed traditional Native American religions in the late 1800s, thus forcing many tribal groups to practice in secret or lose much of their ceremonies. It was not until 1978 that the American Religious Freedom Act officially allowed Native Americans to practice their time-held religions. Unfortunately, because of almost a century of religious oppression, many of the beliefs and practices vanished, though there has been a resurgence of traditional practices in some areas. For the two-thirds of Native Americans who do not live on a reservation full-time and therefore are more likely to come into contact with mainstream mental health services, it is likely that they hold some combination of Christian and Native religious beliefs.

Traditional oral religious practices and beliefs were handed down for centuries, unlike the European and Eastern written traditions. Sacred knowledge was transferred through tribal prayers, observances, and rites. The spiritual knowledge and practices provided a foundation and a framework from which to go about daily living. In other words, Native spirituality is central to other parts of life, and one cannot separate Native American values, beliefs, and rituals from spirituality. In fact, spirituality is one of the common links among the diverse tribes (Trujillo, 2000; Whitbeck, 2006). In Native American cultures, spirituality is a state of being while living on earth. It is a means to keep a balance within the tribe.

Most spiritual beliefs include a higher power that is often referred to as the Great Spirit or the Creator, and there are often other spirit beings that function in other capacities (M. T. Garrett & Wilbur, 1999). These spirits are both good and bad, which will help you or harm you, depending on your actions and your balance with the universe. There exist three worlds, the underworld, the middle world, and the celestial world, which comprise life, death, the earth, and the universe (Halifax, 1982, as described in Trujillo, 2000). In Native American religion there is a spiritual energy that interconnects all things on the earth and in the heavens. This connection is often described by the Circle of Life (spirit, body, mind, and nature) through the Medicine Wheel. Medicine is considered to be our inner being, an energy perhaps equivalent with the Asian *chi*. The Medicine Wheel is represented as the Four Directions (north, south, east, west), where each direction is equated with the four parts of the Circle of Life (J. T. Garrett & Garrett, 1994). There is a continual ebb and flow of this energy, and problems often arise for individuals because they are not balanced in their energy or are in a state of disharmony. Unlike Cartesian philosophy, one cannot separate the mind, body, and spirit; therefore, any imbalance in those systems causes the whole person to become ill. Each person is responsible for his or her own wellness by attempting to find his or her place in the universe and being consistent with and respecting the ways of Native American heritage. Often it is the spiritual leader (e.g., shaman) who passes on the sacred ways that continue to influence tribal communities. Within other U.S. cultural groups, a spiritual leader also influences the community. However, some communities seem to have spirituality interwoven at a deeper level than other communities (e.g., African American versus European American). Counselors cannot treat just the mind or just a spiritual concern in values and beliefs underlying Native American traditions.

VIEWS ON DEATH, SUICIDE, AND THE AFTERLIFE

As indicated previously, most Native Americans, especially non-reservation and assimilated, are Christian or have some form of Christianity within their religious beliefs. Their views may not differ from non-Native Americans who hold Christian views. However, many hold some degree of a mixture of Christian and traditional spiritual beliefs, whereas a minority maintain purely traditional beliefs. This section will consider views on death and an afterlife.

As with some Asian cultures, death is viewed as a natural part of the never-ending cycle of life. It keeps the balance of the universe intact, and is not something to be avoided. This does not mean that Native Americans do not fear death, but they accept that it is not a state separate from life. Life and death must be understood as part of a cycle. Some people fear the dead though, believing that ghosts walk the earth for a short period of time. These ghosts may bring bad luck to the family or to the community if one speaks of the deceased (Langdon, 1993, as described in Stamm & Stamm, 1999).

In most Christian traditions, one must believe that Jesus Christ was the son of God and/or must do good deeds to be accepted into heaven. In Native American culture, all persons go to heaven. A reason that suicide is admonished is that the person who completes suicide is believed to have acted selfishly and has not fulfilled his or her potential. The latter point is similar to the beliefs embedded within Judaism and Hinduism. Both prior to and after death the soul exists. After death, the soul takes a journey to the Spirit Land where all animal and human souls remain. However, a presence of the person remains on the earth (Brokenleg & Middleton, 1993). Some tribes view the human body as devised of life and spirits; thus, if one completes suicide, then the spirit cannot reach the afterlife. This spiritual belief acts as a sanction against suicide.

DEATH RITUALS AND MOURNING

Death and afterlife rituals are extremely varied among Native American tribes. This makes it very difficult for mental health workers to gain appropriate knowledge for the variety of Native Americans seen for counseling. Because it is virtually impossible for counselors to grasp the death customs of Native American tribal groups as a whole, it is recommended that they become familiar with the tribal groups in the area. For example, Mississippi has a fairly large Choctaw population in Philadelphia, and it would be important for counselors to speak with the Philadelphia reservation counselors, or other individuals who live and work there, about the customs of the area.

The reservation at Philadelphia, and many others, are very willing to assist non-Native groups in learning more about cultural norms and philosophies, and to help with interventions when necessary.

Literature is rarely available about specific death and afterlife rituals, so it would be difficult to simply read this material. It is equally difficult to access religious information specific to a tribe, instead garnering general information from references such as those listed in this chapter may be useful. The social sciences literature offers equally few detailed references regarding Native American spirituality and death rituals. Two notable exceptions are Brokenleg and Middleton (1993; Lakota people) and Stamm and Stamm (1999; general rituals). Therefore, it is recommended that the following information, largely summarized from these two references, be used only as a guideline from which to initiate client discussion.

There are numerous rituals that are observed, with nuances as great as the number of tribes and religious traditions that accompany them. Therefore, the information that follows is consistent across many tribes but is also lacking in scope. Ceremonies surrounding death are considered to be sacred and thus are given significant reverence. Just prior to a death, including suicides, the person will give away possessions as a sign of appreciation and respect. The family is revered as the most important part of life, and possessions are viewed throughout life as holding less importance. Upon nonsuicidal death, family members will gather around the body and extended family members from all over the country will join the rest of the family to offer comfort and support in this time of need. All family members will join together, even those who do not have close ties, because of the importance of family cohesiveness within Native American communities. It is common for the family to give away possessions of the deceased as an indication of the respect that the living has for the deceased and to alleviate grief by removing possessions that offer remembrances of the deceased. Giving gifts is seen as an appreciative gesture, and this gesture will be reciprocated at a later date upon the next death in the tribe (Stamm & Stamm, 1999). A variation on giving away possessions is that some tribes may burn some of the possessions of the deceased, a custom that goes back many centuries. Unlike years ago when the home of the deceased may be burned, today it may only be a few small items, if any. The burning may also occur at the first anniversary of the death. Regardless of the manner of letting items go, both gift-giving and burning are seen as symbolic gestures of letting the person go to the afterlife and the living returning to their lives.

After three days of lying in state, funeral services commence. During these three days, certain rituals may be performed such as cutting one's hair, wearing black and tearing clothing, again consistent with Jewish and Hindu cultures. More often than not, a Christian minister or priest will play an important role in the ceremony and the shaman will play a minimal role. Often funerals are a combination of Christian and traditional rituals, and the majority usually takes place on reservation land whether the person lived in the area or not. Food is generally placed outside of the home in order to feed the spirits.

There will be speakers who talk about the deceased and what he or she offered the tribe and community. In the case of a suicide, the tribe may be admonished by the speaker for not being more responsible in saving the individual. After this lecture, normal proceedings will occur, including prayers, Christian and traditional songs, drumming, and reminiscing. Open expressions of grief are permitted from both men and women from the time of death until the funeral, but during the funeral it is generally expected that no one will cry openly. After the funeral proceedings, open mourning is again condoned (Brokenleg & Middleton, 1993). The family is supposed to feed the mourners, and money is frequently given to the deceased's family to offset the costs. It is customary that the person be buried, as cremation is not accepted because the body should not be disturbed from its natural state. Objects relevant to the person will be included in the casket. All close family members and friends partake in filling up the gravesite as a sign of respect. A picture of the person or a lock of hair may be placed in the home, and on the first anniversary of the death family and friends will gather in a joyous occasion. Although less common, ceremonies during other anniversaries can occur throughout the years by individual families.

GAY/LESBIAN/BISEXUAL ("TWO-SPIRIT") ISSUES

For centuries sex between two same-sex partners has been considered acceptable in the Native American community, and even preferable in some tribes. Native American communities did not separate people into male and female, and more than two-thirds of the Native languages spoken today have a term consistent with a third gender (Tafoya & Wirth, 1996). The term *berdache* was an anthropological term that originally meant male sex slave. Because of that inaccurate definition, the term is falling out of favor among many Native American people. Even the terms gay, lesbian, bisexual, and transgendered may not be accurate to describe "gay" Native Americans because they are considered to be European terms. Historically, berdache were also believed to possess a strong spiritual component, something that is lost when using Western terms (e.g., gay). Recently, the term *Two-Spirit,* used to describe the unique features of the Native American gay community and maintain consistency with Native terminology, has gained increased acceptance. Essentially, Two-Spirit people are thought to be multigendered and therefore see the world from a holistic perspective rather than from either a male or a female perspective. In essence, they are not considered entirely male or female (Tafoya, 1997; Tafoya & Wirth, 1996). Historically, in many Native American cultures, Two-Spirit persons were held in high esteem because they possessed a unique worldview with a strong spiritual element, whereas in other tribes they were often scorned. Generally, there has been much broader acceptance of sexuality in multiple forms in the Native American community than in the European American community.

Consistent with Hispanic and Asian cultures, one's sexual identity is defined within oneself, through sexual behaviors rather than by the person's sexual partner. Some Native American male clients, for example, may have sexual intercourse with other men but consider themselves to be straight because they engage in the dominant position. There is less information regarding a female Two-Spirit (sometimes called an "Amazon"; Tafoya & Wirth, 1996). Sexual identity issues can arise in counseling within the Native American community. It is important for counselors not to categorize Native American Two-Spirit people in conventional heterosexual, homosexual, and bisexual terms (and perhaps transgendered), thus increasing the risk of losing the client for failing to understand the Two-Spirit concept. If sexual identity issues arise, it may be beneficial to talk in terms of the benefits and respect given to Two-Spirit people. Tafoya and Wirth (1996) discussed the fact that traditionally a berdache status may not have been as important as whether the individual was a good person and a valuable contributor to the tribe and community.

Some more mainstream gay Native American men and women, like others, are scorned through oppression or nonacceptance from multiple cultural and societal groups. The dominant gay culture tends not to accept Native American GLBTs or views them with less respect than dominant group GLBTs. The European American gay culture has been accused at times of not accepting gays of color regardless of ethnic background. The straight dominant culture still exhibits racism and homophobic behavior. It may be difficult for a Native American gay individual to find a Native American partner because of the limited numbers of gays in the community seeking relationships. However, there is also a general lack of acceptance, or at best a passive acceptance of the Native American gay community. Because of these concerns, there are organizations that have begun specifically for gay Native Americans such as Gay Native Americans and Bay Area Native American Two Spirits (BAAITS). In addition, there are specified Native American organizations that have themes empowering members, such as the National Native American AIDS Prevention Center (Tafoya & Wirth, 1996). These organizations allow for greater acceptance within the community, potentially decreasing suicidal behaviors.

SUICIDE PREVENTION AND INTERVENTION

LaFromboise and Bigfoot (1988) highlighted specific cultural values that should be considered when conducting a suicide assessment. Many Native Americans stress self-control, which leads to some youths internalizing psychological hurt. The self-control is often translated into becoming an active participant in the preparation for death, instead of avoiding death. Also, Native American perspectives often include an interrelationship between human and spirit worlds, aligned with the belief in reincarnation, which may decrease concerns about death.

Very few empirically validated suicide prevention programs specific to Native Americans are available, though a couple are reported later. Part of the concern is whether suicide prevention programs can transfer easily from one tribal group to another given their heterogeneity (LaFromboise & Howard-Pitney, 1994; Novins, Beals, Roberts, & Manson, 1999). However, there are more programs available than found in the African American, Asian American, and Hispanic

American literature. In order to qualify as sensitive to Native Americans they must include culture-specific factors consistent with Native Americans (e.g., spirituality, ethnic-identity loss, acculturation, traditional healing approaches). These types of programs would probably be most appropriate for Native Americans living on or near reservations (40 percent; Middlebrook, LeMaster, Beals, Novins, & Manson, 2001), and those who are not assimilated into mainstream culture. The majority of generic prevention programs typically include common factors such as the relationship between suicide and substance use, depression, firearm access, and relationship stressors. Issues such as self-esteem, problem solving, and communicating with peers and parents are addressed. Many of these programs are included in schools with high Native American populations, usually teenagers, because the general risk factors are typically the same as with other populations. However, some studies have shown differences in the importance of some culturally specific variables that may lead to increased suicide, such as weakened familial structure based on specific cultural gender roles, loss of ethnic identity, and loss of achievement (e.g., Dinges & Duong-Tran, 1992-1993, 1994; Levy & Kunitz, 1987; Novins et al., 1999). At the very least, presenting material that is consistent with clients' surroundings and worldviews may lead to superior results over those that are generic.

Middlebrook et al. (2001) outlined the nine programs that can be considered sensitive to Native American cultural values, with five developed to reverse increased suicide rates and four developed as part of larger programs addressing issues such as substance abuse. For a more detailed analysis of the programs, see Middlebrook et al. (2001), but two of the suicide prevention programs will be briefly presented here as an introduction to culturally sensitive suicide prevention programs.

Bechtold (1994) recommended that communities must present "moral proscriptions against suicide . . . [that are] culturally relevant and consistent with traditional values" (p. 77). The Zuni Pueblo in New Mexico have such a belief as suicide and suicidal ideation are prohibited. However, there was a concern about a fairly high suicide rate within the tribal unit. Based on skills training grounded in social learning theory (Bandura, 1977), LaFromboise and Howard-Pitney (1994) presented an overview of a suicide prevention program for Zuni Pueblo adolescents. Skills training was chosen as the primary approach because of its consistency with many Native American values and beliefs, such as flexibility and collaboration, and the use of modeling and community support. When appropriate, their interventions were structured within Zuni values, as the authors collaborated with community leaders to devise the prevention program. For example, anger management was presented, an area typical of many suicide prevention programs. However, anger management was coupled with feelings of prejudice, intolerance, and oppression. Coping mechanisms consistent with Zuni traditions were associated with substance use rejection and antecedents of self-destruction. Zuni rights were presented. Typical suicide prevention strategies were also utilized, as they appear to be consistent regardless of population (e.g., understanding warning signs), but were couched within a Zuni framework when possible. Zuni-specific scenarios were created and the students responded positively given that they could relate to the situations. Teachers, parents, and community resource people were involved, and the program showed positive empirical results.

The Positive Reinforcement in Drug Education (PRIDE) program was designed for Puyallup Tribe preschool through high school students as an alternative, culturally sensitive approach to substance use. A number of Native American issues such as community support systems, tribal values, and school-sponsored extracurricular events such as festivals and powwows were incorporated into the curriculum. Their regular school curriculum, through input of family, community, and the school board, included presentations and discussions of cultural identity and ethnic pride. Cultural traditions and enhancement activities are included such as drumming and dance rituals. The importance of culturally relevant interventions cannot be overstated, as students will be more receptive to information and activities that are applicable and relevant. Clinicians would do well to consider the cultural nuances in the client's background and incorporate ethnically (religious, sexual orientation, etc.) appropriate approaches with which the client can identify.

SUMMARY

High suicide rates have been well documented among some Native American tribal groups, though there is such variability among the tribes that the data are difficult to extrapolate. The literature indicates that acculturation stress is a significant factor for Native Americans, particularly for youths and young adults. The overwhelming majority of suicides occurs in the adolescent and young adult groups, with virtually no suicides in the older age groups, regardless of tribe. Research indicates that increasing the connections with spiritual roots and the community, traditional rituals, and prevention efforts aimed at the reduction of substance abuse, significantly decreases the likelihood of suicide. Programs aimed at the reduction of prejudice aimed at Native Americans may also diminish the suicide rates, particularly if peers are involved, though research is needed. There are a number of prevention and intervention efforts devised strictly for a few Native American groups, and it is hoped that further interventions are developed. It is hoped also that community efforts to increase awareness of suicide will continue, and that researchers will continue efforts determining which suicide factors may be unique and which may be considered universal.

References

Allport, G. W., & Ross, M. J. (1967). Personal religious orientation and prejudice. *Journal of Personality and Social Psychology, 5*, 432-443.

Almeida, R. (1996). Hindu, Christian, and Muslim families. In M. McGoldrick, J. Giordano, & J. K. Pearce (Eds.), *Ethnicity and family therapy* (2nd ed.) (pp. 395-423). New York: Guilford Press.

Alston, M. H., & Anderson, S. E. (1995). Suicidal behavior in African-American women. In S. S. Canetto & D. Lester (Eds.), *Women and suicidal behavior* (pp. 133-143). New York: Springer Publishing.

Anderson, R. N., Kochanek, K. D., & Murphy, S. L. (1995). Report of final mortality statistics, 1995. *Monthly vital statistics report, 45* (Suppl. 2), table 7. Hyattesville, MD: National Center for Health Statistics.

Andrews, J. A., & Lewinsohn, P. M. (1992). Suicidal attempts among older adolescents: Prevalence and co-occurrence with psychiatric disorders. *Journal of the American Academy of Child and Adolescent Psychiatry, 31*, 655-662.

Bachman, J. G., Wallace, J. M. Jr., & O'Malley, P. M. (1991). Racial/ethnic differences in smoking, drinking, and illicit drug use among American high school seniors, 1976-1989. *American Journal of Public Health, 81*, 372-377.

Bachman, R. (1992). *Death and violence on the reservation.* New York: Auburn House.

Bagley, C., & Greer, S. (1972). "Black suicide": A report of 25 English cases and controls. *Journal of Social Psychology, 86*, 175-179.

Bagley, C., & Ramsay, R. F. (1989). Attitudes toward suicide, religious values and suicidal behavior: Evidence from a community survey. In R. F. W. Diekstra & Maris, R. (Eds.), *Suicide and its prevention: The role of attitude and imitation* (pp. 78-90). Leiden, The Netherlands: E. J. Brill.

Bailey, W. T., & Stein, L.B. (1995). Jewish affiliation in relation to suicide rates. *Psychological Reports, 76*, 561-562.

Bainbridge, W. S., & Stark, R. (1981). Suicide, homicide, and religion: Durkheim reassessed. *Annual Review of the Social Sciences of Religion, 5*, 33-56.

Baker, F. M. (1988). Afro-Americans. In L. Comas-Diaz & E. H. Ezra (Eds.), *Clinical guidelines in cross-cultural mental health* (pp. 151-181). Oxford, England: John Wiley and Sons.

Baker, F. M. (1990). Black youth suicide: Literature review with a focus on prevention. *Journal of the National Medical Association, 82*, 495-507.

Cultural Diversity and Suicide
© 2006 by The Haworth Press, Inc. All rights reserved.
doi:10.1300/5680_07

Baker, F. M. (1994). Suicide among ethnic minority elderly: A statistical and psychosocial perspective. *Journal of Geriatric Psychiatry, 27,* 261-264.

Baker, F. M. (1996). Suicide among ethnic elders. In G. J. Kennedy (Ed.), *Suicide and depression in late life: Critical issues in treatment, research, and public policy* (pp. 51-79). Oxford, England: John Wiley and Sons.

Bandura, A. (1977). *Social learning theory.* Oxford, England: Prentice-Hall.

Barry, R. (1999). The Catholic condemnation of rational suicide. In J. L. Werth Jr. (Ed.), *Contemporary perspectives on rational suicide* (pp. 29-34). Philadelphia: Brunner/Mazel.

Baruth, L. G., & Manning, M. L. (2003). *Multicultural counseling and psychotherapy* (3rd ed.). Upper Saddle River, NJ: Merrill Prentice Hall.

Bechtold, D. W. (1994). Indian adolescent suicide: Clinical and developmental considerations. *Native American and Alaska Native Mental Health Research, 4,* 71-80.

Beck, A. T. (1987). Cognitive models of depression. *Journal of Cognitive Psychotherapy, 1,* 5-37.

Beck, A. T., Brown, G., & Steer, R. A. (1989). Prediction of eventual suicide in psychiatric inpatients by clinical ratings of hopelessness. *Journal of Consulting and Clinical Psychology, 57,* 309-310.

Beck, A. T., Freeman, A. M., & Associates. (1990). *Cognitive therapy of personality disorders.* New York: Guilford Press.

Beck, A. T., Steer, R. A., Beck, J. S., & Newman, C. F. (1993). Hopelessness, depression, suicidal ideation, and clinical diagnosis of depression. *Suicide and Life-Threatening Behavior, 23,* 139-145.

Beck, A. T., Steer, R. A., Kovacs, M., & Garrison, B. (1985). Hopelessness and eventual suicide: A 10-year prospective study of patients hospitalized with suicidal ideation. *American Journal of Psychiatry, 142,* 559-563.

Becker, T. M., Samet, J. M., Wiggins, C. L., & Key, C. R. (1990). Violent death in the west: Suicide and homicide in New Mexico, 1958-1987. *Suicide and Life-Threatening Behavior, 20,* 324-334.

Bell, A. P., & Weinberg, M. S. (1978). *Homosexualities.* New York: Simon and Schuster.

Bender, M. L. (2000). Suicide and older African-American women. *Mortality, 5,* 158-170.

Berlin, I. N. (1987). Suicide among Native American adolescents: An overview. *Suicide and Life-Threatening Behavior, 17,* 218-232.

Berman, A. L. (1991). Suicide cases. *Suicide and Life-Threatening Behavior,* Special issue: Assessment and prediction of suicide, *21,* 18-36.

Berman, A. L., & Jobes, D. A. (1992). *Adolescent suicide: Assessment and prevention.* Washington, DC: American Psychological Association.

Berman, A. L., & Jobes, D. A. (1995). Suicide prevention in adolescents (age 12-18). In M. M. Silverman & R. W. Maris (Eds.), *Suicide prevention: Toward the year 2000* (pp. 143-154). New York: Guilford Press.

Bernal, G., & Guitierrez, M. (1988). Cubans. In L. Comas-Diaz & E. H. Ezra (Eds.), *Clinical guidelines in cross-cultural mental health* (pp. 233-261). Oxford, England: John Wiley and Sons.

Berrill, K. T. (1990). Anti-gay violence and victimization in the United States: An overview. *Journal of Interpersonal Violence, 5,* 274-294.

Berry, J. W. (1990). Acculturation and adaptation: A general framework. In W. H. Holtzman & T. H. Bornermann (Eds.), *Mental health of immigrants and refugees* (pp. 90-102). Austin, TX: Hogg Foundation for Mental Health.

Berry, J. W. (1995). Psychology of acculturation. In N. R. Goldberger & J. B. Veroff (Eds.), *Culture and psychology reader* (pp. 457-488). New York: New York University Press.

Billingsley, A. (1992). *Climbing Jacob's ladder: The enduring legacy of African American families.* New York: Simon and Schuster.

Blatt, S. J. (1995). The destructiveness of perfectionism: Implications for the treatment of depression. *American Psychologist, 50,* 1003-1020.

Blatt, S. J., Quinlan, D. M., & Pilkonis, P. A. (1995). Impact of perfectionism and need for approval on the brief treatment of depression: The National Institute of Mental Health treatment of depression collaborative research program revisited. *Journal of Consulting and Clinical Psychology, 63,* 125-132.

Bliatout, B. T. (1993). Hmong death customs: Traditional and acculturated. In D. P. Irish & K. F. Lundquist (Eds.), *Ethnic variations in dying, death, and grief: Diversity in universality* (pp. 79-100). Philadelphia: Taylor and Francis.

Boergers, J., & Spirito, A. (2003). The outcome of suicide attempts among adolescents. In A. Spirito & J. C. Overholser (Eds.), *Evaluating and treating adolescent suicide attempters: From research to practice* (pp. 261-276). San Diego, CA: Academic Press.

Bongar, B. (2002). *The suicidal patient: Clinical and legal standards of care* (2nd ed.). Washington, DC: American Psychological Association.

Bongar, B., Berman, A. L., Maris, R. W., Silverman, M. M., & Harris, E. A. (1998). *Risk management with suicidal patients.* New York, NY: Guilford Press.

Bonger, B. M. (1991). *The suicidal patient: Clinical and legal standards of care.* Washington, DC: American Psychological Association.

Bouhdiba, A. (1985). *Sexuality in Islam.* London: Routledge and Kegan Paul.

Bourne, P. G. (1973). Suicide among Chinese in San Francisco. *American Journal of Public Health, 8,* 744-750.

Braun, K. L., & Nichols, R. (1997). Death and dying in four Asian American cultures: A descriptive study. *Death Studies, 21,* 327-359.

Brent, D. A., Kerr, M. M., & Goldstein, C. (1991). An outbreak of suicide and suicidal behavior in a high school. In S. Chess & M. E. Hertzig (Eds.), *Annual progress in child psychiatry and child development, 1990* (pp. 532-546). Philadelphia: Brunner/Mazel.

Brokenleg, M., & Middleton, D. (1993). Native Americans: Adapting, yet retaining. In D. P. Irish & K. F. Lundquist (Eds.), *Ethnic variations in dying, death, and grief: Diversity in universality* (pp. 101-112). Philadelphia: Taylor and Francis.

Brown, D. R., & Gary, L. E. (1985). Social support network differentials among married and nonmarried Black females. *Psychology of Women Quarterly, 9,* 229-241.

Brown, H. K. (1987). The impact of suicides on therapists in training. *Comprehensive Psychiatry, 28,* 101-112.

Brown, L. M., Bongar, B., & Cleary, K. M. (2004). A profile of psychologists views of critical risk factors for completed suicide in older adults. *Professional Psychology: Research and Practice, 35,* 90-96.

Buriel, R., & Rivera, L. (1980). The relationship of locus of control to family income and familism among European- and Mexican-American high school students. *Journal of Social Psychology, 111,* 27-34.

Burtt, E. A. (Ed.) (1982). *The teachings of the compassionate Buddha.* New York: Penguin.

Bush, J. A. (1976). Suicide and blacks: A conceptual framework. *Suicide: A Quarterly Journal of Life-Threatening Behavior, 6,* 216-222.

Buzi, R. S., Smith, P. B., & Weinman, M. L. (1988). Incorporating health and behavioral consequences of child abuse in prevention programs targeting female adolescents. *Patient Education and Counseling, 33,* 209-216.

Canetto, S. S. (1991). Gender roles, suicide attempts, and substance abuse. *Journal of Psychology, 125,* 605-620.

Canetto, S. S., & Lester, D. (1995a). The epidemiology of women's suicidal behavior. In S. S. Canetto & D. Lester (Eds.), *Women and suicidal behavior* (pp. 35-57). New York: Springer Publishing Co.

Canetto, S. S., & Lester, D. (1995b). Gender and the primary prevention of suicide mortality. In M. M. Silverman & R. W. Maris (Eds.), *Suicide prevention: Toward the year 2000* (pp. 58-69). New York: Guilford Press.

Canino, G., & Roberts, R. E. (2001). Suicidal behavior among Latino youth. *Suicide and Life-Threatening Behavior, 31,* 122-131.

Carrier, J. M. (1989). Gay liberation and coming out in Mexico. *Journal of Homosexuality, 17,* 225-252.

Casas, J. M., & Pytluk, S. D. (1995). Hispanic identity development: Implications for research and practice. In J. G. Ponterotto & J. M. Casas (Eds.), *Handbook of multicultural counseling* (pp. 155-180). Thousand Oaks, CA: Sage Publications.

Cass, V. C. (1979). Homosexual identity formation: A theoretical model. *Journal of Homosexuality, 4,* 219-235.

Castro, F. G., Furth, P., & Karlow, H. (1984). The health beliefs of Mexican, Mexican American and European American women. *Hispanic Journal of Behavioral Sciences, 6,* 365-383.

Cecchini, T. B. (1998). An interpersonal and cognitive-behavioral approach to childhood depression: A school based primary prevention study. *Dissertation Abstracts International, 58,* 12-B, 6803.

Cervantes, J. M., & Ramirez, O. (1992). Spirituality and family dynamics in psychotherapy with Latino children. In L. A. Vargas & J. D. Koss-Chioino (Eds.),

Working with culture: Psychotherapeutic interventions with ethnic minority children and adolescents (pp. 103-128). San Francisco: Jossey-Bass.

Chan, C. S. (1993). Issues of identity development among Asian-American lesbians and gay men. In L. D. Garnets & D. C. Kimmel (Eds.), *Psychological perspectives on lesbian and gay male experiences* (pp. 376-387). New York: Columbia University Press.

Chan, S. (1989). Issues of identity development among Asian-American lesbians and gay men. *Journal of Counseling and Development, 68,* 16-20.

Chan, S. (1992). Families with Asian roots. In E. W. Lynch & M. J. Hanson (Eds.), *Developing cross-cultural competence: A guide for working with young children and their families* (pp. 181-257). Baltimore: Paul H. Brooks Publishing.

Chance, S. E., Kaslow, N. J., Summerville, M. B., & Wood, K. (1998). Suicidal behavior in African American individuals: Current status and future directions. *Cultural Diversity and Mental Health, 4,* 19-37.

Chandler, C. R. (1979). Traditionalism in a modern setting: A comparison of Anglo and Mexican American value orientations. *Human Organization, 38,* 153-159.

Chandler, C. R., Tsai, Y. M., & Wharton, R. (1999). Twenty years after: Replicating a study of Anglo- and Mexican-American cultural values. *Social Science Journal, 36,* 353-367.

Chandler, M. J., Lalonde, C. E., Sokol, B. W., & Hallett, D. (2003). Personal persistence, identity development, and suicide: A study of Native and non-Native North American adolescents. *Monographs of the Society for Research in Child Development, 68,* vii-130.

Chang, E. C., (1998). Cultural differences, perfectionism, and suicidal risk in a college population: Does social problem solving still matter? *Cognitive Therapy and Research, 22,* 237-254.

Choney, S. K., Berryhill-Paapke, E., & Robbins, R. R. (1995). The acculturation of Native Americans: Developing frameworks for research and practice. In J. G. Ponterotto & J. M. Casas (Eds.), *Handbook of multicultural counseling* (pp. 73-92). Thousand Oaks, CA: Sage Publications.

Chung, C. H. (1990). Death and dying: A Vietnamese cultural perspective. In J. K. Parry (Ed.), *Social work practice with the terminally ill: A transcultural perspective* (pp. 191-204). Springfield, IL: Charles C. Thomas, Publisher.

Chung, Y. B., & Katayama, M. (1998). Ethnic and sexual identity development in Asian American lesbian and gay adolescents. *Professional School Counseling, 1,* 21-25.

The Church of Jesus Christ of Latter-Day Saints (LDS). (1998). *General Handbook of Instructions.* Salt Lake City, Utah: Intellectual Reserve, Inc.

Clark, R. L. (2006). Healing the generations: Urban Indians in recovery. In W. Witko (Ed.), *Mental health care for urban Indians: Clinical insights from Native practitioners* (pp. 83-89). Washington, DC: American Psychological Association.

Clarke, R. V., & Lester, D. (1989). *Suicide: Closing the exits.* New York: Springer-Verlag Publishing.

Clemons, J. T. (1990a). *Perspectives on suicide.* Louisville, KY: John Knox Press.

Clemons, J. T. (1990b). *What does the Bible say about suicide?* Minneapolis, MN: Fortress Press.

Comer, J. P. (1973). Black suicide. *Urban Health, 2,* 21-43.

Comstock, G. D. (1989). Victims of anti-gay/lesbian violence. *Journal of Interpersonal Violence, 4,* 101-106.

Conwell, Y. (2001). Suicide in later life: A review and recommendations for prevention. *Suicide and Life-Threatening Behavior, 31,* 32-47.

Coppen, A. (1994). Depression as a lethal disease: Prevention strategies. *Journal of Clinical Psychiatry, 55,* 37-45.

Coryell, W., Solomon, D., Turvey, C., Keller, M., Leon, A. C., Endicott, J., Schettler, P., Judd, L., & Mueller, T. (2003). The long-term course of rapid-cycling bipolar disorder. *Archives of General Psychiatry, 60,* 914-920.

Croom, G. L. (1998). The effects of a consolidated versus non-consolidated identity on expectations of African-American lesbians selecting mates: A pilot study. *Dissertation Abstracts International, 58,* 12-B, 6804.

Cross, W. E. Jr., & Vandiver, B. J. (2001). Nigrescence theory and measurement. In J. G. Ponterotto, J. M. Casas, L. A. Suzuki, & C. M. Alexander (Eds.), *Handbook of multicultural counseling* (pp. 371-393). Thousand Oaks, CA: Sage Publications.

Dahl, L. E. (1994). Degrees of Glory. In D. H. Ludlow (Ed.), *Jesus Christ and His Gospel: Selections from the Encyclopedia of Mormonism* (pp. 101-104). Salt Lake City: Deseret Book.

Dalton, E. J., Cate-Carter, T. D., Mundo, E., Parikh, S. V., & Kennedy, J. L. (2003). Suicide risk in bipolar patients: The role of co-morbid substance use disorders. *Bipolar Disorders, 5,* 8-61.

Dana, R. H. (1993). *Multicultural assessment perspectives for professional psychology.* Needham Heights, MA: Allyn and Bacon.

D'Augelli, A. R. (2002). Mental health problems among lesbian, gay, and bisexual youths ages 14 to 21. Special issue: Sexual identity and gender identity. *Clinical Child Psychology and Psychiatry, 7,* 433-456.

D'Augelli, A. R., & Hershberger, S. L. (1993). Lesbian, gay, and bisexual youth in community settings: Personal challenges and mental health problems. *American Journal of Community Psychology, 21,* 421-448.

Davidson, L. E., Rosenberg, M. L., Mercy, J. A., Franklin, J., & Simmons, J. T. (1989). An epidemiologic study of risk factors in two teenage suicide clusters. *Journal of the American Medical Association, 262,* 2687-2692.

Davis, R. (1979). Black suicide in the seventies: Current trends. *Suicide and Life-Threatening Behavior, 9,* 131-140.

Davis, R. (1980). Suicide among young blacks: Trends and perspectives. *Phylon, 41,* 223-229.

Davison-Aviles, R. M., Guerrero, M. P., Barajas, H. H., & Thomas, G. (1999). Perceptions of Chicano/Latino students who have dropped out of school. *Journal of Counseling & Development, 77,* 465-473.

Dean, P. J., & Range, L. M. (1999). Testing the escape theory of suicide in an outpatient clinical population. *Cognitive Therapy and Research, 23,* 561-572.

de la Cancela, V., & Martinez, I. Z. (1983). An analysis of culturalism in Latino mental health: Folk medicine as a case in point. *Hispanic Journal of Behavioral Sciences, 5,* 251-274.

De Leo, D., & Spathonis, K. (2003). Do psychosocial and pharmacological interventions reduce suicide in schizophrenia and schizophrenia spectrum disorders? *Archives of Suicide Research, 7,* 353-374.

de Monteflores, C. (1993). Notes on the management of difference. In L. D. Garnets & D. C. Kimmel (Eds.), *Psychological perspectives on lesbian and gay male experiences* (pp. 218-247). New York: Columbia University Press.

Diego, A. T., Yamamoto, J., Nguyen, L. H., & Hifumi, S. S. (1994). Suicide in the elderly: Profiles of Asians and whites. *Asian American and Pacific Islander Journal of Health, 2,* 49-57.

Dinges, N. G., & Duong-Tran, Q. (1992-1993). Stressful life events and co-occurring depression, substance abuse and suicidality among American Indian and Alaska Native adolescents. *Culture, Medicine and Psychiatry, 16,* 487-502.

Dinges, N. G., & Duong-Tran, Q. (1994). Suicide ideation and suicide attempt among American Indian and Alaska Native boarding school adolescents. *American Indian and Alaska Native Mental Health Research, 4* (mono), 167-188.

Domino, G. (1981). Attitude toward suicide among Mexican American and European youth. *Hispanic Journal of Behavioral Sciences, 3,* 385-395.

Donaldson, D. B., Spirito, A., & Farnett, E. (2000). The role of perfectionism and depressive cognitions in understanding the hopelessness experienced by adolescent suicide attempters. *Child Psychiatry and Human Development, 31,* 99- 111.

Donin, H. H. (1972). *To be a Jew: A guide to Jewish observance in contemporary life.* New York: Basic Books.

Downing, N. E., & Roush, K. L. (1985). From passive acceptance to active commitment: A model of feminist identity development for women. *The Counseling Psychologist, 13,* 695-709.

Dunston, P. J. (1990). Stress, coping, and social support: Their effects on black women. In D. S. Ruiz (Ed.), *Handbook of mental health and mental disorder among black Americans* (pp. 133-147). New York: Greenwood Press.

Durkheim, E. (1951). *Suicide: A study in sociology* (J. A. Spaulding & G. Simpson, Trans.). New York: Free Press (Original work published 1897).

Earls, F., Escobar, J. I., & Manson, S. M. (1990). Suicide in minority groups: Epidemiologic and cultural perspectives. In S. J. Blumenthal & D. J. Kupfer (Eds.), *Suicide over the life cycle: Risk factors, assessment, and treatment of suicidal patients* (pp. 571-598). Washington, DC: American Psychiatric Press, Inc.

Early, K. E., & Akers, R. L. (1993). "It's a White thing": An exploration of beliefs about suicide in the African-American community. *Deviant Behavior, 14,* 277-296.

EchoHawk, M. (1997). Suicide: The scourge of Native American people. *Suicide and Life-Threatening Behavior, 27,* 60-67.

El Azayem, G. A., & Hedayat-Diba, Z. (1994). The psychological aspects of Islam: Basic principles of Islam and their psychological corollary. *International Journal for the Psychology of Religion, 4,* 41-50.

Ellis, J. B., & Range, L. M. (1991). Differences between blacks and whites, women and men in reasons for living. *Journal of Black Studies, 21,* 341-347.

Enns, C. Z. (1992). Toward integrating feminist psychotherapy and feminist philosophy. *Professional Psychology: Research and Practice, 23,* 453-466.

Enns, C. Z. (1997). *Feminist theories and feminist psychotherapies: Origins, themes, and variations.* New York: The Haworth Press.

Erdman, J. L., Andrade, N. N., Glipa, J., Foster, J., Danko, G. P., Yates, A., Johnson, R. C., McDermott, J. F., & Waldron, J. A. (1998). Depressive symptoms among Filipino American adolescents. *Cultural Diversity & Mental Health, 4,* 45-54.

Escobar, J. I. (1987). Cross-cultural aspects of the somatization trait. *Hospital and Community Psychiatry, 38,* 174-180.

Espin, O. M. (1984). Cultural and historical influences on sexuality in Hispanic/ Latin women: Implications for psychotherapy. In C. Vance (Ed.), *Pleasure and danger: Exploring female sexuality* (pp. 149-163). London: Routledge and Kegan Paul.

Espin, O. M. (1987). Psychotherapy with Hispanic women: Some considerations. In P. Pedersen (Ed.), *Handbook of cross-cultural counseling and therapy* (pp. 165-171). New York: Greenwood Press.

Farberow, N. L. (1975). *Suicide in different cultures.* Baltimore: University Park Press.

Fawcett, J., Scheftner, W. A., Fogg, L. Clark, D. C., Young, M. A., Hedeker, D., & Gibbons, R. (1990). Time-related predictors of suicide in major affective disorder. *American Journal of Psychiatry, 147,* 1189-1194.

Firestone, R. W. (1997). *Suicide and the inner voice: Risk assessment, treatment, and case management.* Santa Barbara, CA: Sage Publications.

Forbes, N., & Van der Hyde, V. (1988). Suicide in Alaska from 1978 to 1985: Updated data from state files. *Native American and Alaska Native Mental Health Research, 1,* 36-55.

Frankish, C. J. (1994). Crisis centers and their role in treatment: Suicide prevention versus health promotion. In A. A. Leenaars, J. T. Maltsberger, & R. Neimeyer (Eds.), *Treatment of suicidal people* (pp. 33-43). Philadelphia: Taylor and Francis.

Fuertes, J. N., & Gretchen, D. (2001). Emerging theories of multicultural counseling. In J. G. Ponterotto, J. M. Casas, L. A. Suzuki, & C. M. Alexander (Eds.), *Handbook of multicultural counseling* (2nd ed.) (pp. 509-541). Thousand Oaks, CA: Sage Publications.

Fukuyama, M. A., & Sevig, T. D. (1999). *Integrating spirituality into multicultural counseling.* Thousand Oaks, CA: Sage Publications.

Garland, A. F., & Zigler, E. (1993). Adolescent suicide prevention: Current research and social policy implications. *American Psychologist, 48,* 169-182.

Garnets, L. D., & Kimmel, D. C. (Eds.). (2003). *Psychological perspectives on lesbian, gay, and bisexual experiences* (2nd ed.). New York, NY: Columbia University Press.

Garrett, J. T., & Garrett, M. W. (1994). The path of good medicine: Understanding and counseling Native Americans. *Journal of Multicultural Counseling and Development, 22,* 134-144.

Garrett, M. T. (2003). Two Spirit: Counseling Native American gay, lesbian, and bisexual people. *Journal of Multicultural Counseling and Development, 31,* 131-142.

Garrett, M. T., & Wilbur, M. P. (1999). Does the worm live in the ground? Reflections on Native American spirituality. *Journal of Multicultural Counseling and Development, 27,* 193-206.

Garrison, C. Z., McKeown, R. E., Valois, R. F., & Vincent, M. L. (1993). Aggression, substance use, and suicidal behaviors in high school students. *American Journal of Public Health, 83,* 179-184.

Garroutte, E. M., Goldberg, J., Beals, J., Herrell, R., & Manson, S.M. (2003). Spirituality and attempted suicide among American Indians. *Social Science and Medicine, 56,* 1571-1579.

Gibbs, J. T. (1997). African-American suicide: A cultural paradox. *Suicide: Individual, Cultural, International Perspectives, 27,* 68-79.

Gibbs, J. T., & Fuery, D. (1994). Mental health and well-being of Black women toward strategies of empowerment. *American Journal of Community Psychology:* [Special Issue] Empowering the silent ranks, *22,* 559-582.

Gibson, P. (1989). Gay male and lesbian youth suicide. In M. R. Feinleib (Ed.), *Report of the Secretary's Task Force on youth suicide. Volume 3: Prevention and interventions in youth suicide* (pp. 110-142) (DHHS Publication No. ADM 89-1623). Washington, DC: U.S. Government Printing Office.

Glenmullen, J. (2000). *Prozak backlash: Overcoming the dangers of Prozac, Zoloft, Paxil, and other antidepressants with safe, effective alternatives.* New York: Touchstone Books/Simon and Schuster.

Goldring, N., & Fieve, R. R. (1984). Attempted suicide in manic-depressive disorder. *American Journal of Psychotherapy, 38,* 373-383.

Goldston, D. B. (2003). *Measuring suicidal behavior and risk in children and adolescents.* Washington, DC: American Psychological Association.

Goss, R. E., & Klass, D. (1997). Tibetan Buddhism and the resolution of grief: The Bardo-thodo for the dying and the grieving. *Death Studies, 21,* 377-395.

Gould, M. S. (1990). Suicide clusters and media exposure. In S. J. Blumenthal & D. J. Kupfer (Eds.), *Suicide over the life cycle: Risk factors, assessment, and treatment of suicidal patients* (pp. 517-532). Washington, DC: American Psychiatric Association.

Greaney, S. (1995). *Psychologists behaviors and attitudes when working with the non-hospitalized suicidal patient.* Unpublished doctoral dissertation, Pacific Graduate School of Psychology, Palo Alto, CA.

Greene, B. (1994). Lesbian women of color: Triple jeopardy. In L. Comas-Diaz (Ed.), *Women of color: Integrating ethnic and gender identities in psychotherapy* (pp. 389-427). New York: Guilford Press.

Greene, B. (1997). Ethnic minority lesbians and gay men: Mental health and treatment issues. In B. Greene (Ed.), *Ethnic and cultural diversity among lesbians and gay men* (pp. 216-239). Thousand Oaks, CA: Sage Publications.

Greening, L., & Stoppelbein, L. (2002). Religiosity, attributional style, and social support as psychological buffers for African American and White adolescents' perceived risk for suicide. *Suicide and Life-Threatening Behavior, 32,* 404-417.

Grieger, I., & Ponterotto, J. G. (1995). A framework for assessment in multicultural counseling. In J. G. Ponterotto & J. M. Casas (Eds.), *Handbook of multicultural counseling* (pp. 357-374). Thousand Oaks, CA: Sage Publications.

Griffith, E. E., & Bell, C. C. (1989). Recent trends in suicide and homicide among blacks. *Journal of the American Medical Association, 262,* 2265-2269.

Griffith, J. E. (1985). Social support providers: Who are they? Where are they met?—and the relationship of network characteristics to psychological distress. *Basic and Applied Social Psychology, 6,* 41-60.

Griffith, J. E., & Villavicencio, S. (1985). Relationships among acculturation, sociodemographic characteristics and social supports in Mexican American adults. *Hispanic Journal of Behavioral Sciences, 7,* 75-92.

Grossman, D. C., Milligan, B. C., & Deyo, R. A. (1991). Risk factors for suicide attempts among Navajo adolescents. *American Journal of Public Health, 81,* 870-874.

Groth-Marnat, G. (1992). Buddhism and mental health: A comparative analysis. In J. F. Schumaker (Ed.), *Religion and mental health* (pp. 270-280). London: Oxford University Press.

Guarnero, P. A. (2001). Shadows and whispers: Latino gay men living in multiple worlds. *Dissertation Abstracts International, 61,* 11-B, 5796.

Gunnar, A., Guest, A., Immerwahr, G., & Spittel, M. (1998). Joblessness, family disruption, and violent death in Chicago, 1970-1990. *Social Forces, 76,* 1465-1494.

Gutierrez, P. M., Rodriguez, P. J., & Garcia, P. (2001). Suicide risk factors for young adults. *Death Studies, 25,* 319-340.

Haddad, Y., & Lummis, A. (1987). *Islamic values in the United States: A comparative study.* London: Oxford University Press.

Hahn, N. J. (1989). *The study of the contemporary Korean family.* Seoul, Korea: Il Ji Sa.

Hall, D. A. (1997). Self-concept and multiple reference group identity structure in lesbians in black-african descent. *Dissertation Abstracts International: Section B: The Sciences and Engineering, 58*(5-B), 2718.

Hall, G. C. N., & Barongan, C. (2002). *Multicultural psychology.* Upper Saddle River, NJ: Prentice Hall.

Hall, M. (1991). Ex-therapy to sex-therapy: Notes from the margins. In C. Silverstein (Ed.), *Gays, lesbians, and their therapists: Studies in psychotherapy.* New York: W. W. Norton and Co.

Halstead, J. M., & Lewicka, K. (1998). Should homosexuality be taught as an acceptable alternative lifestyle? A Muslim perspective. *Cambridge Journal of Education, 28,* 49-64.

Harris, M., Velasquez, R. J., White, J, & Renteria, T. (2004). Folk healing and curanderismo within the contemporary Chicana/o community. In R. J. Velasquez, L. M. Arellano, & B. W. McNeill (Eds.), *The handbook of Chicana/o psychology and mental health* (pp. 111-125). Mahwah, NJ: Lawrence Erlbaum Associates.

Hayes, C. L., & Kalish, R. A. (1987-1988). Death-related experiences and funerary practices of the Hmong refugee in the United States. *Journal of Death and Dying, 18,* 63-70.

Heacock, D. R. (1990). Suicidal behavior in black and Hispanic youth. *Psychiatric Annals, 20,* 134-142.

Helminiak, D. A. (2000). *What the Bible really says about homosexuality.* New Mexico: Alamo Square Press.

Helms, J. E. (1990). *Black and white racial identity: Theory, research, and practice.* New York and England: Greenwood Press.

Helms, J. E. (1995). An update of Helms's white and people of color racial identity models. In J. G. Ponterotto, J. M. Casas, L. A. Suzuki, & C. M. Alexander (Eds.), *Handbook of multicultural counseling* (pp. 181-198). Thousand Oaks, CA: Sage Publications.

Henriksson, M. M., Aro, H. M., & Marttunen, M. J. (1993). Mental disorders and comorbidity in suicide. *American Journal of Psychiatry, 150,* 935-940.

Herek, G. M., & Berrill, K. T. (1992). *Hate crimes: Confronting violence against lesbians and gay men.* Thousand Oaks, CA: Sage Publications.

Heron, R. L., Twomey, H. B., Jacobs, D. P., & Kaslow, N. J. (1997). Culturally competent interventions for abused and suicidal African American women. *Psychotherapy: Theory, Research, Practice, Training:* [Special Issue] Psychotherapy: Violence and the family, *34,* 410-424.

Hetzel, S., Winn, V., & Tolstoshev, H. (1991). Loss and change: New directions in death education for adolescents. *Journal of Adolescence, 14,* 323-334.

Hewitt, P. L., Newton, J., Flett, G. L., & Callander, L. (1997). Perfectionism and suicide ideation in adolescent psychiatric patients. *Journal of Abnormal Child Psychology, 25,* 95-101.

Hickman, L. C. (1984). Descriptive differences between black and white suicide attempters. *Issues in Mental Health Nursing, 6,* 293-310.

Hinsch, B. (1990). *Passions of the cut sleeve: The male homosexual tradition in China.* Berkeley: University of California Press.

Hirayama, K. K. (1990). Death and dying in Japanese culture. In J. K. Parry (Ed.), *Social work practice with the terminally ill: A transcultural perspective* (pp. 159-174). Springfield, IL and England: Charles C. Thomas.

Hlady, W. G., & Middaugh, J. P. (1988). The understanding of suicides in state and national records, Alaska, 1983–1984. *Suicide and Life-Threatening Behavior, 18,* 237-244.

Holinger, P. C., Offer, D., Barter, J. T., & Bell, C. C. (1994). *Suicide and homicide among adolescents.* New York: Guilford Press.

Hovey, J. D., & King, C. A. (1997). Suicidality among acculturating Mexican Americans: Current knowledge and directions for research. *Suicide and Life-Threatening Behavior, 27,* 92-103.

Howard-Pitney, B., LaFromboise, T. D., Basil, M., September, B., & Johnson, D. (1992). Psychological and social indicators of suicide ideation and suicide attempts in Zuni adolescents. *Journal of Consulting and Clinical Psychology, 60,* 473-476.

Hunter, J. (1990). Violence against lesbian and gay male youths. *Journal of Interpersonal Violence:* [Special Issue] Violence against lesbians and gay men: Issues for research, practice, and policy, *5,* 295-300.

Hunter, J. (1992). Violence against lesbians and gay male youths. In G. M. Herek & K. T. Berrill (Eds.), *Hate crimes: Confronting violence against lesbians and gay men* (pp. 76-82). Thousand Oaks, CA: Sage Publications.

Ialongo, N., McCreary, B. K., Pearson, J. L., Koenig, A. L., Wagner, B. M., Schmidt, N. B., Poduska, J., & Kellam, S. G. (2002). Suicidal behavior among urban, African American young adults. *Suicide and Life-Threatening Behavior, 32,* 256-271.

Icard, L. (1985-1986). Black gay men and conflicting social identities: Sexual orientation versus racial identity [Special Issue]. *Journal of Social Work and Human Sexuality, 4,* 83-93.

Icard, L. D. (1996). Assessing the psychological well-being of African American gays: A multidimensional perspective. In J. F. Longres (Ed.)., *Men of color: A context for service to homosexually active men* (pp. 25-49). New York: Harrington Park Press.

Ivey, G. (1999). Transference-counter-transference constellations and enactments in the psychotherapy of destructive narcissism. *British Journal of Medical Psychology, 72,* 63-74.

Jacobs, D. G. (Ed.) (1999). *Harvard Medical School guide to suicide assessment and intervention.* San Francisco: Jossey-Bass.

Joe, S., & Kaplan, M. S. (2001). Suicide among African American men. *Suicide and Life-Threatening Behavior, 31,* 106-121.

Joe, S., & Marcus, S. C. (2003). Datapoints: Trends by race and gender in suicide attempts among U.S. adolescents, 1991-2001. *Psychiatric Services, 54,* 454.

Johnson, D. (1994). Stress, depression, substance abuse, and racism. *Native American and Alaska Native Mental Health Research, 6,* 29-33.

Jones, J. M. (1991). Psychological models of race: What have they been and what should they be? In J. D. Goodchilds (Ed.), *Psychological perspectives on human diversity in America* (pp. 7-46). Washington, DC: American Psychological Association.

Juon, H., Nam, J. A., & Ensminger, M. E. (1994). Epidemiology of suicidal behavior among Korean adolescents. *Journal of Child Psychology and Psychiatry and Allied Disciplines, 35,* 663-676.

Kachur, S. P., Potter, L. B., James, S. P., & Powell, K. E. (1995). *Suicide in the United States, 1980-1992.* Atlanta: Centers for Disease Control and Prevention, National Center of Injury Prevention.

Kalafat, J., & Elias, M. J. (1995). Suicide prevention in an educational context: Broad and narrow foci [Special Issue]. *Suicide and Life-Threatening Behavior, 25,* 123-133.

Kalish, R. A. (1968). Suicide: An ethnic comparison in Hawaii. *Bulletin of Suicidology,* December, 37-43.

Kalish, R. A. (1980). *Death, grief, and caring relationships.* Monterey, CA: Brooks Cole.

Kaslow, N. J., Reviere, S. L., Chance, S. E., Rogers, J. H., Hatcher, C. A., Wasserman, F., Smith, L., Jessee, S., James, M. E., & Seelig, B. (1998). An empirical study of the psychodynamics of suicide. *Journal of the American Psychoanalytic Association, 46,* 777-796.

Kaslow, N. J., Thompson, M. P., Brooks, A. E., & Twomey, H. B. (2000). Ratings of family functioning of suicidal and nonsuicidal African American women. *Journal of Family Psychology, 14,* 585-599.

Kaslow, N. J., Webb-Price, A., Wyckoff, S., Grall, M. B., Sherry, A., Young, S., Scholl, L., Upshaw, V. M., Rashid, A., Jackson, E. B., & Bethea, K. (2004). Person factors associated with suicidal behavior among African American women and men. *Cultural Diversity and Ethnic Minority Psychology, 10,* 5-22.

Kelleher, M. J., Chambers, D., Corcoran, P., Williamson, E., & Keeley, H. S. (1998). Religious sanctions and rates of suicide worldwide. *Crisis, 19,* 78-86.

Keller, R. R. (2000). Religious diversity in North America. In P. S. Richards & A. E. Bergin, (Eds.), *Handbook of psychotherapy and religious diversity* (pp. 27-55). Washington, DC: American Psychological Association.

Kelly, D. L., Shim, J. C., Feldman, S. M., Yu, Y., & Conley, R. R. (2004). Lifetime psychiatric symptoms in persons with schizophrenia who died by suicide compared to other means of death. *Journal of Psychiatric Research, 38,* 531-536.

Kennedy, G. J., & Tanenbaum, S. (2000). Suicide and aging: International perspectives. *Psychiatric Quarterly, 71,* 345-362.

Kerkhof, A. J., & Bernasco, W. (1990). Suicidal behavior in jails and prisons in The Netherlands: Incidence, characteristics, and prevention. *Suicide and Life-Threatening Behavior, 20,* 123-137.

Kerwin, C., & Ponterotto, J. G. (1995). Biracial identity development: Theory and research. In J. G. Ponterotto & J. M. Casas (Eds.), *Handbook of multicultural counseling* (pp. 199-217). Thousand Oaks, CA: Sage Publications.

Kettl, P., & Bixler, E. O. (1991). Suicide in Alaska Natives, 1979-1984. *Psychiatry: Journal for the Study of Interpersonal Processes, 54,* 55-63.

Kettl, P., & Bixler, E. O. (1993). Alcohol and suicide in Alaska Natives. *Native American and Alaska Native Mental Health Research, 5,* 34-45.

Khan, A., Leventhal, R. M., Khan, S., & Brown, W. A. (2002). Suicide risk in patients with anxiety disorders: A meta-analysis of the FDA database. *Journal of Affective Disorders, 68,* 183-190.

Kimmel, D. C. (1993). Adult development and aging: A gay perspective. In L. D. Garnets & D. C. Kimmel (Eds.), *Psychological perspectives on lesbian and gay male experiences*. New York: Columbia University Press.

King, C. A., Hovey, J. D., Brand, E., Wilson, R., & Ghaziuddin, N. (1997). Suicidal adolescents after hospitalization: Parent and family impacts on treatment follow-through. *Journal of the American Academy of Child and Adolescent Psychiatry, 36*, 85-93.

Kirk, A. R., & Zucker, R. A. (1979). Some sociopsychological factors in attempted suicide among urban black males. *Suicide and Life-Threatening Behavior, 9*, 76-86.

Koenig, A. L., Ialongo, N., & Wagner, B. M. (2002). Negative caregiver strategies and psychopathology in urban, African American young adults. *Child Abuse and Neglect, 26*, 1211-1233.

Kok, Lee-peng (1988). Race, religion and female suicide attempters in Singapore. *Social Psychiatry and Psychiatric Epidemiology, 23*, 236-239.

Kourany, R. F. (1987). Suicide among homosexual adolescents. *Journal of Homosexuality, 13*, 111-117.

Kral, M. J., & Sakinofsky, I. (1994). A clinical model for suicide risk assessment. In A. A. Leenaars, & J. T. Maltsberger (Eds.), *Treatment of suicidal people* (pp. 19-31). Philadelphia, PA: Taylor and Francis.

Krug, E. G., Dahlberg, L. L., Mercy, J. A., Zwi, A., & Lozano, R. (Eds.) (2002). *World Report on Violence and Health*. Geneva, Switzerland: World Health Organization.

Kurz, A., Moller, H. J., Baindl, G., Burk, F., Torhorst, A., Wachtler, C., & Lauter, H. (1987). Classification of parasuicide by cluster analysis: Types of suicidal behavior, therapeutic, and prognostic implications. *British Journal of Psychiatry, 150*, 520-525.

Kushner, H. I. (1995). Women and suicidal behavior: Epidemiology, gender and lethality in historical perspective. In S. S. Canetto and D. Lester (Eds.), *Women and suicidal behavior* (pp. 11-34). New York: Springer Publishing.

LaFleur, N. K., Rowe, W., & Leach, M. M. (2002). Reconceptualizing white racial consciousness. *Journal of Multicultural Counseling and Development, 30*, 148-152.

LaFromboise, T. D., & Bigfoot, D. S. (1988). Cultural and cognitive considerations in the prevention of Native American adolescent suicide. *Journal of Adolescence, 11*, 139-153.

LaFromboise, T. D., & Howard-Pitney, B. (1994). The Zuni Life Skills Development curriculum: A collaborative approach to curriculum development. *American Indian and Alaska Native Mental Health Research, 4*, 98-121.

Lambert, M. T., & Fowler, D. R. (1997). Suicide risk factors among veterans: Risk management in the changing culture of the Department of Veterans Affairs. *Journal of Mental Health Administration, 24*, 350-358.

Lamke, L. K. (1982a). The impact of sex-role orientation on self-esteem in early adolescence. *Child Development, 53*, 1530-1535.

Lamke, L. K. (1982b). Adjustment and sex-role orientation in adolescence. *Journal of Youth and Adolescence, 11*, 247-259.

Lamm, M. (1969). *The Jewish way in death and mourning.* Middle Village, NY: Jonathan David Publishers, Inc.

Lang, L. T. (1990). Aspects of the Cambodian death and dying process. In J. K. Parry (Ed.), *Social work practice with the terminally ill: A transcultural perspective* (pp. 205-221). Springfield, IL: Charles C Thomas Publisher, Ltd.

Laungani, P. (1997). Death in a Hindu family. In C. M. Parkes, P. Laungani, & B. Young (Eds.), *Death and bereavement across cultures* (pp. 52-72). New York: Routledge.

Leach, M. M., & Carlton, M. A. (1997). Toward defining a multicultural training philosophy. In D. B. Pope-Davis & H. L. K. Coleman (Eds.), *Multicultural counseling competencies: Assessment, education and training, and supervision* (pp. 184-208). Thousand Oaks, CA: Sage Publications.

Leach, M. M., Levy, J., Denton, L., & Owens, S. (April 2004). *Pickin' and choosin' religious beliefs to justify social attitudes.* Paper presented at the annual Division 36 conference of the American Psychological Association, Baltimore, MD.

Leach, M. M., & Sullivan, A. (2001). The intersection of race, class, and gender on diagnosis. In D. B. Pope-Davis & H. L. K. Coleman (Eds.), *The intersection of race, class, and gender in multicultural counseling.* Thousand Oaks, CA: Sage Publications.

Leenaars, A. A. (1994). Crisis intervention with highly lethal suicidal people. In A. A. Leenaars, J. T. Maltsberger, & R. A. Neimeyer (Eds.), *Treatment of suicidal people* (pp. 45-59). Philadelphia: Taylor and Francis.

Leenaars, A. A. (1999). Rational suicide: A psychological perspective. In J. L. Jr. Werth (Ed.), Contemporary perspectives on rational suicide (pp. 135-141). Philadelphia, PA: Brunner/Mazel, Inc.

Leenaars, A. A., Maltsberger, J. T., & Neimeyer, R.A. (Eds.) (1994). *Treatment of suicidal people.* Washington, DC: Taylor and Francis.

Lester, D. (1990). The regional variation of suicide by different methods: A problem for Durkheim's theory of suicide. *Crisis, 11*, 32-37.

Lester, D. (1990-1991). Mortality from suicide and homicide for African Americans in the USA: A regional analysis. *Omega: Journal of Death and Dying, 22*, 219-226.

Lester, D. (1994a). Challanges in preventing suicide. *Death Studies, 18*, 623-639.

Lester, D. (1994b). Differences in the epidemiology of suicide in Asian Americans by nation of origin. *Omega: Journal of Death and Dying, 29*, 89-93.

Lester, D. (1994c). Psychotherapy for suicidal clients. *Death Studies:* [Special Issue] Suicide assessment and intervention, *18*, 361-374.

Lester, D. (1994d). Suicide rates in Native Americans by state and size of population. *Perceptual and Motor Skills, 78*, 954.

Lester, D. (1997a). Suicide in America: A nation of immigrants. *Suicide and Life-Threatening Behavior:* [Special issue] Suicide: Individual, cultural, international perspectives, *27*, 50-59.

Lester, D. (1997b). Suicide in an international perspective. *Suicide and Life-Threatening Behavior, 27*, 104-111.

Lester, D. (1998). *Suicide in African Americans.* Commack, NY: Nova Science Publishers.

Lester, D. (2001). *Suicide in American Indians.* Hauppauge, NY: Nova Science Publishers.

Levine, E. (1998). Jewish views and customs on death. In C. M. Parkes, P. Laungani, & B. Young (Eds.), *Death and bereavement across cultures* (pp. 98-130). New York: Routledge.

Levy, J. E., & Kunitz, S. J. (1987). A suicide prevention program for Hopi youth. *Social Science & Medicine, 25*, 931-940.

Lewinsohn, P. M., Rhode, P., & Seeley, J. R. (1996). Adolescent suicidal ideation and attempts: Prevalence, risk factors, and clinical implications. *Clinical Psychology: Science and Practice, 3*, 25-46.

Links, P. S., Gould, B., & Ratnayake, R. (2003). Assessing suicidal youth with antisocial, borderline, or narcissistic personality disorders. *Canadian Journal of Psychiatry, 48*, 301-310.

Lipschitz, A. (1995). Suicide prevention in young adults (age 18-30). In M. M. Silverman & R. W. Maris (Eds.), *Suicide prevention: Toward the year 2000* (pp. 155-170). New York: Guilford Press.

Lipschitz, D. S., Bernstein, D. P., & Winegar, R. K. (1999). Hospitalized adolescents' reports of sexual and physical abuse: A comparison of two self-report measures. *Journal of Traumatic Stress, 12*, 641-654.

Liu, W. T., & Lu, E. (1985). Asian/Pacific American elderly. Mortality differentials, health status, and use of services. *Journal of Applied Gerontology, 4*, 35-64.

Liu, W. T., Yu, E. E. H., Chang, C. F., & Fernandez, M. (1990). The mental health of Asian American teenagers: A research challenge. In A. Rubin & L. Davis (Eds.), *Ethnic issues in adolescent mental health* (pp. 92-112). Thousand Oaks, CA: Sage Publications.

Llorente, M. D., Eisdorfer, C., Loewenstein, D. A., & Zarate, Y. A. (1996). Suicide among Hispanic elderly: Cuban Americans in Dade County, Florida 1990-1993. *Journal of Mental Health and Aging, 2*, 79-87.

Loiacano, D. K. (1993). Gay identity issues among Black Americans: Racism, homophobia, and the need for validation. In L. D. Garnets & D. C. Kimmel (Eds.), *Psychological perspectives on lesbian and gay male experiences* (pp. 364-375). New York: Columbia University Press.

Lopez, S. J., Snyder, C. R., & Pedrotti, J. T. (2003). Hope: Many definitions, many measures. In S. J. Lopez & C. R. Snyder (Eds.), *Positive psychological assessment: A handbook of models and measures* (pp. 91-106). Washington, DC: American Psychological Association.

LoPresto, C. T., Sherman, M. F., & DiCarlo, M. A. (1994-1995). Factors affecting the unacceptability of suicide and the effects of evaluator depression and religiosity. *Omega: Journal of Death and Dying, 30*, 205-221.

Madsen, T. G. (1992). Distinctions in the Mormon approach to death and dying. In S. J. Palmer (Ed.), *Deity and death* (pp. 61-74). Provo, Utah: BYU Religious Studies Center.

Manalansan, IV, M. F. (1990). *Tolerance or struggle: Male homosexuality in the Philippines today.* Paper presented at the American Anthropological Association Annual Meeting, New Orleans, LA.

Marion, M. S., & Range, L. M. (2003a). African American college women's suicide buffers. *Suicide and Life-Threatening Behavior, 33*, 33-43.

Marion, M. S., & Range, L. M. (2003b). Do extenuating circumstances influence African American women's attitudes toward suicide? *Suicide and Life-Threatening Behavior, 33*, 44-51.

Maris, R. M. (1981). *Pathways to suicide: A survey of self-destructive behaviors.* Baltimore: Johns Hopkins University Press.

Maris, R. W. (1969). *Social forces in urban suicide.* Homewood, IL: Dorsey Press.

Maris, R. W., Berman, A. L., & Silverman, A. L. (2000). *Comprehensive textbook of suicidology.* New York, NY: Guilford Press.

Marrero, D. N. (1998). Suicide attempts among Puerto Ricans of low socioeconomic status. *Dissertation Abstracts International, 58*, 7-B, 3929.

Martin, W. T. (1984). Religiosity and United States suicide rates, 1972-1978. *Journal of Clinical Psychology, 40*, 1166-1169.

Marzuk, P. M., & Mann, J. J. (1988). Suicide and substance abuse. *Psychiatric Annals: [Special Issue] Suicide, 18*, 639-645.

Marzuk, P. M., Tardiff, K., & Leon, A. C. (1992). Prevalence of cocaine use among residents of New York City who committed suicide during a one-year period. *American Journal of Psychiatry, 149*, 371-375.

May, P. A. (1990). A bibliography on suicide and suicide attempts among American Indian and Alaska natives. *Omega: Journal of Death & Dying, 21*, 199-214.

May, P. A., Van Winkle, N. W., Williams, M. B., McFeeley, P. J., DeBruyn, L. M., Serna, P. (2002). Alcohol and suicide death among American Indians of New Mexico: 1980-1998. *Suicide and Life-Threatening Behavior, 32*, 240-255.

McBee, S. M., & Rogers, J. R. (1997). Identifying risk factors for gay and lesbian suicidal behavior: Implications for mental health counselors. *Journal of Mental Health Counseling, 19*, 143-155.

McBee-Strayer, S. M., & Rogers, J. R. (2002). Student award paper: Lesbian, gay, and bisexual suicidal behavior: Testing a constructivist model. *Suicide and Life-Threatening Behavior, 32*, 272-283.

McDaniel, J. S., Purcell, D., & D'Augelli, A. R. (2001). The relationship between sexual orientation and risk for suicide: Research findings and future directions for research and prevention. *Suicide and Life-Threatening Behavior, 31*, 84-105.

McKenzie, K., Serfaty, M., & Crawford, M. (2003). Suicide in ethnic minority groups. *British Journal of Psychiatry, 183*, 100-101.

Melton, J. G. (1996). *Encyclopedia of American religions.* Detroit, MI: Gale Research.

Mena, F. J., Padilla, A. M., & Maldonado, M. (1987). Acculturative stress and specific coping strategies among immigrant and later generation college students. *Hispanic Journal of Behavioral Sciences, 9,* 207-225.

Middlebrook, D. L., LeMaster, P. L., Beals, J., Novins, D. K., & Manson, S. M. (2001). Suicide prevention in Native American and Alaska Native communities: A critical review of programs. *Suicide and Life-Threatening Behavior, 31,* 132-149.

Miller, L., & Lovinger, R. J. (2000). Psychotherapy with conservative and reform Jews. In P. S. Richards & A. E. Bergin (Eds.), *Handbook of psychotherapy and religious diversity* (pp. 259-286). Washington, DC: American Psychological Association.

Miller, M. (1985). *Information center: Training workshop manual.* San Diego: The Information Center.

Mirowsky, J., & Ross, C. E. (1984). Mexican culture and its emotional contradictions. *Journal of Health and Social Behavior, 25,* 2-13.

Mishara, B. L. (1999). Conceptions of death and suicide in children ages 6-12 and their implications for suicide prevention. *Suicide and Life-Threatening Behavior, 29,* 105-118.

Montgomery, S. A., Montgomery, D. B., Green, M., Bullock, T., & Baldwin, D. (1992). Pharmacotherapy in the prevention of suicidal behavior. *Journal of Clinical Psychopharmacology, 12,* 27S-31S.

Moscicki, E. K. (1995). Epidemiology of suicidal behavior. *Suicide and Life-Threatening Behavior:* [Special Issue] Suicide prevention: Toward the year 2000, *25,* 22-25.

Muehrer, P. (1995). Suicide and sexual orientation: A critical summary of recent research and directions for future research. *Suicide and Life-Threatening Behavior, 25*(Suppl), 72-81.

Murphy, S. L. (2000). Deaths: Final data for 1998. *National Vital Statistics Report, 48*(11). Hyattsville, MD: National Center for Health Statistics. DHHS Publication No. (PHS) 2000-1120.

Nakajima, G. A., Chan, Y. H., & Lee, K. (1996). Mental health issues for gay and lesbian Asian-Americans. In R. P. Cabaj & T. S. Stein (Eds.), *Textbook of homosexuality and mental health* (pp. 563-581). Washington, DC: American Psychiatric Association.

National Center for Injury Prevention and Control (1999). Center for Disease Control. Retrieved from http://www.cdc.gov/ncipc/default.htm.

National Center for Injury Prevention and Control (2000). Center for Disease Control. Retrieved from http://www.cdc.gov/ncipc/default.htm.

Neeleman, J., Wessley, S., & Lewis, G. (1998). Suicide acceptability in African and White Americans: The role of religion. *Journal of Nervous and Mental Disease, 186,* 12-16.

Negy, C., & Eisenman, R. (2005). A comparison of African American and White college students' reactions to lesbian, gay, and bisexual individuals: An exploratory study. *Journal of Sex Research, 42,* 291-298.

Nelson, S. H., McCoy, G. F., Stetter, M., & Vanderwagen, W. C. (1992). An overview of mental health services for Native Americans and Alaska natives in the 1990s. *Hospital and Community Psychiatry, 43,* 257-261.

Ng, B. (1996). Characteristics of 61 Mexican American adolescents who attempted suicide. *Hispanic Journal of Behavioral Sciences, 18,* 3-12.

Nisbet, P. A. (1996). Protective factors for suicidal black females. *Suicide and Life-Threatening Behavior, 26,* 325-341.

Nisbet, P. A., Duberstein, P. R., Cornwell, Y., & Seidlitz, L. (2000). The effect of participation in religious activities on suicide versus natural death in adults 50 and older. *Journal of Nervous and Mental Disease, 188,* 543-546.

Norris, W. P. (1992). Liberal attitude and homophobic acts: The paradoxes of homosexual experience in a liberal institution. *Journal of Homosexuality, 22,* 81-120.

Novins, D. K., Beals, J., Roberts, R. E., & Manson, S. M. (1999). Factors associated with suicide ideation among Native American adolescents: Does culture matter? *Suicide and Life-Threatening Behavior, 29,* 332-346.

O'Donnell, L., Stueve, A., Wardlaw, D., & O'Donnell, C. (2003). Adolescent suicidality and adult support: The Reach for Health study of urban youth. *American Journal of Health Behavior, 27,* 633-644.

Ohberg, A., Vuori, E., Ojanpera, I., & Loennqvist, J. (1996). Alcohol and drugs in suicides. *British Journal of Psychiatry, 169,* 75-80.

Oquendo, M. A., Ellis, S. P., Greenwald, S., Malone, K. M., Weissman, M. M., & Mann, J. J. (2001). Ethnic and sex differences in suicide rates relative to major depression in the United States. *American Journal of Psychiatry, 158,* 1652-1658.

Ossana, S. M., Helms, J. E., & Leonard, J. E. (1992). Do 'womanist' identity attitudes influence college women's self-esteem and perceptions of environmental bias? *Journal of Counseling & Development, 70,* 402-408.

Padilla, A. M., Alvarez, M., & Lindholm, K. J. (1986). Generational status and personality factors as predictors of stress in students. *Hispanic Journal of Behavioral Sciences, 8,* 275-288.

Padilla, A. M., Wagatsuma, Y., & Lindholm, K. J. (1985). Acculturation and personality as predictors of stress in Japanese and Japanese-Americans. *Journal of Social Psychology, 125,* 295-305.

Paniagua, F. A. (1998). *Assessing and treating culturally diverse clients: A practical guide* (2nd ed.). Thousand Oaks, CA: Sage Publications.

Pastore, D. R., Fisher, M., & Friedman, S. B. (1996). Violence and mental health problems among urban high school students. *Journal of Adolescent Health, 18,* 320-324.

Peterson, L. G., & Bongar, B. (1989). The suicidal patient. In A. Lazare (ed.), *Outpatient psychiatry: diagnosis and treatment* (2nd ed., pp. 569-584). Baltimore: Williams & Wilkins.

Phillips, D. P., & Ruth, T. E. (1993). Adequacy of official suicide statistics for scientific research and public policy. *Suicide and Life-Threatening Behavior, 23,* 307-319.

Phinney, J. S. (1996). Understanding ethnic diversity: The role of ethnic identity. *American Behavioral Scientist, 40,* 143-152.

Ponterotto, J. G., Fuertes, J. N., & Chen, E. C. (2000). Models of multicultural counseling. In S. D. Brown & R. W. Lent (Eds.), *Handbook of counseling psychology* (3rd ed.) (pp. 639-669). New York: John Wiley.

Prochaska, J. O., & DiClemente, C. C. (1992). The transtheoretical approach. In J. C. Norcross & M. R. Goldfried (Eds.), *Handbook of psychotherapy intergration* (pp. 300-334). New York: Basic Books.

Queralt, M. (1984). Understanding Cuban immigrants: A cultural perspective. *Social Work, 29,* 115-121.

Rabinowitz, A. (2000). Psychotherapy with Orthodox Jews. In P. S. Richards & A. E. Bergin (Eds.), *Handbook of psychotherapy and religious diversity* (pp. 237-258). Washington, DC: American Psychological Association.

Radomsky, E. D., Haas, G. L., Mann, J. J., & Sweeney, J. A. (1999). Suicidal behavior in patients with schizophrenia and other psychotic disorders. *American Journal of Psychiatry, 156,* 1590-1595.

Radov, C. G., Masnick, B. R., & Hauser, B. B. (1977). Issues in feminist therapy: The work of a women's study group. *Social Work, 22,* 507-509.

Range, L. M., Leach, M. M., & McIntyre, D. (1999). Multicultural perspectives on suicide. *Aggression and Violent Behavior, 4,* 413-430.

Rasmussen, K. M., Negy, C., Carlson, R., & Burns, J. M. (1997). Suicide ideation and acculturation among low socioeconomic status Mexican American adolescents. *Journal of Early Adolescence, 17,* 390-407.

Rawlings, S. W. (1995). Households and families. *U.S. Census Bureau.* Washington, DC.

Remafedi, G. (1987). Male homosexuality: The adolescent's perspective. *Pediatrics, 79,* 326-330.

Remafedi, G., Farrow, J. A., & Deisher, R. W. (1993). Risk factors for attempted suicide in gay and bisexual youth. In L. D. Garnets & D. C. Kimmel (Eds.), *Psychological perspectives on lesbian and gay male experiences* (pp. 486-499). New York: Columbia University Press.

Resnick, H. L. P. (1980). Suicide. In H. I. Kaplan & B. J. Sadock (Eds.), *Comprehensive textbook of psychiatry* (3rd ed.). Baltimore: Williams and Wilkins.

Rew, L., Thomas, N., Horner, S. D., Resnick, M. D., & Beuhring, T. (2001). Correlates of recent suicide attempts in a triethnic group of adolescents. *Journal of Nursing Scholarships, 33,* 361-367.

Reynolds, A. L., & Pope, R. L. (1991). The complexities of diversity: Exploring multiple oppressions. *Journal of Counseling and Development, 70,* 174-180.

Rich, C. L., & Runeson, B. S. (1992). Similarities in diagnostic comorbidity between suicide among young people in Sweden and the United States. *Acta Psychiatrica Scandinavica, 86,* 335-339.

Richards, P. S., & Bergin, A. E. (2000). *Handbook of psychotherapy and religious diversity.* Washington, DC: American Psychological Association.

Ritter, D. R. (1990). Adolescent suicide: Social competence and problem behavior of youth at high risk and low risk for suicide. *School Psychology Review, 19,* 83-95.

Robinson, T. L. (1999). The intersections of dominant discourses across race, gender, and other identities, *Journal of Counseling and Development, 77,* 73-79.

Rodriguez, F. I. (1996). Understanding Filipino male homosexuality: Implications for social services. In J. F. Longres (Ed.), *Men of color: A context for service to homosexually active men* (pp. 93-113). New York: Harrington Park Press.

Rogers, J. R. (1992). Suicide and alcohol: Conceptualizing the relationship from a cognitive-social paradigm. *Journal of Counseling and Development, 70,* 540-543.

Rogers, J. R., Alexander, R. A., & Subich, L. M. (1994). Development and psychometric analysis of the Suicide Assessment Checklist. *Journal of Mental Health Counseling, 16,* 352-368.

Rose, D. T., & Abramson, L. Y. (1992). Developmental predictors of depressive cognitive style: Research and theory. In C. Cicchetti & S. L. Toth (Eds.), *Developmental perspectives on depression* (pp. 323-349). Rochester, NY: University of Rochester Press.

Rotheram-Borus, M. J. Hunter, J., & Rosario, M. (1994). Suicidal behavior and gay-related stress among gay and bisexual male adolescents. *Journal of Adolescent Research, 9,* 498-508.

Roy, A. (2003). Distal risk factors for suicidal behavior in alcoholics: Replications and new findings. *Journal of Affective Disorders, 77,* 267-271.

Ryan, A. S. (1985). Cultural factors in casework with Chinese-Americans. *Social Casework, 66,* 333-340.

Saleem, R. (2002). Comparison of suicidal risk factors among Mexican-American and European-American adolescents. *Dissertation Abstracts International, 63,* 5-B, 2601.

Sanchez-Barker, T. N. (2003). Coping with depression: Adpated for use with incarcerated Hispanic youth. *Dissertation Abstracts International: Section B: The Sciences and Engineering, 64,* 5-B, 2403.

Sanyika, A. M. (1995). Distinguishing suicide from parasuicide among African Americans. *Dissertation Abstracts International, 56,* 4-B, 2340.

Sarason, I. G., & Sarason, B. R. (2002). *Abnormal psychology: The problem of maladaptive behavior.* Upper Saddle River, NJ: Prentice Hall.

Saunders, J. M., & Valente, S. M. (1987). Suicide risk among gay men and lesbians: A review. *Death Studies, 11,* 1-23.

Savin-Williams, R. C. (1990). *Gay and lesbian youth: Expressions of identity.* Washington, DC: Hemisphere Publishing.

Savin-Williams, R. C., & Ream, G. L. (2003). Suicide attempts among sexual-minority male youth. *Journal of Clinical Child and Adolescent Psychology, 32,* 509-522.

Saynor, J. K. (1988). Existential and spiritual concerns of people with AIDS. *Journal of Palliative Care:* [Special Issue] AIDS, *4*, 61-65.

Schild, M. (1992). Islam. In A. Schmitt & J. Sofer (Eds.), *Sexuality and eroticism among males in Moslem societies* (pp. 179-188). New York: Harrington Park Press.

Schneider, S. G., Farberow, N. L., & Krucks, G. N. (1989). Suicidal behavior in adolescent and young adult gay men. *Suicide and Life-Threatening Behavior, 19,* 381-394.

Schulte, L. J., & Battle, J. (2004). The relative importance of ethnicity and religion in predicting attitudes towards gays and lesbians. *Journal of Homosexuality, 47,* 127-141.

Schwartz, R. C., & Smith, S. D. (2004). Suicidality and psychosis: The predictive potential of symptomatology and insight into illness. *Journal of Psychiatric Research, 38,* 185-191.

Shaffer, D., Garland, A., Gould, M., Fisher, P., & Trautman, P. D. (1998). Preventing teenage suicide: A critical review. *Journal of the American Academy of Child and Adolescent Psychiatry, 27,* 675-687.

Shaffer, D., Gould, M., & Hicks, R. C. (1994). Worsening suicide rate in black teenagers. *American Journal of Psychiatry, 151,* 1810-1812.

Shiang, J. (1998). Does culture make a difference? Racial/ethnic patterns of completed suicide in San Francisco, CA 1987-1996 and clinical applications. *Suicide and Life-Threatening Behavior, 28,* 338-354.

Shiang, J., Blinn, R., Bonger, B., Stephens, B., Allison, D., & Schatzberg, A. (1997). Suicide in San Francisco, CA: A comparison of Caucasian and Asian groups, 1987-1994. *Suicide and Life-Threatening Behavior, 27,* 80-91.

Shneidman, E. S. (1987). A psychological approach to suicide. In G. R. VandenBos & B. K. Bryant (Eds.), *Cataclysms, crises, and catastrophes: Psychology in action* (pp. 147-183). Washington, DC: American Psychological Association.

Shneidman, E. S. (1989). Overview: A multidimensional approach to suicide. In D. G. Jacobs & H. N. Brown (Eds.), *Suicide: Understanding and responding* (Harvard Medical School Perspectives on suicide, pp 1-30). Madison, CT: International Universities Press.

Shneidman, E. S. (1991). Key psychological factors in understanding and managing suicidal risk. *Journal of Geriatric Psychiatry, 24,* 153-174.

Shneidman, E. S. (1993). *Suicide as psychache: A clinical approach to self-destructive behavior.* Northvale, NJ: Jason Aronson, Inc.

Shneidman, E. S. (1999). Perturbation and lethality: A psychological approach to assessment and intervention. In D.G. Jacobs (Ed.), *The Harvard Medical School guide to suicide assessment and intervention* (pp. 83-97). San Francisco, CA: Jossey-Bass.

Shopshire, J. M. (1990). Sociological perspectives. In J. T. Clemons (Ed.), *Perspectives on suicide* (pp. 22-39). Louisville, KY and England: Westminster and John Knox Press.

Silverman, M. M., & Maris, R. W. (1995). *Suicide prevention: Toward the year 2000.* New York: Guilford Press.

Simonds, J. F., McMahon, T., & Armstrong, D. (1991). Young suicide attempters compared with a control group: Psychological, affective, and attitudinal variables. *Suicide and Life-Threatening Behavior, 21,* 134-151.

Slaby, A. E. (1994). Psychopharmacology of suicide. *Death Studies, 18,* 483-495.

Smith, H. (1991). *The world's religions.* New York: Harper Collins.

Smith, K., & Crawford, S. (1986). Suicidal behavior among "normal" high school students. *Suicide and Life-Threatening Behavior, 16,* 313-325.

Smith, J. C., Mercy, J. A., & Rosenberg, M. L. (1986). Suicide and homicide among Hispanics in the southwest. *Public Health Report, 101,* 265-270.

Smith, J. C., Mercy, J. A., & Warren, C. W. (1985). Comparison of suicides among Europeans and Hispanics in five southwestern states. *Suicide and Life Threatening Behavior, 15,* 14-26.

Snyder, C. J. (2004). Hope and depression: A light in the darkness. *Journal of Social and Clinical Psychology, 23,* 347-351.

Sodowsky, G. R., Kwan, K. K., & Pannu, R. (1995). Ethnic identity of Asians in the United States. In J. G. Ponterotto & J. M. Casas (Eds.), *Handbook of multicultural counseling* (pp. 123-154). Thousand Oaks, CA: Sage Publications.

Sohng, S., & Icard, L. D. (1996). A Korean gay man in the United States: Toward a cultural context for social service. In J. F. Longres (Ed.), *Men of color: A context for service to homosexually active men* (pp. 115-137). New York: Harrington Park Press.

Sommers-Flanagan, J., & Sommers-Flanagan, R. (2002). *Clinical interviewing* (3rd ed.). Hoboken, NJ: John Wiley and Sons.

Sorenson, S. B., & Golding, J. M. (1988a). Prevalence of suicide attempts in a Mexican-American population: Prevention implications of immigration and cultural issues. *Suicide and Life-Threatening Behavior, 18,* 322-333.

Sorenson, S. B., & Golding, J. M. (1988b). Suicide ideation and attempts in Hispanics and non-Hispanic whites: Demographic and psychiatric disorder issues. *Suicide and Life-Threatening Behavior, 18,* 205-218.

Spaights, E., & Simpson, G. (1986). Some unique causes of black suicide. *Psychology: A Journal of Human Behavior, 23,* 1-5.

Spilka, B., Hood, R. W., Jr., Hunsberger, B., & Gorsuch, R. (2003). *The psychology of religion: An empirical approach.* New York: Guilford Press.

Spinelli, M. G. (1999). Prevention of postpartum mood disorders. In L. J. Miller (Ed.), *Postpartum mood disorders* (pp. 217-235). Washington, DC: American Psychiatric Association.

Stack, S. (1980). Religion and suicide: A reanalysis. *Social Psychiatry, 15,* 65-70.

Stack, S. (1983). The effect of religious commitment on suicide: A cross-national analysis. *Journal of Health and Social Behavior, 24,* 362-374.

Stack, S. (1996). The effect of marital integration on African American suicide. *Suicide and Life-Threatening Behavior, 26,* 405-414.

Stack, S. (1998). The relationship between culture and suicide: An analysis of African Americans. *Transcultural Psychiatry, 35,* 253-269.

Stamm, B. H., & Stamm, H. E. (1999). Trauma and loss in native North America: An ethnocultural perspective. In K. Nader & N. Dubrow (Eds.), *Honoring differences: Cultural issues in the treatment of trauma and loss* (pp. 49-75). Philadelphia: Brunner/Mazel.

Sue, D. W., & Sue, D. (2003). *Counseling the culturally diverse: Theory and practice* (4th ed.). New York: John Wiley and Sons, Inc.

Swanson, J. W., Linskey, A. O., Quinter-Salinas, R., Pumariega, A. J., & Holzer, C. E. (1992). A binational school survey of depressive symptoms, drug use, and suicidal ideation. *Journal of the American Academy of Child and Adolescent Psychiatry, 31,* 669-678.

Tafoya, T. (1997). Native gay and lesbian issues: The Two-Spirited. In B. Greene (Ed.), *Ethnic and cultural diversity among lesbians and gay men*: Vol. 3. Psychological perspectives on lesbian and gay issues (pp. 1-10). Thousand Oaks, CA: Sage Publications.

Tafoya, T., & Wirth, D. A. (1996). Native American two-spirit men. In J. F. Longres (Ed.), *Men of color: A context for service to homosexually active men* (pp. 51-67). New York: Harrington Park Press.

Takahashi, Y. (1989). Suicidal Asian patients: Recommendations for treatment. *Suicide and Life-Threatening Behavior, 19,* 305-313.

Tan, M. L. (1995). From bakla to gay: Shifting gender identities and sexual behaviors in the Philippines. In R. G. Parker & J. H. Gagnon (Eds.), *Conceiving sexuality: Approaches to sex research in a postmodern world* (pp. 85-96). Florence, KY: Taylor and Frances/Routledge.

Teague, J. B. (1992). Issues relating to the treatment of adolescent lesbians and homosexuals. *Journal of Mental Health Counseling, 14,* 422-439.

Thompson, M. P., Kaslow, N. J., Lane, D. B., & Kingree, J. B. (2000). Childhood maltreatment, PTSD and suicidal behavior among African American females. *Journal of Interpersonal Violence, 15,* 3-15.

Travis, R. (1984). Suicide and economic development among the Inupiat Eskimo. *White Cloud Journal, 3,* 14-21.

Tremble, B., Schneider, M., & Appathurai, C. (1989). Growing up gay or lesbian in a multicultural context. *Journal of Homosexuality, 17,* 253-267.

Trivino, J. E. (2000). Characteristics of Hispanic Seventh-day Adventist adolescents who attempted suicide. *Dissertation Abstracts International, 60,* 12-B, 6351.

Troiden, R. R. (1979). Becoming homosexual: A model of gay identity acquisition. *Psychiatry: Journal for the Study of Interpersonal Processes, 42,* 363-373.

Truitner, K., & Truitner, N. (1993). Death and dying in Buddhism. In D. P. Irish & K. F. Lundquist (Eds.), *Ethnic variations in dying, death, and grief: Diversity and universality* (pp. 125-136). Philadelphia: Taylor and Francis.

Trujillo, A. (2000). Psychotherapy with Native Americans: A view into the role of religion and spirituality. In P. S. Richards & A. E. Bergin (Eds.), *Handbook of psychotherapy and religious diversity* (pp. 445-466). Washington, DC: American Psychological Association.

Tueth, M. J. (1994). Revisiting fluoxetine (Proxac) and suicidal preoccupations. *Journal of Emergency Medicine, 12,* 685-687.

Ulrich, W. L., Richards, P. S., & Bergin, A. E. (2000). Psychotherapy with Latter-Day Saints. In P. S. Richards & A. E. Bergin (Eds.), *Handbook of psychotherapy and religious diversity* (pp. 185-209). Washington, DC: American Psychological Association.

Vajda, J., & Steinbeck, K. (2000). Factor associated with repeat suicide attempts among adolescents. *Australian and New Zealand Journal of Psychiatry, 34,* 437-445.

Valle, R. (1986). Hispanic social networks and prevention. In R. L. Hough, P. A. Gongla, V. B. Brown, & S. E. Goldston (Eds.), *Psychiatric epidemiology and prevention: The possibilities* (pp. 131-157). UCLA Neuropsychiatric Institute.

Van Winkle, N. W., & May, P. A. (1986). Native American suicide in New Mexico, 1957-1979: A comparative study. *Human Organization, 45,* 296-301.

Van Winkle, N. W., & May, P. A. (1993). An update on Native American suicide in New Mexico, 1980-1987. *Human Organization, 52,* 304-515.

Vega, W. A., Gil, A. G., Warheit, G. J., Apospori, E., & Zimmerman, R. (1993). The relationship of drug use to suicide ideation and attempts among African American, Hispanic, and white non-Hispanic male adolescents. *Suicide and Life-Threatening Behavior, 23,* 110-119.

Vega, W. A., Kolody, B., Aguilar-Gaxiola, S., Alderete, E., Catalano, R., & Caraveo-Anduaga, J. (1998). Lifetime prevalence of DSM-III-R psychiatric disorders among urban and rural Mexican Americans in California. *Archives of General Psychiatry, 55,* 771-778.

von Schulthess, B. (1992). Violence in the streets: Anti-lesbian assault and harassment in San Francisco. In G. M. Herek & K. T. Berrill (Eds.), *Hate crimes: Confronting violence against lesbians and gay men* (pp. 65-75). Thousand Oaks, CA: Sage Publications.

Walker, R. L. (2003). An investigation of acculturative stress and ethnic identification as risk factors for suicidal ideation in African-American vs. European-American men and women: The moderating effects of religiosity and social support. *Dissertation Abstracts International: Section B: The Sciences and Engineering, 63,* 8-B, 3945.

Wasserman, D. (1988). Separation: An important factor in suicidal actions. *Crisis, 9,* 9-63.

Wasserman, I., & Stack, S. (1993). The effect of religion on suicide: An analysis of cultural context. *Omega: Journal of Death & Dying, 27,* 295-305.

Watson, J. L., & Rawski, E. S. (1988). *Death rituals in late imperial and modern China.* Berkeley, CA: University of California Press.

Watt, T. T., & Sharp, S. F. (2002). Race differences in strains associated with suicidal behavior among adolescents. *Youth and Society, 34,* 232-256.

Wells, T. L. (1995). Learned effectiveness: The role of self-efficacy, racial identity and perceptions of racism in the adaptive functioning of African American youth. *Dissertation Abstracts International: Section B: The Sciences and Engineering, 56,* 5-B, 2907.

Westefeld, J. S., & Furr, S. R. (1987). Suicide and depression among college students. *Professional Psychology: Research and Practice, 18,* 119-123.

Westefeld, J. S., Maples, M. R., Buford, B., & Taylor, S. (2001). Gay, lesbian, and bisexual college students: The relationship between sexual orientation and depression, loneliness, and suicide. *Journal of College Student Psychotherapy, 15,* 71-82.

Westefeld, J. S., Range, L. M., Rogers, J.R., Maples, M. R., Bromley, J. L., & Alcorn, J. (2000). Suicide: An overview. *The Counseling Psychologist, 28,* 445-510.

Whitbeck, L. B. (2006). Some guiding assumptions and a theoretical model for developing culturally specific preventions with Native American people. *Journal of Community Psychology, 34,* 183-192.

White, T. W. (1999). *How to identify suicidal people: A systematic approach to risk assessment.* Philadelphia: Charles Press.

Whitehead, P. C., Johnson, F. G., & Ferrence, R. (1973). Measuring the incidence of self-injury: Some methodological and design considerations. *American Journal of Orthopsychiatry, 43,* 142-148.

Wingate, L. R., Bobadilla, L., Burns, A. B., Cukrowicz, K. C., Hernandez, A., Ketterman, R. L. et al. (2005). Suicidality in African American men: The roles of southern residence, religiosity, and social support. *Suicide and Life-Threatening Behavior, 35,* 615-629.

Wooden, W. S., Kawasaki, H., & Mayeda, R. (1983). Lifestyles and identity maintenance among gay Japanese-American males. *Alternative Lifestyles, 5,* 236-243.

Yeung, I., Kong, S. H., & Lee, J. (2000). Attitudes toward organ donation in Hong Kong. *Social Science and Medicine, 50,* 1643-1654.

Yoffie, E. (March 2000). *Same gender officiation.* Resolution adopted at the 111th Convention of the Central Conference of American Rabbis. Greensboro, NC. Retrieved from http://www.uahc.org/yoffie/gender.shtml.

Young, T. J., & French, L. A. (1993). Suicide and social status among Native Americans. *Psychological Reports, 73,* 461-462.

Young, T. J., & French, L. A. (1995). Status integration and suicide among Native American women. *Social Behavior and Personality, 23,* 155-157.

Yuen, N. C., Noelle, C., Nahulu, L. B., Hishinuma, E. S., & Miyamoto, R. H. (2000). Cultural identification and attempted suicide in native Hawaiian adolescents. *Journal of the American Academy of Child and Adolescent Psychiatry, 39,* 360-367.

Zamora-Hernandez, C. E., & Patterson, D. G. (1996). Homosexuality active Latino men: Issues for social work practice. In J. F. Longres (Ed.), *Men of color: A context for service to homosexually active men* (pp. 69-91). New York: Harrington Park Press.

Zayas, L. H. (1989). A retrospective on the "suicidal fit" in mainland Puerto Ricans: Research issues. *Hispanic Journal of the Behavioral Sciences, 11,* 46-57.

Zayas, L. H., & Dyche, L. A. (1995). Suicide attempts in Puerto Rican adolescent females: A sociocultural perspective and family treatment approach. In J. K. Zimmerman & G. M. Asnis (Eds.), *Treatment approaches with suicidal adolescents* (pp. 203-218). Oxford, England: John Wiley and Sons.

Zayas, L. H., Kaplan, C., Turner, S., Romano, K., & Gonzalez-Ramos, G. (2000). Understanding suicide attempts by adolescent Hispanic females. *Social Work, 45,* 53-63.

Zhang, J., & Jin, S. (1996). Determinants of suicide behavior: A comparison of Chinese and American college students. *Adolescence, 31,* 451-467.

Zimmerman, J. K., & Zayas, L. H. (1995). Suicidal adolescent Latinas: Culture, female development, and restoring the mother-daughter relationship. In S. S. Canetto & D. Lester (Eds.), *Women and suicidal behavior* (pp. 120-132). New York: Springer Publishing.

Zinnbauer, B. J., Pargament, K. J., & Scott, A. B. (1999). The emerging meanings of religiousness and spirituality: Problems and prospects. *Journal of Personality, 67,* 889-919.

Zuckerman, M. (1990). Some dubious premises in research and theory on racial differences: Scientific, social, and ethical issues. *American Psychologist, 45,* 1297-1303.

Index

Immersion/emersion status, 44
Impulsiveness, as suicide risk factor, 27-28
India
   caste system, 149-150
   funeral rituals, 149-151
   treatment of widows, 150
Indian Child Welfare Act of 1978, 192
Indians. *See* Native Americans
Insurance, no benefits paid for suicide, 7
Integrated/bicultural individuals, 45
Integrative awareness status, 44
Internal acculturation, 45-46
Internalization status, 44
Interpersonal dynamics, 7
Intervention. *See* Prevention of suicide
Intrapsychic dynamics, 7
Intrinsic religiosity, 63-65
Inwardness, 23
Iscariot, Judas, suicide, 58
Islam
   African Americans, 102-107, 120-121
   afterlife views, 105-106
   Allah, 103-104
   angels, 106-107
   the Hadith, 102-106
   jinns, 107
   lesbianism, 120
   likelihood of suicide, 14
   Muhammad, 102
   Muslim, defined, 103
   paradise, 106
   pillars of faith, 103
   purgatory, 106
   Quran (Koran), 102-108, 121
   suicide views, 103-105
Isolation, as suicide risk factor, 29

Jackson, E. B., 27
Jacobs, D. P., 124
James, M. E., 40
James, S. P., 129

Japanese Americans
   as Asian Americans, 127, 134-135, 156-157
   Buddhism, 130, 148
   death and funerals, 156-157
   euthanasia, 148
   GLBT issues, 140
   suicide rates, 128
   suicide views, 134-135
Jessee, S., 40
Jin, S., 129, 133
Jinns, 107
Joe, S., 96
Johnson, D., 195, 197
Johnson, R. C., 135
Jonah's attempted suicide, 59
Judaism
   afterlife, 70-71
   aninut, 68
   autopsies, 71-72
   avelut, 69
   burial, 68-69, 71-72
   Central Conference on American Rabbis, 89-90
   Conservative, 65, 69
   denominations, 65-66
   European Americans, 65-72
   GLBT views, 88-91
   Kaddish, 69-70
   minyan, 69
   mourning, 67-70
   Orthodox. *See* Orthodox Jews
   rabbinic rulings on autopsies, 72
   rabbinic rulings on causes of death, 67, 68
   Reform, 65, 69, 71, 90-91
   shiva, 68, 69, 72
   shloshim, 69
   suicide beliefs, 66-67
   suicide risk, 25
   Talmud, 66, 71, 89
   Torah, 66, 70, 88-89
   Union of American Hebrew Congregations, 90
   Yahreit, 69
Juon, H., 137

Order a copy of this book with this form or online at:
http://www.haworthpress.com/store/product.asp?sku=5680

CULTURAL DIVERSITY AND SUICIDE
Ethnic, Religious, Gender, and Sexual Orientation Perspectives

_____in hardbound at $49.95 (ISBN-13: 978-0-7890-3018-4; ISBN-10: 0-7890-3018-7)

_____in softbound at $34.95 (ISBN-13: 978-0-7890-3019-1; ISBN-10: 0-7890-3019-5)

241 pages plus index

Or order online and use special offer code HEC25 in the shopping cart.

COST OF BOOKS_____	☐ **BILL ME LATER:** (Bill-me option is good on US/Canada/Mexico orders only; not good to jobbers, wholesalers, or subscription agencies.)
	☐ Check here if billing address is different from
POSTAGE & HANDLING_____	shipping address and attach purchase order and
(US: $4.00 for first book & $1.50	billing address information.
for each additional book)	
(Outside US: $5.00 for first book	Signature_____
& $2.00 for each additional book)	
SUBTOTAL_____	☐ **PAYMENT ENCLOSED: $**_____
IN CANADA: ADD 6% GST_____	☐ **PLEASE CHARGE TO MY CREDIT CARD.**
STATE TAX_____	☐ Visa ☐ MasterCard ☐ AmEx ☐ Discover
(NJ, NY, OH, MN, CA, IL, IN, PA, & SD	☐ Diner's Club ☐ Eurocard ☐ JCB
residents, *add appropriate local sales tax)*	Account # _____
FINAL TOTAL_____	
(If paying in Canadian funds,	Exp. Date_____
convert using the current	
exchange rate, UNESCO	Signature_____
coupons welcome)	

Prices in US dollars and subject to change without notice.

NAME_____

INSTITUTION_____

ADDRESS_____

CITY_____

STATE/ZIP_____

COUNTRY_____ COUNTY (NY residents only)_____

TEL_____ FAX_____

E-MAIL_____

May we use your e-mail address for confirmations and other types of information? ☐ Yes ☐ No
We appreciate receiving your e-mail address and fax number. Haworth would like to e-mail or fax special
discount offers to you, as a preferred customer. **We will never share, rent, or exchange your e-mail address
or fax number.** We regard such actions as an invasion of your privacy.

Order From Your Local Bookstore or Directly From

The Haworth Press, Inc.

10 Alice Street, Binghamton, New York 13904-1580 • USA
TELEPHONE: 1-800-HAWORTH (1-800-429-6784) / Outside US/Canada: (607) 722-5857
FAX: 1-800-895-0582 / Outside US/Canada: (607) 771-0012
E-mail to: orders@haworthpress.com

For orders outside US and Canada, you may wish to order through your local
sales representative, distributor, or bookseller.
For information, see http://haworthpress.com/distributors

(Discounts are available for individual orders in US and Canada only, not booksellers/distributors.)

PLEASE PHOTOCOPY THIS FORM FOR YOUR PERSONAL USE.

http://www.HaworthPress.com   BOF06